IT-Driven Business Models

IT-Driven Business Models

Global Case Studies in Transformation

HENNING KAGERMANN
HUBERT OSTERLE
JOHN M. JORDAN

WILEY
John Wiley & Sons, Inc.

Published by John Wiley & Sons, Inc., Hoboken, New Jersey.
Published simultaneously in Canada.

For general information on our other products and services or for technical support,
please contact our Customer Care Department within the United States at
(800) 762-2974, outside the United States at (317) 572-3993 or fax (317) 572-4002.

Wiley also publishes its books in a variety of electronic formats. Some content that
appears in print may not be available in electronic books. For more information about
Wiley products, visit our web site at www.wiley.com.

Library of Congress Cataloging-in-Publication Data:

Kagermann, Henning.
  IT-driven business models : global case studies in transformation /
Henning Kagermann, Hubert Osterle, John M. Jordan.
      p. cm.
  Includes index.
  ISBN 978-0-470-61069-5; ISBN 978-0-470-94425-7 (ebk);
  ISBN 978-0-470-94426-4 (ebk); ISBN 978-0-470-94427-1 (ebk)
  1. Information technology—Management.   2. Technological
innovations—Management.   3. Industrial management.   I. Osterle, Hubert.
II. Jordan, John M. III. Title.
  HD30.2.K32 2010
  658.4′012—dc22

                                                              2010032746

Printed in the United States of America.

10 9 8 7 6 5 4 3 2 1

Contents

Foreword

It's no secret that the rules of competition are changing in pretty dramatic ways. Globalization is not just a word; it's a dynamic, ever-changing reality in all of our business decisions at LEGO. Customer expectations have reshaped some of our core operating assumptions. And information technology is not only reshaping our internal systems but also, and more important, the ability of our customers and fans to connect, to collaborate, and to coordinate.

The LEGO group, a small but global company that I happen to know well, had been a vertically integrated enterprise like many other organizations. We are one of the best-known brands in the world, but we cannot afford a big infrastructure footprint or an organization with a large head count. In order for us to actually achieve global reach, we decided that we needed to open up our business. Inviting partners from across the business landscape gave us access to the scale and entrepreneurship that we couldn't drive out of our own small organization.

As a result, we have invited partners into every stage of our value chain. We work with partners at retail to bring products to market through franchises and so forth. In production, we work with partners on the manufacturing side. Logistics is run by partners, including Deutsche Post—Germany's mail carrier—and DHL. Finally, in innovation, we work with 120,000 LEGO fans across the world to innovate new products alongside our 120 or so designers. In this way, we're capturing incredible leverage.

I think the special nature of LEGO drives us to be more focused on what we really do best, so the inclusion of more partners will only accelerate. I also think being orchestrators of that dialogue with numerous partners will be extremely challenging on corporations, especially if you operate on a global scale. The risk to us is that we lose our global touch because managing between Dubai, China, New York, and Frankfurt is a huge challenge.

We've received a lot of attention for doing things in this community, this way of co-creation. But people should realize it was not our intent. Traditionally, we had not tracked Net Promoter Score as a measure of customer loyalty. We found out quite by accident that our affinity numbers and affection numbers were off the charts. Once we realized there was an asset right there, mobilizing that loyalty became important.

Make no mistake—that customer loyalty is a two-edged sword. IP (intellectual property) protection is a huge issue when you do co-creation. How much would you let people run with your brand? At the same time, these people don't get paid, and don't expect to be, for their contributions. They work for free and they literally work hundreds of hours for free. We found they respond best to rewards other than financial ones, typically things like recognition. So we now actually launch products where we say, This product was built by Fan So-and-So and you can go to his or her Web site and see all the things this person has done and the like. It's a model that we're still struggling to execute exactly, but it's been an exciting journey.

Our journey is not unique, as readers will see in this book. Several phenomena can be seen across the business landscape. Customers are playing new roles, both in relation to a company and in their interactions with each other on such social networks as Facebook, Twitter, and blogs. Supply chains are being reinvented, with new scales of time and space to manage. Risk, opportunity, innovation, and capital each must be understood in new ways. Simultaneously managing inside an organization and coexisting with outside ecosystem partners requires new tools and new attitudes. Business models are being reinvented in some fascinating ways. Strategic agility has been forced on us in some ways by the state of the economy. In every one of these examples, information technology is enabling, complicating, and disrupting managers' lives. Thinking systematically about the key issues is an important first step in capturing some of the value of these technologies.

Jørgen vig Knudstorp
CEO, LEGO Group

Preface

Information Technology and Business Model Innovation

We wrote this book to inform a debate that is of critical importance: How can information technology (IT) contribute to business model innovation?

The global economy remains unsteady, despite unprecedented government intervention. Currencies and cultures, workforces and welfare systems, shopping and saving are all undergoing foundational change. Business leaders are competing in a new market—in a new *kind* of market—in which organizational assumptions, capital requirements, and tools for execution are being challenged and reinvented.

Honored brands, such as General Motors, Encyclopedia Britannica, and Sony are trying to reinvent themselves across every facet of their operations. Global economic growth is being driven by neither Europe, Japan, nor the United States, but by China, by Brazil, by South Korea. Google is at once a force in advertising and media, in computing, in software, in mapping and location-related services, and in telephony. One's vertical industry is no longer destiny.

Given that so many elements of the business environment are in a state of uncertainty or transition, new ways of managing are proving their worth. The importance of a coherent, adaptable business model has been amply demonstrated by both the past decade's failures and successes, particularly in the tech sector. As the dynamism of the mobile phone market is illustrating, new technologies can reshape personal behavior, social life, and business opportunity with unprecedented speed. Finally, the availability of more data than ever before is at once providing new opportunities and imposing new requirements on managers to better use information to make decisions.

Drawing on decades of experience in academia, consulting, and executive leadership, the authors begin from a simple premise: Enterprise value relates directly to the value created for one's customers. Value for the customer, in turn, derives from knowledge of the customer's key processes. Great business models build on this foundation.

We have worked to bring a truly global perspective to the book's examples. Thus we have included Economist Intelligence Unit (EIU) case studies from Apple and ABB, Nokia and Li Ning, Endress+Hauser and Saudi Aramco. All told, companies from five continents and virtually every industry vertical are represented.

It is our hope that the reader can take two key messages from the book. First, the challenges of global business demand robust business models, well executed. Second, the pace of innovation and adoption of information technologies is creating new opportunities for margin enhancement, increased customer satisfaction, capital efficiency, and agile organizational behavior. Those companies that can combine the former with the latter will continue to prosper, regardless of the macro forces of uncertainty and volatility.

CEO Agenda

This book is intended to inform an agenda for CEOs and executive managers. It builds on an Economist Intelligence Unit study, on face-to-face interviews of several hours with nearly 50 global CEOs and board members, and on findings from the academic world, consulting firms, the software industry, and market research companies.

The CEO agenda includes analyses of innovative business concepts as well as practical advice for realizing them. The book's chapters each illustrate an agenda item:

Chapter 1: Enterprise Value from Customer Value
Chapter 2: Customer Value from the Customer Process
Chapter 3: More Customers and More for the Customer
Chapter 4: Innovation and Personalization Trump Commoditization
Chapter 5: Silent Commerce
Chapter 6: Strategy-Compliant Management
Chapter 7: Value Chain Redesign
Chapter 8: IT's Role in Business Model Transformation

Enterprise Value from Customer Value: An Overview

This chapter explains how customer value determines enterprise value. Chapter 2 shows how the customer perceives the advantages added to its process by a particular provider. Chapters 3 to 6 introduce innovative business concepts for the core business processes and the management process. Chapter 7 looks at broadening the enterprise's view of the value chain, while Chapter 8 describes how information technologies support or hinder business model change.

Customer Value from the Customer Processes

As CEOs position their firms for both short-term profitability and long-term viability, most will find that customer value relates to a supplier's impact on a customer's process. Customers want to concentrate on the outcomes of their processes, retailers on merchandising and selling, banks on granting loans, and brand owners on positioning their label. With increasing frequency, they expect suppliers to understand and support the customer processes. In practice, this means that suppliers have to relieve customers of the factors that put a strain on their processes, while delivering services that meet customer needs, potentially at any time and any place.

The majority of the companies we surveyed want to migrate from product providers to solution providers and thus bring more value to the customer process than their competitors. In Chapter 2, case studies from COSCO, Hilti, and ABB Turbo show that IT can open new possibilities for catering to customer processes, but also that management must follow this strategic line of attack over the long term.

A company that wants to provide for key aspects of a customer process must concentrate on what it does best and look to partners to deliver any expertise it may lack itself—but it must not leave the customer to coordinate activities. Learning to manage in networks, where persuasion replaces formal lines of authority, represents an organizational challenge for most companies.[1]

> The customer process is beginning to drive an economic shake-up, as the transforming relationship between automotive OEMs and tier 1 suppliers is illustrating.

More Customers and More for the Customer

According to the Economist study, customer access is the area where managers expect to see most change. This is confirmed by our CEO interviews as well as by several surveys of IT investment.[2] The goal in this domain is to reach every important potential customer and serve his needs as fully as possible. This aspiration demands broad, in-depth knowledge of prospective and existing customers, and of their requirements. Integrated customer support structures use and improve on this information each time contact is made with a customer, whether in a search, sales, after-sales, or product development context.

The switch from product to solution sales calls for new price structures (for instance, the sale of the customer's process objective—broken rock—rather than explosives) that until recently would have generated far too much administrative outlay. More important, the entire sales process and value proposition must be rethought and restructured. In nearly every case that we have seen, merging products and services into solutions requires a change to the business model and the supporting business concepts.

Case studies from Telefónica and the chemicals industry are included to demonstrate these concepts.

> The battle is on for customer ownership as companies want unprecedented access to and knowledge about customers.

Innovation and Personalization Trump Commoditization

The majority of the CEOs we surveyed cited product and service innovation as pivotal to their company's success and a major reason for remaining in high-wage countries. Case studies from Procter & Gamble, LEGO, and the Swiss precision instrumentation company Endress+Hauser illustrate this reasoning, while Tata provides another perspective, that of disruptive innovation from the developing world.

Despite all the teething troubles with electronics in vehicles and other devices, companies are competing to provide the most functionally advanced products and services built upon the development of embedded software and electronic services. A vehicle without an antilock brake system, electronic stability program, or navigation system with up-to-the-minute traffic and weather news is virtually unsalable in some customer segments. The challenge from the Tata Nano, meanwhile, lies in exactly the opposite orientation.

The low marginal costs associated with electronic services (such as cash terminals and online social networks) have opened the way for countless new services that human staff alone would never have been able to deliver cost effectively. In every industry sector, electronic services and other IT-based business solutions are driving the personalization of products and services, from mileage-related motor insurance to customer-designed building maintenance packages.

> IT is a necessary but not sufficient condition for a differentiated customer experience that supports profitable businesses.

Silent Commerce

It is taken for granted today that an order will be processed quickly, securely, and cost efficiently to the required level of quality. Ideally, customers will be completely unaware of the fulfillment process—thus the focus on silent commerce—because the necessary products and services they require for their processes will be available exactly when they need them. As we will see in case studies from the linen supplier CWS-boco and Li Ning, the Chinese athletic apparel firm, suppliers can fulfill this ideal quite ingeniously.

In the 1990s, the desire to fulfill orders efficiently prompted companies to restructure their internal processes; in the future, the same desire will also drive inter-enterprise collaboration. Since the IT required for closer electronic cooperation was not available or was too expensive in the past, this area still holds tremendous potential.

Capturing data automatically provides a more accurate and up-to-date picture of the flow of goods. Sensors embedded in everything from uniforms to cell phones to locomotives can trigger various business processes. Standardization, say in the way design drawings are created or in global branding, means that once captured, data can be used by anybody involved in the process. Companies can replace the physical flow of goods and manual activities with a flow of information at many stages in the fulfillment process, but synchronization across the value chain remains challenging: different trading partners have competing objectives and optimization targets.

> The best kind of fulfillment is one where the customer need not attend to anything.

Strategy-Compliant Management

IT cannot replace people. For the foreseeable future, leadership, decisiveness, and creativity will remain the preserve of human intelligence. Management methods are being challenged to respond swiftly to market changes, global management, and external transparency demands from the fast-close concept, corporate social responsibility bodies, Basel II, and the International Financial Reporting Standards (IFRS). New regulatory requirements will undoubtedly emerge from the credit shortage and market turmoil of 2008, putting an additional premium on the intangibles of leadership and decision making.

Quality management follows through the strategy in day-to-day activities. Starting with the winning propositions in the business model, it sets targets and cascades them across all management levels and business areas down to the level of individual employees. For the first time in memory, managers can draw on an integrated data foundation as a "single source of truth" that is binding and up to date for all employees, even in widely distributed enterprises. Such a data environment thus promises the ability to keep activities aligned with the overall strategy, as we will see at such varied companies as Saudi Aramco, SAP, and Vestas, the world's largest installer of wind turbines.

> The integrated data foundation promotes strategy-compliant management.

Value Chain Redesign

ERP systems helped start a wave of business process redesign.[3] Seamless, real-time processes are already the status quo in both individual plants and entire companies. The next wave of business process redesign addresses interplant and inter-enterprise processes, known as collaborative processes. Such processes hold far more potential than the first wave because companies are only just beginning to exploit the concept's possibilities. Our case study companies—IKEA, De Beers, Nokia, Lindt & Sprüngli, Sharp, Virgin Mobile, and Amazon Web Services—provide varied examples of value chain redesign.

Although electronic collaboration actually began in 1980s with electronic data interchange (EDI) and gained momentum in the 1990s with the arrival of Internet portals, until now it has been far too expensive and too time-consuming to connect businesses to businesses and IT applications to IT applications. Steady progress in this area will come from standardization, online service providers, and business process platforms for linking IT applications flexibly across enterprises.

From management's perspective, this emerging capability will necessitate dismantling and rebuilding value chains. Globalization, specialization, aggregation, mergers and acquisitions, outsourcing and outtasking, and a new industry of electronic services and online exchanges mean that each and every company must be able to defend or strengthen its position in different value chains.

Redesigned value chains are effecting a fundamental change in the balance of power between market players. Standards such as RosettaNet for collaboration in the computer industry can create exclusive clubs. Software companies are banking on their ecosystem, on a network of partners involved in developing and marketing their software and providing support for customers. Owning customer data—such as details of the components installed in chemical plants—can help determine the partnerships an enterprise needs to cultivate.

> Standards and platforms are initiating a wave of value chain redesign.

IT's Role in Business Model Transformation

Executives are often more concerned with the costs and risks of information technology than with the benefits. This attitude is understandable, given recent history. The 1990s saw unprecedented growth in IT investment. Companies started reorganizing their processes on the basis of integrated ERP systems, implemented new software ready for the year 2000, and pursued ambitious e-business plans to drive stock prices higher.

This period of intense investment in IT was followed by one of disenchantment, and a huge clean-up operation began. The cost-cutting programs of recent years have shown that measures such as consolidation, harmonization, and outsourcing can significantly reduce IT expenditure without compromising the quality of service delivered by the Information Services department. Leading information services organizations, including those at the British government, Intel, and Valero Energy, are discussed in detail.

At the same time, the decisive factor is not the absolute amount of IT expenditure or a percentage of revenues, but the alignment of each individual investment and business solution with the overarching strategy.[4] In short, only the business model can dictate the direction and amount of investment. Are investments in new, IT-based business concepts really a source of competitive advantage? In many cases, the answer is no, if competitors adopt the same concepts. But a company that does not stay current can fall behind. The company that implements a new solution first can set itself apart from competitors until they catch up by implementing the same solution or a better one.

Building on the idea of business concepts, many of which are driven or supported by IT, process visibility is a common precondition of business model innovation; package tracking at overnight shippers such as DHL or FedEx is a common example. Better awareness of skills, both internally and in the ecosystem, provides a further example of IT facilitating business model change. At the same time, IT organizations are being called upon to better understand and manage the various forms of risk with which they engage.

> While certain technologies may become commoditized, good information and information processes remain distinctive and valued.

At the end of each chapter, we have included a short checklist to help CEOs and other business managers assess their own enterprise's situation.

Acknowledgments

This book would not have been possible without the collaboration of Dr. Oliver Christ, Dr. Enrico Senger, and Oliver Wilke. Their careful research into the examples used in the book, both for their dissertations and for the book itself, is much appreciated and their studies were a valuable source of information. Together with the authors and Prof. Dr. Thomas Gutzwiller, they participated in the 26 in-depth interviews with CEOs and other executive managers. We are extremely grateful for their contribution. Our thanks go also to the interviewees for giving us an insight into their companies, challenges, solutions, and visions.

CHAPTER 1

Enterprise Value from Customer Value

Business executives confront numerous uncertainties as they cross into the second decade of the new century. Consider:

- "Free" is a common price point in information industries, such as newspapers or music, leaving firms to find new models for profitability.
- Apart from free, pricing pressure is intensified by the rapid rise of developing economies, which are home to a steady stream of new low-cost providers serving many markets.
- The traditional model of the firm has been joined by other organizational possibilities: quasi-governmental capitalist entities (Thales Group, General Motors, AIG), business ecosystems that link capabilities from multiple organizational "homes" (Apple's iPhone software development network), and dispersed pools of volunteer talent with no revenue streams but category-leading products (Linux, Wikipedia).
- The attractive size of Asian markets is made problematic by cultural issues, language barriers, the wide variation in intellectual property protection, and risks—everything from influenza outbreaks to terrorism and extreme weather.

In short, what firms deliver, how much they charge, how they organize to deliver it, and the constraints under which they do so are all in transition.

Perhaps the only certainty lies in the necessity of serving customers better. As these customers have more complex needs, increased competition of their own, and more suppliers to choose among, successful businesses are returning to the ground truth of profitably delivering value across multiple geographies, in the context of rapid and unpredictable change. Accordingly, an enterprise's financial health is largely a function of the value its customers derive from the seller's products and services.

Aligning the delivery of superior customer value with increasing enterprise value derives from strategy, from operational excellence, and from the *business model,* which articulates the differentiated ways that an enterprise delivers value to its customers. While the term is widely used, we follow coauthor Kagermann's definition:

> *A business model consists of four interlocking elements that, taken together, create and deliver value.*
>
> **Customer value proposition,** *including target customer, the customer's job to be done, and the offering which satisfies the problem or fulfills the need.*
> **Profit formula,** *including the revenue model, cost structure, margin model, and resource velocity (lead times, turns, etc.).*
> **Key resources** *to deliver the customer value proposition profitably, potentially including people, equipment, technologies, partnerships, brand, etc.*
> **Key processes** *also include rules, metrics, norms of behavior that make repeated delivery of the customer value proposition repeatable and scalable.*[1]

The great business models have become familiar icons. King Gillette gave away razors to sell an annuity stream of replacement blades. American Airlines pioneered the use of Sabre, a computerized reservations network that became so strategically important it was spun out as a separate entity; Bloomberg's financial information service followed along similar lines. IKEA combined Nordic design, expertise in flat packaging, and large retail footprints to reinvent the furniture industry.

Because it is fundamental to a firm's success, however, changing a business model can be difficult. General Motors' template for labor costs, model changeovers, and brand management dates to the 1960s and did not adapt to new dynamics of competition and consumer behavior. The music industry's bundling of songs into LP records worked for a few decades, but the model failed in the digital era, leaving the labels' economics and practices out of step with the market. Established air carriers' inattention to the low end of the market, and to their cost structures, left them vulnerable to a new wave of budget airlines such as EasyJet, Ryan Air, and Southwest.

With this history in mind, our focus in this book will be on business model innovation, specifically on the role of information technology in driving and enabling changes to the fundamental facets of the business: the offer and customer, the value chain and its players' margin structures, and the ecosystem and the business processes it performs. A particular emphasis will fall on what we call business concepts. Business concepts, which frequently utilize technology in innovative ways, can be seen as building blocks in the creation or revision of business models.

> The business model determines the value of a company by facilitating the profitable delivery of value to the firm's customers.

Customer Value and Enterprise Value

To see how customer value shapes enterprise value, let's do a thought experiment involving search. Before the World Wide Web, according to Kevin Kelly (founding editor of *Wired*), U.S. searches added up to a staggering 111 billion a year, most of them directory assistance telephone calls, but also counting librarian queries. After the advent of search engines, people appear to be asking more questions: the measurement firm comScore estimated 2 billion searches per day, worldwide, as of December 2007.

In Kelly's admittedly rough estimate, an unnamed Google employee hypothetically and unscientifically values these searches as follows. Let's assume, he says, that

1/4 of all searches are really easy ones (like "american airlines") that save the user maybe 30 seconds.

1/4 are a little hard and save maybe 5 minutes.

1/4 are just wasting time.

1/4 are hard ones that lead to substantial savings—like diagnosing your serious disease, or choosing the right college, or the right vacation destination.

Suppose it takes 10 searches on average to get one of these "hard" answers, but when you get it, you've saved maybe 3 hours. That averages out to 6 minutes saved/search. Figure average income of $25,000/year, or $12.50/hr. So we get a value of $1.25/search by this metric.[2]

Assuming the U.S. audience as 1.2 billion searches per day at that $1.25 per search, and Google's market share of roughly 65 percent, that would mean that Google creates $1.5 billion of value for its U.S. users per day.

Now, these are unofficial numbers, and this is only a thought experiment, but even if the numbers are off by a factor of five, that still means that Google creates 25 cents of value with the average search, at a cost to serve in the range of .2 cents. That would represent a 100-fold ratio of customer well-being to cost, a stunning value proposition by any measure. Google's share price is a direct reflection of both this calculus and the advertising business model that allows it to be converted into revenue.

While stressing the role of customer value in enterprise value may sound like a truism, recent academic research suggests that theory and practice converge. The logic for moving from product or service provision into solution-centric business models is not only intuitive. In the past several decades, accounting-based value of a company's assets has reflected less and less of the stock market capitalization. In fact, as of 2003, the market value of the Fortune 500 was fully six times the book value.[3] If physical capital and similar assets fail to explain the value of a company, the reasoning went, intangibles such as brand equity, goodwill, and intellectual property must be responsible.

A landmark study published in 2004 explored one such intangible, customer satisfaction, which the authors hypothesized was related to increased "share of wallet," improved customer retention and therefore cash flows, positive word of mouth, and other benefits. The research showed that a one point gain in customer satisfaction using standard metrics correlated to a 2.75 percent gain in shareholder value.[4]

More recently, a 2008 study used customer satisfaction metrics as a guide to portfolio creation, and the customer-satisfying portfolio outperformed groups of companies with either low or decreasing customer satisfaction scores.[5] In both cases, positive customer experiences translated both to the bottom line and to stock market performance.

> Our assertion that enterprise value derives from customer value is founded in experience, logic, and quantitative models.

Context

Because of the recent economic turmoil, business model innovation has never been more difficult—or more necessary. Six new or reconstituted macro forces will reshape the global context for business decisions in the coming years.[6]

1. *The changing shape of globalization.* As the world enters the second decade of the millennium, the process of globalization is in flux. China's role in military and economic affairs, while not yet fully clear, will be larger and different from what most observers predicted. Exhibit 1.1

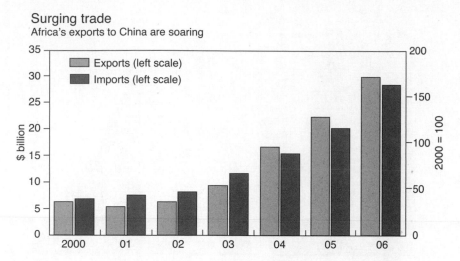

Surging trade
Africa's exports to China are soaring

EXHIBIT 1.1   Increased Trade between Africa and China Comprises One Facet of the Changing Shape of Globalization

Sources: International Monetary Fund (IMF), *Direction of Trade Statistics*; and authors' calculations.

shows but one facet of this expansion: dramatic increases in Chinese trade with Africa.[7] Global problems such as climate change and capital mobility are exposing the limits of existing governance structures.[8] The shift from a bipolar world dominated by the United States and USSR and their associated spheres to a multipolar world has broad implications. Among these are the rise of nonstate actors (whether Doctors without Borders or Al Qaeda) and new trade patterns between the BRIC (Brazil, Russia, India, China) countries and the developing world.

2. *Demographics and urbanization.* The aging of industrial workforces is occurring against the backdrop of a foundational shift to a services-based economy. In addition, cities around the world are growing bigger as agriculture declines in economic impact. Both employer- and employee-managed retirement portfolios have lost substantial value, complicating the demographic picture further. Developing economies typically have much higher population growth, and thus different age pyramids, compared to OECD countries, as Exhibit 1.2 illustrates.[9] Older people consume more health care resources than do younger ones, and those resources are becoming more expensive every year. In addition, elders constitute a distinctive market, one that requires new channels

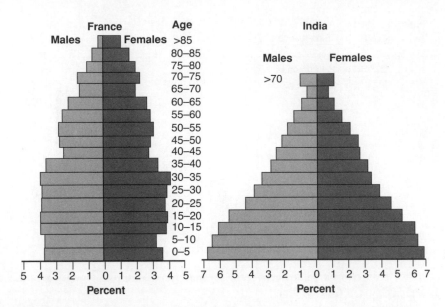

EXHIBIT 1.2 Workforce and Social Welfare Projections in France and India Vary Considerably Because of Demographic Differences, Shown Here on Age Pyramids

Source: Age pyramids available at U.S. Census Bureau, International Data Base (IDB).

to market, more support to make use of products and services, and a variety of aids to handle the growing complexity of modern life.

3. *Environmental concerns and resource shortages.* After the Kyoto protocols were either unratified or frequently ignored, worldwide sentiment regarding the reality of climate change has shifted in light of evidence of the sort presented in Exhibit 1.3.[10] Substantial policy commitments are emerging from many countries, and the cost of these mandates will ultimately fall on business. In addition, critical resources including water and key metals can become scarce for either natural or political reasons. Meanwhile, the countless opportunities that will emerge from greater environmental awareness—whether in the areas of power generation, lighting, packaging, local farming, or many others—could well contribute to a new era of prosperity.

4. *Increased governmental presence.* Financial services scandals, new kinds of infrastructure vulnerability (as in the power grid for example), and new standards for drug and medical device approvals will ratchet up the regulatory burden. Whether in mortgage origination and packaging, end-of-life requirements for electronics, or efforts to increase financial transparency, expect to see governments increase their presence—and

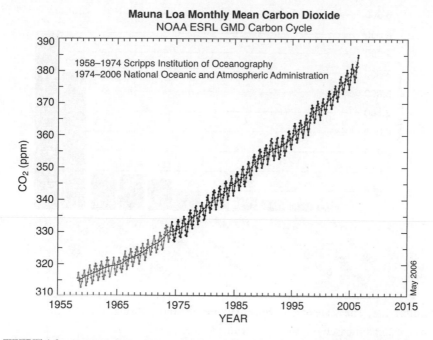

Mauna Loa Monthly Mean Carbon Dioxide
NOAA ESRL GMD Carbon Cycle

1958–1974 Scripps Institution of Oceanography
1974–2006 National Oceanic and Atmospheric Administration

EXHIBIT 1.3 By Many Measures Including Readings at This Hawaiian Observatory, Environmental Indicators of Global Climate Change Are Driving Responses by National and International Agencies

Source: National Oceanographic and Atmospheric Administration long-term carbon dioxide readings at Mauna Loa observatory.

thus reporting requirements—in most industries. Finally, stimulus packages in many countries (see Exhibit 1.4)[11] are partially reversing the trend toward privatization of major industries as governments purchase damaged assets. In almost every U.S. industry vertical, the government is competing with, taxing, regulating, and/or subsidizing a given company, shaping the range of strategic possibilities. Other governments play similarly critical roles.

5. *Digital trust.* Various digital connections have made possible new kinds of relationships and arrangements, but they have also opened the door to innovative forms of fraud, data loss (see Exhibit 1.5), and other violations of trust such as electronic voting machine miscounting. Search technologies, which have become ubiquitous, are generally taken as objective when in fact their results reflect multiple agendas. At both the consumer and business-to-business levels, watch for new forms of trust to be required and enforced.

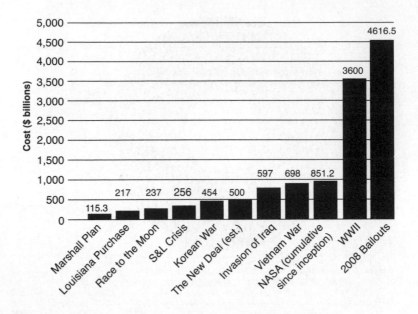

EXHIBIT 1.4 The Scale of Governmental Intervention Is Rising

Source: Exhibit based on data from Bianco Research.

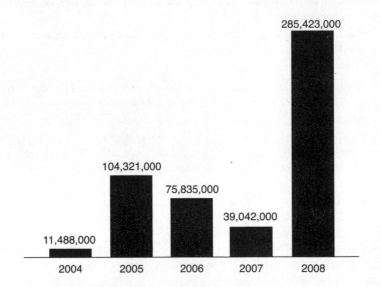

EXHIBIT 1.5 Commercial Firms Investigating Data Breaches Saw a Sudden Upturn in Compromised Data Records in 2008

Source: Verizon Business 2009 Data Breach Investigations Report, p. 32.

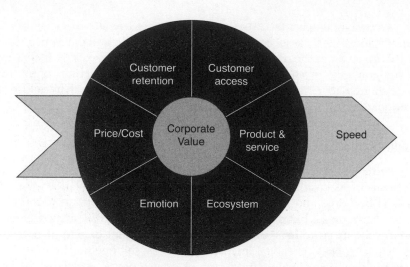

EXHIBIT 1.6 Corporate Value Derives from Both Market Relationships and Internal Processes, and Both Tangible and Intangible Factors

6. *Risk management*. Whether in the 2008 terror attacks in Mumbai, the rogue trader at Société Générale, or AIG's missteps with collateralized debt obligations, we have seen the substantial impact of insufficient attention to risk. While the pendulum may swing too far in the opposite direction, almost every business activity will operate under increased scrutiny as the practice of risk management in its many forms is intensified.

Shaping a Response

Ample evidence suggests that the factors determining customer value (see Exhibit 1.6) are in flux. Our CEO studies,[12] numerous detailed case studies, and analyses by other authors verify that the market rules are being rewritten by many factors, including:

- Blurring enterprise boundaries
- Product commoditization
- Volatility and interconnectedness of financial markets
- Personalization of electronic services
- Intelligence in products
- Actionable knowledge about customers, markets, and products
- Transparency in the value chain

We conclude that after 2010 the following factors will be crucial for customer value and, by association, drive market success and enterprise value. At the same time, the world is moving fast and complexity is increasing, so the converse of each statement is also worth considering: opportunities continue to emerge, but each one also carries risks that cannot be overlooked.

Product and Service Integration

In selected markets, an intelligent enterprise understands the needs and problems of its customers and, when appropriate, offers them leading services at any time and in any location. It presents itself not as a company that sells products, but as a solution provider that delivers comprehensive services for its customers' unique processes.[13] Aircraft engine manufacturers, whose process is capital intensive, not only sell engines but also have started operating them for the customer as a monthly service, paid as a monthly expense.[14] The need for new pricing models presents both upside potential and operational challenges across the enterprise.

Caveat: Making the transition from product manufacturer to solution provider requires that an enterprise reinvent its business model from the foundation. Margin structure, balance sheet analysis, and financing can be problematic. Sales forces need new compensation models, and the cultural shift to solution selling can be wrenching. Finally, risk management becomes a newly required core competency as customers for product-service hybrids differ from their product-centric counterparts.

Customer Access

An intelligent enterprise finds target customers worldwide, beyond its traditional region and industry. It knows the customers, their requirements, and their decision makers. A family hotel in Denmark reaches customers via the Internet that it could not access through print advertising, tour operators, or travel agents.

Caveat: Borderless competition both increases market access and exposes formerly local concerns to global competitive pressures. Currency changes are a simple example. More critically, the hypothetical hotel in Denmark now must compete with not only other properties in its town and nation, but also vacation destinations worldwide.

Customer Retention

An intelligent enterprise strengthens its partnership with a customer by building up expertise in the customer's specific area then using IT applications to support cooperation. The customer benefits from low trans-action costs and in turn accepts the higher switching costs for moving to a different supplier. A retail bank may get its customers used to convenient Internet services so that they find it difficult to move to a different provider.

Caveat: Lock-in behaves differently in the age of the Internet.[15] When proprietary solutions stop delivering added value, customers can share ex-periences in online forums and defect if necessary. Furthermore, competi-tion can often come from outside the traditional domain: eBay stunned the credit card industry by acquiring PayPal and functioning much like a bank.

Ecosystem

If a company's product is part of a broader solution for the customer, its success depends on the quality of the partner companies which together form the ecosystem. The more complicated a product or service becomes, the more specialists a customer needs. In other words, a customer no longer focuses on just the individual product but on the supplier's entire ecosystem. For instance, a skier is not looking for the best ski lift but rather the best ski resort complete with hotels, ski schools, restaurants, and more: accordingly, the resort must bundle offers that come from a network of suppliers and contractors, presenting a single face to the customer.

Caveat: Managing partners in an ecosystem is an entirely new discipline compared with running a functional or geographic group in an enterprise.[16] If a firm in a company's or a competitor ecosystem is acquired or sold, for example, the ripple effect could be significant. Operating in a networked environment means both gaining access to more capabilities but also being influenced by more parties. The size and quality of a company's ecosystem may define part of its market value: the number of application developers aligned with a given platform, and the caliber of independent financial advisors who represent a given investment, matter both to customers and investors.

Less powerful players within an ecosystem may lose brand equity, for example: both Intel and Microsoft were better recognized than many hardware manufacturers and computer retailers. Alternatively, a unique assemblage of capabilities may enable an ecosystem or brand to transcend its members: airline alliances such as Star or Skyteam are one potential example.

Emotion

Customers enjoy working with a company because it offers a specific brand, reliability, and convenience. A customer purchases from a particular manu-facturer because he associates a certain image with the brand, appreciates the service crew's reliability, or has come to rely on the convenience, ease of use, or trustworthiness of the company's IT-driven interfaces. Employee loyalty, shareholder confidence in management, and trust in trading partners are other examples of the place of emotion.

Caveat: Only a few brands have proven adept at maintaining emotional bonds at scale. Compare Disney to Vivendi in entertainment, or Volkswagen to GM in automotive. A company's internal perception of its brand is often not that of its customers or the market at large. The emotional connection to a brand can also be impaired by poor usability, lack of availability, and errors in online interactions.

Costs

Companies sometimes opt for high production volumes in order to better allocate fixed costs, especially research and development. They move facilities to cost-saving locations and coordinate global production activities in seamless, lean processes. Particularly in information-rich settings, marginal costs in many cases approach zero.

Caveat: In an age of tight credit, preservation of working capital can be more important than amassing excess inventory. Understanding the total cost implications of a given decision, such as plant expansion, adding sales channels, or opening a new geography, can be challenging in many companies that lack sophisticated financial systems.

Price

A company understands the value of its products and services and also knows what alternatives are available to the customer. It uses an intelligent revenue model to find the best long-term price. The manufacturer of a humidity sensor bases the price of the product on whether it is being sold as a series part for a large-scale production car, as a discrete product for an electrician, or as a spare part for a plant operator. As we have seen, new pricing models will apply to solutions rather than products. Dynamic pricing, long practiced in the airline industry, is moving to more products and services, whether parking spaces or tickets to sporting events.

Caveat: Many markets, such as pharmaceuticals, have become substantially more transparent in the past 15 years. Charging higher prices for a device based on its application only works if customers fail to do research, or if the supplier adds sufficient value to the customer relative to the demands of the device's use: brand, price, and customer experience must reinforce each other. Finally, given the extreme volatility of such commodities as copper, "long-term" prices aren't what they used to be either.

Speed

Speed dictates how long a company holds the prize for the best business model. Speed in this context refers not only to delivery speed, but to how quickly an enterprise recognizes market changes and responds with an innovative business concept. In some industries, time to market is less important than time to volume, which implies economies of scale and potentially market share improvement. Many examples like that of the music industry verify that the swiftness with which a business model is implemented can be more important than the model itself.

Caveat: Speed is one thing, jumpiness another. Knowing the fundamental facets of the company, its industry, and its business model will prevent executives from chasing fads in the name of speed.

To summarize, many business models beyond 2010 will be characterized by solution offerings rather than product offerings, new routes to customers, close customer relationships, ecosystems, convenience, more flexible price structures, and rapid transformation.

Business Models, Business Concepts, and the Role of IT

The innovativeness of the business model is more important than the innovativeness of the products. This finding was the result of a study in which the Economist Intelligence Unit surveyed 3,700 executive board members and senior managers from European, Asian, and American companies.[17] New research published in 2008 confirms the assertion.[18]

We argue that business models in turn require a sophisticated *operationalization* of several parts, what we call business concepts; they turn abstract theory into measurable actions. Examples include:

- Handling a sales order within 24 hours
- Being accessible around the clock to customers worldwide over the Internet
- Manufacturing goods in different countries but managing processes centrally
- Coordinating global research and development activities
- Accommodating the regional needs of customers on all continents and still leveraging the economies of scale that a global market leader can provide

Business models are built by combining business concepts.

What distinguishes an enterprise in 2010 from an enterprise in 1970? More "intelligent" business concepts. All the examples of business concepts mentioned above were unheard of in 1970. Why? Because competition has become stiffer? Because people have become more intelligent or work harder? These reasons may explain some of the changes. Other explanations include deregulation, global logistics, and new materials and production procedures. But the key trigger for most new business concepts is information technology.[19]

An effective corporate information environment instantiates the skills and intelligence of the company's people, serving as a persistent institutional memory. New technologies for search and data exploration as well as enterprise social networking can find either answers or people with answers. In addition, an organization's electronic intelligence (in the form of processes, databases, and visualizations, for example) "amplifies" human intelligence. Such an environment has several distinguishing characteristics, all of which bear on the enablement of effective business concepts:

- Electronic intelligence does not depend on a particular person (for instance, in product catalogs, customer databases, or maintenance manuals).
- Interactions through search, visualization, and other mechanisms allow humans to manage the scale and complexity of modern information environments.
- Effective corporate information environments record data faster (often in real time), cheaper, more reliably (automatically), and in more detail (for instance, clicks in a webpage or temperature data for the manufacture of silicon wafers).
- Effective environments route data immediately and to any location (such as stock market data or traffic information).
- Effective environments store huge amounts of data (such as orders, articles, and performance data) for any desired period of time.
- Effective environments have extremely powerful processing capabilities and can generate new value and insight by combining existing data (for example, delivery date determination, salary schedules, or product simulation).

This organizational intelligence in the form of processes, software, customer databases, and other such elements has become so important that the IFRS7 require parts of this intelligence to be evaluated and shown in financial statements. Financial Accounting Standards Board (FASB) disclosure standards remain different, however.

The euphoria surrounding the Internet at the end of the nineties and the ensuing hangover brought on by a series of broken promises were followed by a systematic and more market-oriented search for new, IT-based business concepts. The recession has intensified the quest for enterprise IT value: new technologies and management practices have forced pragmatism to be the byword of the entire industry.

Business managers are not concerned with IT per se, but they are concerned with new business concepts based on IT. Unless managers understand what a new business concept can bring to customers and their own company, they cannot make sound investment decisions.

> The answer to the market's challenges is to be found not in IT but in the business model that uses the IT.

Case Study: Apple

The history of Apple in the first decade of the twenty-first century encapsulates many of this book's key messages. Time and again, CEO Steve Jobs and his leadership team have combined key elements of strategy and execution to reinvent both Apple's business model and an entire industry sector. In doing so, the company's success during a turbulent period illustrates both the necessity and the impact of business model transformation.

Context

In a garage not far from where Bill Hewlett and David Packard got their start, Apple Computer began operation in April 1976. Founded by Steve Jobs and Steve Wozniak, the company helped launch the hobbyist movement that later helped drive the rise of the personal computer. The Apple II sold more than 100,000 units, after which the company went public in 1980.

In contrast to the IBM PC architecture, Apple embraced a proprietary model in which the company supplied both hardware and software. In 1984, this approach helped create the Macintosh, an elegant combination of design and usability, featuring the first widely commercialized WIMP (windows, icons, mouse, pointer) user interface. The proprietary operating system slowed the development of compatible application software, however, and the huge investment in the Mac was perceived to have failed to pay off, so Jobs was removed from operational responsibility by Apple's board in 1985, and he left the firm shortly thereafter.

From Jobs' departure until 1997, Apple hired three CEOs, each of whom directed a different corporate strategy and positioning. With the launch of Windows 3.1 in the early 1990s, meanwhile, the Microsoft-Intel platform achieved a considerable increase in ease of use compared to the command-line DOS interface that preceded it. Then in 1995, Microsoft capitalized on, and helped drive, the rise of the consumer Internet with the launch of its

Windows 95 operating system, which included support for remote dialup, TCP/IP networking, and CD-ROM drives.

Thus when Jobs rejoined Apple in late 1997, the company had experimented with high-volume low-margin products, an early PDA called the Newton, and a return to high-margin products including Internet appliances and servers. Apple also supported, for a time, third-party "clones" that licensed the Mac operating system. None of these moves succeeded: Jobs' predecessor as CEO, Gil Amelio, had lost $1.6 billion in about two years at a time when many tech firms were thriving. Global market share was 3 percent.[20]

At a major technology conference a month after Jobs returned as CEO, Michael Dell was asked what he would do to fix the many problems at Apple. His response illustrates the severity of the situation: "What would I do? I'd shut it down and give the money back to the shareholders."[21]

Jobs and Apple in the Twenty-First Century

Upon his return, Steve Jobs put in place a number of building blocks for later success. With the launch of the self-contained iMac in 1998, Apple returned to the themes of simplicity, ease of use, and striking visual design that had been the hallmark of the original Mac. In addition to commanding higher margins, the new generation of Apple products interoperated with both PC hardware (via USB) and software in the wake of a $150 million investment by Microsoft that also came with a commitment to maintain its Office suite for Mac OS and other applications.

Just as important, the company underwent a house-cleaning in back-office and supply-chain processes. Product lines were discontinued. Vendors were rationalized, distribution channels were pruned and moved into higher-volume retailers, and manufacturing was moved to third parties. Apple launched direct-to-consumer web commerce in 1997. Perhaps most critically, R&D spending was ramped up and internal lines of communication were simplified.

In 2001, Apple opened its first retail store and by 2009 there were 255 worldwide. Public and critical response was extremely positive. New customers could experiment with the products, while a "Genius Bar" provided hip and accessible tech support both pre- and post-purchase. Along with a series of well-designed products, the stores' architecture reinforced Apple's reemergence as a culturally "cool" brand. A string of strong branding and advertising campaigns also succeeded in differentiating Apple from the Microsoft environment.

Later in 2001, Apple launched the iPod, a high-margin version of an MP3 music player. The "ecosystem" around the iPod began to take shape about a year and a half later, however, with the introduction of the iTunes

Music Store for Apple hardware and, six months later, for Windows users. Sales of iPods skyrocketed after the release of the Music Store, with gross margins for the hardware of 30 to 35 percent.[22]

Throughout the following years, Apple (eventually changing its name from Apple Computer in 2007) rapidly refreshed the iPod product line, making some smaller, others with large hard-drive capacity, some with video, and still others without any user interface apart from a "play" switch. Competitors appeared from Dell, Microsoft, and storage manufacturers such as SanDisk, but Apple's franchise became the dominant worldwide leader, with a peak of 90 percent global market share as measured by dollar volume.[23] Nearly 200 million units had been shipped as of mid-2009.

After a failed attempt by Motorola to include iPod functionality in a mobile phone, Apple bundled its music player into a handheld computing platform somewhat misleadingly called the iPhone, which came to market in 2007. It quickly became a major force in the global smartphone market, representing 1.1 percent market share as a premium-priced product competing against traditional voice-only devices in markets around the world.

In mid-2008, Apple built further on the iPhone/iTunes ecosystem with the unveiling of the App Store, a marketplace for third party software developers to end users. In only 9 months 37,000 applications became available, most of them free downloads. Some applications became huge moneymakers for both Apple (which kept 30% of the sale price) and independent software developers. One developer, Ethan Nicholas, taught himself the necessary coding skills using online documentation and wrote a tank shooter game that earned him $600,000 in one month—after taxes—and a reported $900,000 in total before the release of version 2.0.[24]

Business Model Innovation at Apple

ENTERPRISE VALUE FROM CUSTOMER VALUE Less than 10 years after Michael Dell recommended shutting down Apple, the company's market value eclipsed that of Dell in early 2006. Three years later, the ratio of market capitalization was over 5:1 in Apple's favor. The company has created customer value with such emotion-driven factors as good design, ease of use, and powerful branding. Dell, meanwhile, competes in increasingly commoditized markets, having lost its advantage in personalization: the build-to-order model that customized desktop PCs does not create as much advantage in laptops. Now constituting the majority of the market, laptops and netbooks are primarily built in bulk overseas and have few customization options.

Apple also creates customer value by seamlessly blurring products and services with both the iPhone and iPod product lines. These digital hybrids typically commend higher margins than either products or services considered independently. Under Jobs during both of his CEO tenures, Apple has also consistently led the industry in innovation. The instant download model at 99 cents (and up) created unmatched convenience for customers who want a song, movie, iPhone application, podcast, or other content without having to go to a store or wait for physical goods to ship. That same model created a viable, legal alternative to peer-to-peer file-sharing networks such as Napster.

CUSTOMER VALUE FROM THE CUSTOMER PROCESS   When Apple introduced the iPod, MP3 files were widely available on peer-to-peer file sharing networks; compact disc sales had already begun their long decline. A variety of players, beginning with Diamond Multimedia's Rio, had come to market. But Apple reinvented both the music management metaphor and the physical form factor, the latter with a careful mix of design cues. The white case is actually clear over a white base layer, for example, and the case has no visible screws or fasteners.[25]

The net effect of so many careful decisions was to make music an entirely new experience: distinctive white earbuds made it private rather than public (and a fashion statement on the subway and metro), the digital format (albeit a proprietary one in some cases) made carrying a large music library simple and portable, and the software made it searchable, or random, and easily managed. Apple simplified the consumer's process of buying songs out of millions available via iTunes. In short, the iPod addressed and arguably improved the whole of the customer's music- and, later, spoken-word-listening experience. The iPhone later did the same for a much broader set of needs and behaviors.

MORE CUSTOMERS AND MORE FOR THE CUSTOMER   The iPod trained millions of customers to use the iTunes interface, to dock their devices to a computer, and to combine physical products with value-adding updates and downloads via the Internet. While the introduction and the commercialization of an entirely new product type is traditionally a very challenging task, the iPhone's launch was considerably facilitated by a sizeable market ready to explore and maximize the product's utility.

Podcasts, movies, and videos could be delivered through the same interface and management layer as was used for music. Porting iTunes to Windows shortly after introduction overcame some of Apple's historically limited market share by acknowledging the dominant platform. Finally, the iPod shortly became a platform in and of itself as newer models maintained compatibility with older ones. Each one of these management decisions served to increase both the addressable market and the value a given customer could choose to purchase.

Contrary to other suppliers like Diamond Multimedia, Apple could reach out globally using its existing sales channels. Additionally Apple distributed its products via big retail chains. Apple also increased the share of wallet at its customers selling not just a music player or a phone, but music and other content, games, and other applications.

INNOVATION AND PERSONALIZATION TRUMP COMMODITIZATION Following the success of the iPod, numerous competitors introduced devices with better specifications and generally lower prices. None have gained a foothold as Apple continued to innovate on the basic product, with new capabilities, colors, shapes, and capacities. None of the competitors' music management applications has dented iTunes, proving that in some product categories, effective design and a strong brand can help sustain premium pricing.

Enabling customers to gain access to a vast selection of songs gave Apple the power of the so-called "long tail" of Internet content: while a small number of hits attract very large audiences, an effectively infinite number of obscure tracks are available for audiences of any conceivable niche taste.[26] With thousands of songs on any given device, the odds of any two iPods being identically used are nearly zero.

Thus each iPod is by definition personalized: not only are person A's playlists different from person B's, the metadata regarding last played, most popular, and other aspects of a given file will be unique as well. Finally, Apple has managed the supply chain well enough to allow personalized engraving on the back of many iPods, enhancing their attractiveness as gifts.

SILENT COMMERCE iPods and iPhones are manufactured in China, available via multiple retail channels, and can be custom-engraved at the factory. The integration of the products with value-added services is nearly seamless, allowing the devices to continue to address customer needs as those needs change: the product capability has expanded from music to podcasts to videos to software applications and data services all on the same billing and fulfillment platform.

The best supply chain is no supply chain. Comparing Apple's available music downloads to any physical store highlights the difference: zero physical inventory means no stock-outs, no excess stock to sell at a loss, no merchandise damaged in transit, no product returns, and no delay in meeting customer demand.

In the physical manufacture of iPods, the company is equally astute. Apple has managed its suppliers expertly, negotiating not only the rights to an extensive music catalog but locking up a large percentage of the market for various components: in mid-2005 Apple reportedly bought 40 percent of Samsung's total output of flash memory, which both cut supply and raised prices for competitors.[27] That deal later came under investigation, so

Apple prepaid $1.25 billion for future purchases of flash memory from five suppliers in late 2005.

Such long-term planning translates into lower component prices and therefore higher margins at the same time that it avoids product shortages. Product launches are typically handled extremely smoothly, with few stock-outs and little excess inventory of previous models to be sold at discount.

STRATEGY-COMPLIANT MANAGEMENT   The Harvard professor Michael Porter has long contended that the essence of strategy lies in a unique combination of activities that create a differentiated value proposition.[28] Apple's experience shows the truth of this assertion: the market contains competing devices, most with lower prices; competing music services; and competing music management software applications. But nowhere can customers obtain a smoother integration of device, user interaction, and a wide selection of easily navigable content.

As good as the products are, the management of the iPod and later iPhone franchises may be more impressive still. For over eight years, no product release has failed to meet expectations. Products have launched in timely fashion, quality issues have been minimal, and the consistency of branding from billboards to television commercials to product packaging to the products themselves has been exemplary. Thus every functional area at Apple from R&D to manufacturing to marketing to supply chain has played a role, and played it at a sustained, high level of execution.

In addition to its own significant margin and revenue contributions, the iPod has served as a "halo" product and served to reinvigorate the company's desktop and particularly laptop franchises. Computer sales for fiscal 2007 surpassed $10 billion, a 40 percent increase over the previous year, or roughly three times the sectoral growth of 14 percent.[29] Such performance makes Apple a rare beneficiary of the often-promised "synergy" that so often fails to emerge from corporate strategy.

VALUE CHAIN REDESIGN   As of the mid-1990s, music was sold on physical media in music stores and big-box retailers and played back on consumer electronics consisting of a compact disc player, amplifier or receiver, and loudspeakers. Radio served as a means by which listeners could discover new music, which was bought at physical retail outlets on physical media.

Less than 15 years later, that model has been transformed. Music is moved over the Internet, stored on hard drives, and played back either through headphones, computers, or MP3 player peripherals. Bands are discovered by search or word of mouth. Virtual inventory and broadband distribution make iTunes' "logistics" more efficient than any supply chain.

Apple has been central to this redesign, whether in its assembling of the iPod design and engineering team, its management of offshore third-party manufacturing, its ecosystem of contributors such as the Grace-note system that automatically fetches CD song track data upon loading, or its negotiation of contracts with music labels. Podcasts have reshaped broadcast radio, the iPod has contributed to the slow adoption of satellite radio, and the iTunes music store has helped displace music retailers. At the same time, Apple's high-profile stores and online presence have altered existing models of electronics retailing.

Most recently, the App Store has reinvented the role of third party soft-ware developers in the wireless industry, forcing the likes of RIM, Microsoft, and Nokia to scramble in response. For music, television shows, games, and other forms of content as well as for entire categories of devices, Apple has forced fundamental change on several industry sectors.

IT'S ROLE IN BUSINESS MODEL TRANSFORMATION   Perhaps the highest tribute to Apple's IT organization is that it is invisible. Unlike Airbus, whose A380 super-jumbo jet was delayed by incompatible CAD data, Apple shares elec-tronic design documents effectively and securely across numerous partners. The iTunes music store runs reliably, never having logged a major outage. Billions of micropayments are handled at a scale unmatched anywhere else on line via an enterprise resource planning (ERP) backbone, and the mul-titude of transactions are handled seamlessly from an audit and accounting perspective. The high-profile commerce site has never been hacked at scale or suffered a data breach of any magnitude. Logistics and procurement are executed at a high level, contributing directly to brand reputation, sustained margins, and enterprise value.

Considering how many of Apple's peers have suffered one or more of these types of mishaps, the company's performance should in part be credited to its robust IT processes and infrastructure.

Realizing the Information Vision: The Technology Dimension

Enterprise value depends in large measure on how quickly a company iden-tifies and realizes a superior business model's four elements. To reiterate, these are:

1. The customer value proposition
2. The profit formula
3. The key resources
4. The key processes

This list begs the question of what has prevented companies realizing "more intelligent" business concepts in the past and what leads us to expect they will achieve them in coming years.

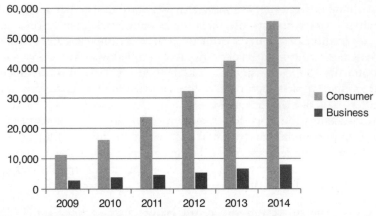

Note: The unit of measurement is petabytes per month

EXHIBIT 1.7   The IP Traffic Projection for 2009–2014 Is One of Many Indicators of Growing Information Overload

Source: Cisco.

Barriers

People's skills and attitudes, regulatory constraints, managerial skills, and not least the complexity of the organization usually present the highest barriers. Amid the many well-known management strategies, very few prescriptions address exactly how to surmount these obstacles. This section deals only with those barriers in the information and technology domains where we expect a progress to come from technological developments.

- *Information overload.* Data is accumulating at many points in an organization: enterprise databases, documents in office software, datasets for technical design and realization, data from intelligent devices, floods of e-mails, voice mails, and management broadcasts in multiple forms. In particular, Internet access to almost any information outside of the company has caused an information overload (see Exhibit 1.7)[30] that has already been described in detail and lamented in many places.[31] As organizations grow in size and complexity, managers find themselves spending more and more of their limited time coordinating activities in discussions and meetings.

   Recently, there have been a growing number of reports about organizations at risk of choking on their communication and information overload. The symptoms include missed opportunities and risks, misjudged priorities, inflexibility, long working hours, and employee burnout.[32] One major company in the consumer goods industry saw its volume of data increase more than seven-fold in five years, from 34 terabytes to 250 terabytes. Let us put this in context: To digitize all the books in the U.S. Library of Congress in text format without graphics, it is generally accepted that around 20 terabytes of storage would be required.[33]

- *Information deficiency.* The fact that people are simultaneously crying out for more information in the midst of such reported overload almost sounds absurd. But it is true that many processes could be accelerated and countless inefficiencies avoided (relating to inventory levels or targeting the wrong customers, for instance) if capturing data were not so expensive, if companies could access all data recorded somewhere electronically already, and if the significance of existing data were clear to all involved.

The final three barriers share a common thread, in that they all contribute to unmanageable system complexity:

- *Stand-alone systems.* Islands create integration gaps—situations in which *people* form the interface between IT applications, say by entering an email into the order entry system or by copying product information from an article database to a product catalog. Integration gaps slow down the flow of information, render processes more prone to error, and increase the complexity of procedures because people have to make inquiries and resolve problems.

  The CEOs we surveyed saw harmonizing stand-alone systems as the most urgent task of the coming years; "silos" still impede the creation of a uniform business process platform. Best-of-breed approaches, where companies take the best solutions from different vendors' software packages, entail persistently high outlay for machine interfaces and integration gaps, which is why many organizations look for flexible application architectures wherever possible (see Chapter 8). Many new business concepts start with integrating processes and applications or enabling cooperation between them. Their goal is seamless, real-time processes without borders.

- *Inadequate networkability.* This term refers to the ability of any number (m) of suppliers to speak the "same language" with any number (n) of customers at the interfaces between processes and systems. Heterogeneous worlds have particularly serious implications when enterprises start to collaborate electronically. For instance, an automotive supplier has to adapt to the development and production practices of the individual vehicle manufacturers, mastering multiple collaborative processes and different IT applications: many inter-organizational interfaces are one-off efforts, unique 1:1 mappings. But different manufacturers demand different collaborative development processes, to which serial 1:1 efforts do not scale. Inadequate m:n capabilities loom as the biggest hurdle on the way to more efficient inter-enterprise processes, and to date IT is only of limited use in addressing the issue.

- *Insufficient flexibility.* Many companies complain of losing flexibility. Process and office software can present barriers, for example, if customer data cannot be changed in different IT applications in parallel without becoming inconsistent. If the outlay required to standardize article data stands in the way of an enterprise-wide product catalog, potentially artificial budget priorities may impede the pursuit of agility.

Enablers

A small number of basic information technologies (including ERP and the Internet) have enabled the level of information intensiveness we know today along with the associated economic changes. Joining these are a few technologies (like social software and content management) currently migrating into enterprise adoption, while another group of new technologies (such as the "Internet of things" made possible by cheap sensors, or new forms on information display) is about to be realized on a broad scale.

"What is the next big thing?" The answer to this question is clearly expected to be a new information technology that will revolutionize the world. But rather than look for a single breakthrough, we believe it is the integration of these technologies that is likely to provide the main impulse for business model change, as demonstrated by the business concepts described in the next chapters of this book. Enterprise IT is getting closer to the Apple model: technology should "just work" and be transparent to the user, who is trying to solve a business problem rather than learn to use a complex system.

SECOND GENERATION SOA   Starting in 2002 or so, vendors invested heavily in the development of service-oriented architectures (SOA). This effort involved systematic approaches to standards-based interfaces across operating environments, applications, and data in both technology organizations and business processes. The ideal of SOA was simultaneously to deliver the cost and efficiency benefits of standardization and to support the need for flexibility required by local change and rapid adaptation. Interoperable, reusable services would be made available to support agile development of new capability, all the while enforcing management mandates including security, performance, and cost of ownership.

While much progress was made in realizing the potential of SOA, it was often regarded with disappointment.[34] In common with all other technology innovations, SOA did not provide a "silver bullet," solving challenges of cost, performance, flexibility, and robustness. As the name suggests, an "orientation" required many changes to mindsets, budgeting, expectation management, and other behaviors in and across enterprises. Few products could deliver the promised benefits without the more subtle and difficult changes to code-writing, data-handling, and business processes: no enterprise has ever purchased a realized architecture, much less an orientation.

In the credit and jobs crisis following 2008, IT budgets were cut dramatically, customer expectations changed (sometimes overnight), and corporate priorities were focused on essential matters of economic survival. In this environment, many facets of SOA proved their worth: sound data structures, well-designed code, and flexible architectures paid off in M&A spinouts or combinations, budget discipline, and competitive nimbleness. New technologies, including software as a service, mashups, and cloud computing, built on many SOA premises. As the economy improves, the lessons will persist, and what might be called "deployed SOA," often in the form of services-based business suites, will continue to deliver competitive and operational benefits.

MOBILITY The ability to capture and process data where it originates or is used would radically change many processes. The price/performance ratio of technology for mobile communications, or "mobility" for short, is improving at a rapid pace, and contributing to national economic competitiveness across the globe (see Exhibit 1.8). The Apple iPhone, RIM BlackBerry, and several Nokia devices currently lead a pack of highly capable handheld mobile computing platforms, but in addition to smartphones, netbook PCs represent another fast-growing market segment poised to drive, and capitalize on, mobility.

SENSORS, NETWORKS, AND "THE INTERNET OF THINGS" Distributed systems can perform many tasks, mimicking an animal in their collective capability. Inexpensive sensors (analogous to eyes or ears) can measure temperature, noise, vibration, dampness, geographic position, color, odor, pressure, weight, and radiation. Data about events in the physical world can now be recorded in a form that is more detailed, timely, reliable, and economical than ever before; processing at the edge of the network (like a spine or brain) can often perform basic association and sense-making at the point of collection. Actuators (electronic nerves) can implement automatic decisions without delay and without human intervention, for instance to preempt traffic lights or to control heating or brake systems. Networks (the system's voice) can tell other entities what is happening or what to do.

Connected sensors and processors are rapidly increasing the functions of technical devices, most notably in cars, but also in measuring devices, lamps, sneakers, and medical apparatus. While most of the technology

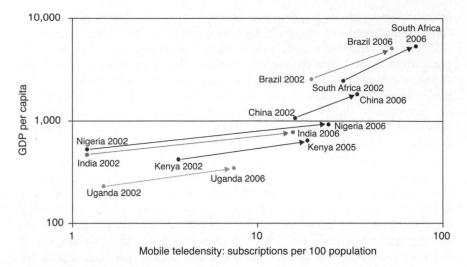

EXHIBIT 1.8 Increases in Mobile Phone Adoption Often Coincide with Increases in Economic Well-being in Developing Nations, Accelerating the Trend toward a "Flatter" World

Source: United Nations Millennium Development Goals Indicators, http://unstats.un. org/unsd/mdg/Default.aspx.

for embedded systems (sometimes called ubiquitous computing) is already available today, it is still too expensive for many applications. Miniaturization, standardization, changes in basic technology, and above all, the large quantities produced (at some point sensors will be made by the billion) will make an almost infinite range of applications profitable in the coming years. At the same time, considerable work remains to be done at the level of standards and applications to make all these billions of devices work properly and work together.

CLOUD COMPUTING The combination of cost and environmental concerns related to low server utilization in data centers, better network infrastructure, and economies of scale in the management of very large data centers is leading to greater interest in offsite computing resources, provided by the likes of Amazon, Google, IBM, and Microsoft. Rather than invest in the capital required for a server cluster or data center, small and medium enterprises in particular may find it more economical, with lower investment risk, to pay for computing commodity cycles with operational budgets. Large companies, on the other hand, may realize many of the same benefits with well-managed data center consolidations that might result in so-called "private clouds."

A simple definition has been offered that states "Cloud computing is on-demand access to virtualized IT resources that are housed outside of your own data center, shared by others, simple to use, paid for via subscription, and accessed over the Web."[35] As this definition is refined, businesses of every size will find benefits in increasing efficiency, lowering cost, and reducing environmental impact by utilizing various styles of cloud computing, whether in software as a service, hardware virtualization, or third-party provision of commodity computing cycles.

KNOWLEDGE MANAGEMENT, INCLUDING WEB 2.0 Data warehouses, content management solutions, search engines, and applications for teamwork are gradually beginning to meet at least some of the high expectations regarding the way existing knowledge is used and how the information overload is managed. The field of analytics and visualization is advancing in particularly promising directions: such technologies as exploratory search, 3-D, and animation make large volumes of data more easily accessible and consumable.

In addition, so-called "enterprise 2.0" solutions exploit the same power of crowds that has proven itself in Wikipedia, delicious, YouTube, and Flickr.[36] Information markets, corporate social networks, automated document discovery, touch and gesture interfaces, and other tools are reinventing enterprise knowledge management.

NEW APPLICATION AREAS The primary use of the new technologies mentioned earlier is not in business processes, but in products and services for the intelligent home, entertainment (from TV to games), health care, retired people, traffic management, vehicles, and location-based services. Many companies are finding new business areas for these IT applications. As more and more enterprises begin to use the new IT applications in their processes, there will be a greater need for integration and networking capabilities.

Checklist

- [ ] Who in your sector exploits the potential of IT most consistently to enhance its business?
- [ ] When did you last check whether new IT developments would enable you to revamp your business model?
- [ ] Do you offer the right products and services for the value chains with the most potential?
- [ ] Which three value chains will determine your business five years from now? Is your enterprise positioned in the right value chains?
- [ ] Do you have globally standardized business processes?

☐ Do you know the profit margin generated by your key customers?

☐ Can you get all the information about a customer and your activities with them—globally, up to date, and in real time?

☐ Do you know which customers you are about to lose and why?

☐ Do you recognize changed market conditions faster than your main competitor? How quickly can you respond to your competitors' marketing campaigns?

☐ How long does your company need to get a product off the drawing board and onto the shelves? What is the quickest you could manage?

☐ How long does your organization need to integrate a unit it has taken over?

☐ How mature is your information architecture compared to your toughest competitor's?

☐ How many processes and systems do you use for processing orders?

☐ What are the critical success factors for your business? Which key figures do you use to assess your achievement of objectives?

☐ Are your managers aware of innovative business concepts in their sectors?

☐ Does IT drive sufficient innovation in your business?

☐ Who is responsible for the quality of the three most important business processes?

☐ Is your company aware of its IT-related duties?

☐ Do you, as a manager, deal with the right IT issues?

CHAPTER 2

Customer Value from the Customer Process

Management Summary

Nearly every transaction begins with a customer's perception of a problem or challenge. Accordingly, customers assess a provider's market offer on the basis of how usefully it helps address that need. In many cases, they expect suppliers to offer a comprehensive range of products and services covering all relevant facets of their process; in many sectors, customers are finding total solution offers more compelling than straightforward products. Customers can and often do expect the products and services to be personalized and available 24/7, immediately, in any place, and through any channel. In short, customers ask for more every year:

- Everything (comprehensive selection)
- Everywhere (any part of the enterprise, any geography)
- Anytime (on short notice, on holidays, in any time zone)
- One Stop (comprehensive coverage; vendor manages partner network transparently)
- Segment of One (customization of products as well as terms and mode of delivery)
- One Face to the Customer ("one throat to choke": accept full responsibility for the outcomes provided by an ecosystem of suppliers and partners)
- Anyhow ("find a way": no such thing as one standard model of interaction in a global, creative business landscape)

These tendencies are emerging in both commercial and consumer markets. Consider the parental process of organizing a birthday party. As Jim Gilmore and Joe Pine noted in their book *The Experience Economy*, as of

1960, a mother could buy eggs, cocoa, milk, butter, and flour to bake a cake for roughly 30 cents or thereabouts. The grocery store's margins were low on commodity items. Shortly thereafter, Procter & Gamble (Duncan Hines) and General Mills (Betty Crocker) pre-packaged the dry ingredients into boxes and the frosting into cans. The cost was now measured in dollars rather than dimes, margins rose, and the home baker both saved time and required less skill.

While stand-alone bakeries were an option as cake suppliers, the cost was often prohibitive. In the 1970s, however, grocery stores began integrating in-store bakeries that used pre-mixed ingredients, commercial ovens, and other tools that allowed them to deliver birthday cakes at competitive prices. The price had risen to perhaps triple that of the Betty Crocker/ Duncan Hines solution, and margins rose again. Parents' willingness to pay rose as well, in part because the continuing rise of the two-income household had the dual effect of increasing disposable income and making time scarcer.

By the 1980s, a new birthday solution was emerging, as Nolan Bushnell (the founder of the pioneering Atari video game firm) rolled out Chuck E. Cheese restaurant franchises. These venues competed not on the quality of their food, but on the comprehensiveness of their party orchestration: pizza, balloons, cake, cartoons, game arcades, and entertaining costumed waiters came as a package deal. The price now ran into dozens or hundreds of dollars, a far cry from the 30 cents for raw ingredients.

Other businesses sought to compete, and by 2000 the time-challenged parent could outsource an entire birthday experience to an ecosystem of bounce-castle rental yards, hotel swimming pools, magicians, skating rinks, pony ride vendors, piñata fabricators, caricaturists, laser tag/climbing wall venues, minor league baseball games, movie theaters, and themed restaurants such as Rainforest Cafe as well as McDonald's. Birthday parties had emerged as an industry subsegment.

Several points are relevant for our purposes here. First, business models often co-evolve with demographics and economics. Second, combining component products (commonly known as *kitting*), then combining product and service, can be seen as steps toward a more comprehensive offer, which Gilmore and Pine call an *experience*. It frequently combines logistics, food, emotion, theatrics, group dynamics, and other nonrational elements. Not surprisingly, such companies as Harrah's casinos, Disney, Apple, Cabelas, and Carnival Cruise Lines have achieved success delivering on the experience formula: each takes a customer process and orchestrates multiple elements into a coherent, engaging solution.[1]

Meeting the demands of addressing a customer's processes presents suppliers with a series of formidable challenges: negotiation, investment,

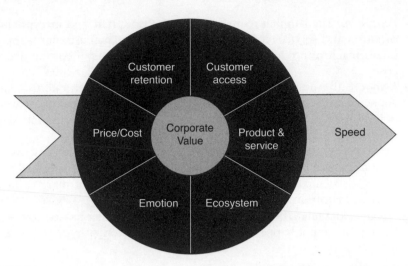

EXHIBIT 2.1 Addressing a Customer's Process Involves Multiple Perspectives on Product and Service Delivery

skills and staffing, execution, profitability, and sustainability (in both the business and environmental senses). The answers lie in networks: very few companies can go it alone any more. In this way, specialization and diversification can sit side by side in a customer process, provided that the supplier focuses its own services on one aspect of the customer process and looks to the ecosystem to provide additional services.

Delivering value within the customer process tests every facet of a company's business model, as Exhibit 2.1 shows:

- *Product and service.* For the customer, support for its process means less complexity because he or she can hand over tasks such as the coordination of suppliers. For the supplier, this expectation represents both an opportunity to generate additional revenues, and an additional risk factor, as more things can go wrong.
- *Customer access.* For some categories of goods, the more customers buying from the same supplier, the more secure the customer's investment, as so-called network externalities emerge: more spare parts depots, compatible aftermarket accessories, and shorter learning curves are three examples among many.
- *Customer retention.* The more comprehensively the supplier serves the customer, the more closely they can collaborate; switching costs increase on both sides of the transaction. The customer can reduce complexity; the supplier can retain customers better.

- *Ecosystem.* The supplier focuses on what it does best and incorporates products and services it lacks into its offerings. The customer wants a broad reach of products and services as well as simplified transaction costs.
- *Emotion.* Business customers and consumers alike often rate the convenience of a business relationship above the price. Customers want brands, reliability, and the comfort of knowing their needs are met with a high level of fit.
- *Price/cost.* When suppliers reliably address customers' process needs, customers gain better control of their life-cycle costs. The supplier generates a sustainable flow of revenues and higher profit margins from services than from products.[2]
- *Speed.* Cooperation between the customer and supplier has to grow step by step. It cannot happen with a big bang, as Internet hype suggested.

Depending on the product and market, a deciding factor in the customer process can be emotion (for instance, when choosing a bank account), quality (when buying a video camera), or price (when choosing a gas station). But if we look closely, we see that the buyer's decision is influenced by all three factors in all three cases, for instance, the bank charges, the camera's brand, or the convenient location of the gas station.

> At the end of the day, it is not abstract, economically rational firms that decide on an order, but human beings with all their imperfect information, individual emotions, limited working time, energy, and taste for risk.

Vision

In certain key markets, an enterprise cannot merely supply products; it must solve customers' problems. Its people know the company's customers and their needs well. It looks to the customer's process—to the tasks the customer has to complete—to determine which products and services are needed. It delivers process-specific services (such as text messages in the case of delayed shipments) and coordinates the problem-solving process using information technology (say, to make complex payment arrangements). Integration with customer processes results in customer retention and provides new knowledge about customer needs and capabilities, driving a feedback loop of innovation and satisfaction.

From Product to Solution Provider

Three companies in widely varied industries each have moved from supplying manufactured products or commodity services to become more comprehensive solution providers. Each of these examples illustrates both the potential for fuller coverage of the value chain and the execution challenges that accompany such a transition.

ABB Turbo Systems

ABB Turbo Systems Ltd., part of the ABB Group, is the global market leader for turbo-charging diesel and gas engines in the over-500 kW power range. Over 180,000 ABB turbochargers are used worldwide on ships (representing 62 percent market share), in power stations, on locomotives, and on heavy-duty vehicles in the construction and mining industries. The company generates about half of its revenues from selling and servicing turbochargers. Although the products have a service life of up to 20 years, they also contain parts that are subject to wear and tear and that have to be replaced on a regular basis.

Some customers requiring service tasks are shipping companies. Since these companies want to spend as little time servicing turbochargers as possible, ABB Turbo Systems has over 100 service stations worldwide to take care of the maintenance process for the ship owners. If its turbocharger fails, the diesel engine on a ship can generate just 25 percent of its usual power. Most ship owners base their selection of a turbocharger supplier partly on the available servicing options. ABB Turbo Systems' global network of service stations, with access to the same product and customer data in Switzerland, guarantees a service within 48 hours, regardless of location.

The head office of ABB Turbo Systems looks upon the service stations that control the "turbocharger service" process as the actual "customers." ABB Turbo Systems provides support to the service stations via a service portal. ATURB@WEB stores the configuration of the different turbochargers in a database and triggers the maintenance process on the basis of defined service cycles. For this, service stations use a tool called the "Maintenance Scheduler." It summarizes the maintenance data so that sales and service staff can alert customers to convenient maintenance times, or, if maintenance periods have elapsed, approach customers to discuss servicing issues.

If a turbocharger develops problems or if the company knows that a ship is going to call at a port with a service station, the ATURB@WEB service portal provides the service employee with the ship's turbocharger configuration, including any modifications from previous service visits and helps them with the selection of spare parts. Finally, the employee can use ATURB@WEB to check the availability and storage location of parts and create the actual order. In addition, the portal provides service technicians with technical drawings and assembly instructions, helps them document any work that has been carried out, initiates the invoicing process, and enables communication between the service stations.

ABB Turbo Systems does not rely solely on the information it gathers in house—turbocharger configurations, assembly instructions, customer histories—but also incorporates external services, such as an insurance database from Lloyd's ship insurers, which uniquely identifies every ship by its policy number even if its name changes. Since Lloyd's insures almost every commercial ship, every account manager at ABB Turbo Systems receives an indication of how many ships have been fitted with ABB turbochargers by the ship owners they advise.

Until the 1990s, mainframe computer technology and transmission costs prevented the development of a solution with such capabilities. It was not until the arrival of the Internet that the services described here became economical in all the service stations worldwide, whether in Hamburg, Singapore, or Vladivostok.

ABB Turbo Systems has a highly integrated and efficient maintenance process. The company can now handle 50 percent more service requests with the same workforce. Throughout the various approval stages, the lead time of an order—from receiving it to completing it in the central spare parts warehouse—is reduced from 24 hours to 2 hours. At the same time, the new solution has cut stocks by 12 percent, enabling the company to save roughly US$1 million annually in interest charges. The configuration data and transparency within the warehouse allow ABB Turbo Systems to process service jobs quickly and reliably, despite lower stocks of spare parts.

Another shipping company in a different part of the world blends products and services in a completely different way.

COSCO

With $17 billion in revenues, the China Ocean Shipping Company Group (COSCO) ranks as the largest shipping company in China. A conglomerate consisting of more than 1,000 enterprises, its businesses include international shipping of both passengers and freight, comprehensive and integrated logistics services, and ship building and repairing. COSCO Group is ranked second in the world based on fleet size and shipping capacity.[3] Since 1998, the group has been led by Capt. Wei Jiafu, a strong and visible leader with a doctorate in marine engineering who prefers and retains the nautical designation from his career at the helm.

Also in 1998, COSCO made a strategic decision to expand from simple cargo capacity in its freight business into logistics services such as container terminals, warehousing, and freight forwarding. The move into such services ancillary to shipping exposed the need for increased integration of information handling processes, especially as the Group built an ecosystem of global partners, some of them highly specialized.

A year after COSCO expanded its scope of operations and altered its business model from owning to controlling shipping capacity, the firm began building a digital backbone, called IRIS-2 (short for "Integrated Regional Information System"), which enables COSCO to better support customer processes with timely information. This system makes operational processes, transportation information, and customer information internally and consistently visible. At the same time, the IRIS-II transaction engine underlies Web-based customer-facing applications, such as automated rate estimation tools.

Customer-facing systems and internal customer service systems based on IRIS-2 have helped COSCO build its brand reputation as it has won trade and other awards for best shipping line, best customer service, and best schedule reliability. Real-time container tracking, for example, represents a substantial improvement over manual process that could take days. The firm's Container Management System has been repeatedly upgraded to support a full range of customer needs ranging from finance to customer service to logistics to regulatory compliance.

In addition to transaction processing, COSCO built analytical capabilities with a data warehouse initiative to support better decision-making. Six facets are supported:

1. Headquarters requirements (corporate and departmental evaluations)
2. Regional Branch requirements (overseas locations)
3. Port Offices requirements (including container-related metrics and documentation compliance)
4. Key Performance Indicators (including process specification relative to customer data and fleet and facilities capacity)
5. e-Business (customer history, quantity, and value by channel)
6. Other requirements (such as standardized report templates)[4]

As COSCO looks ahead to still broader integration of logistics services, including air and land capabilities, effective IT systems have increased its competitive advantages over foreign competitors. COSCO Group currently has representative offices or subsidiaries in many parts of China and 38 countries. Its global operational network extends from Beijing to its agents and partners in 1,500 ports in 160 countries.

Hilti

Hilti manufactures measuring systems, drills, and other tools for professional contractors. From its headquarters in Liechtenstein, the company addresses markets all over the world. It recently has reinvented its business model: instead of only selling tools, it can also provide tool fleets as a service, paid for in monthly fees rather than large capital expenditures. The service comprises six elements:

1. *Financing.* Low monthly payments free up working capital.
2. *Repair.* Tools are maintained to a high standard at no additional charge, including batteries for cordless tools.
3. *Loaner tools.* When a tool fails and is being repaired, Hilti provides a replacement to maintain the contractor's productivity.
4. *Exchange.* Tool fleets are monitored and refreshed as necessary.
5. *Labeling.* Each tool bears a customized label with the contractor's name and logo. Theft is reduced and customers are assured as to the identity of the individual performing the work.
6. *Insurance.* If tools are stolen, financial liability is limited as tools are quickly replaced.

The offering grew from Hilti's direct sales approach: customers made it clear that managing capital infrastructure was not their core competency. At Hilti, the model forces alignment of every function from R&D to logistics to finance to sales and service. Product quality, pricing, and customer responsiveness all have to contribute to the contractor's total experience. An Internet portal unifies all facets of the leasing experience in one place, saving time for the customer.

By so attentively addressing customers' processes, Hilti's tool fleet management consistently scores higher in satisfaction surveys than the standalone product line (see Exhibit 2.2).

Process Focus: Waste Disposal and Management

A number of new business models are emerging in the area of waste disposal, many related to compelling examples of a supplier taking control of a complex customer process. Deriving treasure from trash appears to be a growth industry for the foreseeable future: Nickolas Themelis of Columbia University projects worldwide waste to double in the next 20 years.[5] Both emerging markets, experiencing rapid growth in consumer spending, and developed countries, which are mandating higher-margin, more complex waste treatments, are contributing to the industry's growth.

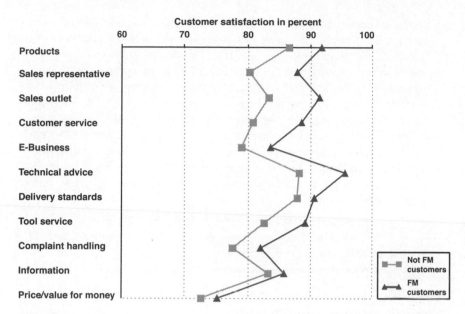

EXHIBIT 2.2 Hilti's Tool Fleet Management Customers Consistently Exhibit Higher Satisfaction

Source: Hilti.

Specialist firms are appearing, but the sector is also home to giant companies such as Suez and Veolia, the latter of which employs roughly 320,000 people. In addition, carbon-footprint and other goals often drive heavy taxation on waste and CO_2, so the core technologies of the industry are being reexamined in a wave of R&D spending. Three brief examples suggest the potential scope and size of the opportunity:

1. If narcotics are out of date or must for other reasons be destroyed, detailed procedures must be followed to comply with law enforcement and environmental regulations: the owner of the drugs is supposed to witness their destruction, for instance, and prevent leakage into either criminal channels or watersheds. Vendors such as Clean Harbors Environmental Services will assume responsibility for the entire process, including complete documentation.
2. Before the economic slowdown dropped demand for cardboard in China, recyclers of office paper had an attractive business model for helping customers save space and comply with document-retention regulations: They would get paid for shredding a customer's documents, then sell the scrap paper for export in largely empty shipping containers returning to China.

3. Municipalities that operate waste disposal and water treatment facilities must meet ever-changing regulatory requirements at the same time that volumes are increasing and funding is under pressure. Vendors such as Veolia Environmental Services can offer a broad range of services including curbside trash pickup, biomass recovery, electronic waste separation, commodity recycling, waste-to-heat conversion, and water treatment facility sludge disposal. The knowledge advantage is substantial, given Veolia Environmental's global scale as opposed to each town having to learn everything on its own. Veolia developed detailed knowledge of the customer processes in waste disposal. In addition, the company's reach allows waste to be understood as a system rather than as isolated tasks.

> The more complex a customer's process for which a vendor assumes responsibility, the higher the margins.

Concepts of the Customer Process

In recent years, scholars around the world have compiled numerous case studies that confirm the increasing tendency among businesses to focus on the customer process. Many enterprises see it as a way of reducing their own process costs, supplementing product revenues with service revenues, and boosting customer retention through better services.[6] Many enterprises are trying to position themselves as system suppliers or solution providers for a specific customer process.

A system provider supplies customers with entire systems such as fuel delivery systems or car interiors instead of individual components (gas tanks or dashboards) and thus relieves the customer of the subprocess of integrating components during both the design and production phases. In the financial services industry, individual products such as pension insurance, stock portfolios, and savings accounts are being replaced by integrated retirement provisions. Addressing the customer process thus spans multiple product life cycles, product and service integration points, and revenue streams (operating expenses and capital investment).

Addressing customer processes, while delivering value to both sides of the interaction, demands flexibility, excellence in execution, astute financial and HR management, and negotiation skills. Attempting to combine products and services, coordinate ecosystem partners, and achieve everything else required, particularly in unstable economic times, constitutes a "stress test" of an organization's capabilities. Many have stumbled; some have failed.

Everything

Many of today's customers are looking for integrated solutions that combine products and services. The companies aiming to meet this demand need to answer the following questions:

- Which customers have similar processes (perhaps requiring new dimensions of customer segmentation)? Do newspaper printers' requirements differ from those of book printers?
- What does the customer process entail? Which tasks does it involve? Which of these could we do better than the customer? Codesign, outsourcing, embedding, and other options may need to be explored.
- Which third-party products and services can we integrate? It is often better for the customer if one vendor takes over the role of system supplier or prime contractor so that the customer does not have to coordinate multiple suppliers.

Integrated solutions are more than the total of their individual elements. They can help customers to reduce complexity or may provide convenience.

Integrated services are at least as important for consumers as they are for business customers. The consumer usually wants to deal with just one bank and expects the bank to provide a full range of services, from managing a current account through trading securities and supplying a tax report for all financial income. As we have seen at Citibank and elsewhere, however, such integration can be difficult to bring to fruition.

"Everything" can also be assumed to equate to broad selection in consumer markets. When looking at some leaders in online commerce, despite many other differences, Amazon, Apple's iTunes and App stores, eBay, and Netflix share a focus on extreme selection.

> A company that makes life easier for its customers retains them.

Everywhere

Customers can receive a product or service wherever they may be completing their process (for instance, buying a book can now be achieved via electronic download). The Internet, GPS, and mobile technology transport the requisite information. Navigation can be a component of business process in industries ranging from public safety to logistics to travel and tourism.

For a long time, the "telephony" service was limited to the telephones in the fixed network. Today, cell phone users expect a full range of communications and information services anywhere in the world, from telephony to messaging, gaming, and Internet access. They are not interested in the integration aspects such as network access or interchange formats that the service provider has to deal with. Frequent travelers, for example, will switch providers if they can access services from more locations by doing so.

Global companies are often expert at arbitraging currencies, labor rates, and other variables such as weather. Accordingly, suppliers to such firms must be nimble, able to shift supply, expertise, and financial tools across geographies at short notice.

> A company must provide its services wherever the customer needs them.

Anytime

Long gone are the times when customers would stand in line to collect cash from the bank between 9 A.M. and 4 P.M., Monday to Friday. Efficiency, convenience, and above all, different time zones demand services such as payment transactions, travel reservations, and refueling at gasoline pumps to be available around the clock. In addition, information must always be current: "anytime" implies "real-time."

Effective IT systems can make fully electronic, cost-effective services available 24/7. When services are to be provided for business customers in the same time zone, it is often sufficient for them to be available during normal business hours. As companies grow accustomed to the 24-hour work day, such practices as overnight batch-mode processing grow less and less feasible.

> Customers must always be able to contact a company whenever they need products and services.

One Stop

Customers expect more and more solutions instantly and without interruption so that once they have started booking a trip or a repair service, for instance, they can finish the job immediately. The fewer people involved in a solution and the more services available electronically, the fewer delays can be expected.

For example, the travel agent business model has undergone considerable change in the past 15 years. Formerly, an employee of the travel agency might be co-located in a customer location to handle the printing of tickets on site; otherwise, large call centers were common. With the Internet, self-service, and e-ticketing, the overhead costs of the previous model became untenable. Corporate travel providers had to evolve or be acquired, as was the case with Rosenbluth.

Now, such providers as American Express or Carlson Wagonlit not only book travel, they can manage the entire set of customer processes associated with travel. In doing so, they answer a broad range of questions, truly taking responsibility for all facets of a customer process:

- Where should we hold our annual sales meeting to minimize days out of the market?
- Is manager Schmidt authorized to book international flights without VP-level approval?
- Is it safe to travel to country X in terms of terror or disease threats?
- Should we renegotiate with our preferred airline and hotel vendors or are the current contracts advantageous?
- What was the Asia–Pacific division's travel spend this year compared to two years ago?
- Vice-president Jones is in country Y with no luggage the day before a major client presentation. Who should she call?
- How can we find hot-air balloon rides for our customer appreciation conference?

IT cuts process times by exchanging information in real time between the parties involved and by automating process steps. One-stop has become a reality because information systems use tools such as workflows to notify and coordinate numerous people efficiently, and to take care of many tasks that previously required time-consuming manual input (such as calculating credit alternatives).

> Companies that make their customers wait lose them.

Segment of One

Ideally, a company would treat each customer as though it were the only one, truly a segment of one. It would understand its customer's needs, problems and processes, background, conditions, deciders and decision-making practices.

IT makes it possible to record, aggregate, and convert knowledge about customers automatically. The computer scans huge amounts of data looking for behavior patterns, business opportunities, and areas in need of action. The Maintenance Scheduler at ABB Turbo Systems, for example, informs the sales team about ship owners whose turbochargers are overdue a service. Like many contemporary plant and machine constructors, ABB Turbo Systems chiefly supplies custom-made turbochargers. One of the company's key strengths is its database containing the configuration data of over 180,000 turbochargers currently in use.

> The customer expects a personalized solution and is often willing to pay extra for it.

One Face to the Customer

The customer expects a supplier to allocate it one contact team for all its concerns. One face to the customer means that the customer always receives the same level of service with complete information across all channels, product groups, and regions. Channels can be stores, the mobile sales force, agents, call centers, and portals. The supplier integrates the organizational units and subcontractors involved so that the customer is unaware of the individual processes.

For this to happen, all information about the customer has to be merged. This is the only way of ensuring that every employee who deals with the customer has comprehensive, up-to-date information about the customer's requirements, the history of the business relationship, and all contact through electronic channels or with different departments in the company.

Canada's ScotiaBank held the unique distinction of that country's lowest expense ratio and highest customer satisfaction among banks. Loans and deposits, credit cards and home mortgages, call centers and branches: all interactions relating to an individual customer were integrated. The company's interactive voice response (IVR) tree was regularly updated to reflect current customer behavior and business conditions, as was Web site navigation. A deposit at an ATM was soon visible via the Internet, and vice versa. ScotiaBank made such reliable, well-designed interactions look simple, though the rest of the industry has yet to catch up, both in Canada and elsewhere.

> The customer wants a supplier who acts as a coherent enterprise.

Anyhow

The customer may have a preferred device or access medium for interacting with the supplier, such as fax, telephone, or portal. "Anyhow" refers to a company's freedom to choose how it communicates with the real world—people, enterprises, machines, and objects. The goal is to realize a customer process in which the customer can concentrate on the job at hand, such as organizing repairs, because machines should take care of the burdensome tasks such as capturing the data, invoicing and coordinating the service providers, in short, the entire administrative side (we call this "silent commerce" in Chapter 5).

Sensors, actuators, intelligent devices, and wireless communication enable such services to be delivered without human input. As components fall in price, many private and commercial customer processes will be fundamentally transformed.

A simple formulation for the customer process might read: "The more automated, the lower the cost on both sides." The less human work is involved, the simpler and more convenient it is for the customer and the lower the communication costs for the supplier. Exhibit 2.3 shows only communication costs; it does not show the value of personal contact with the customer.

Besides the cost aspect, automatic communication has the advantage of being free from the limitations of time and location as well as being fast

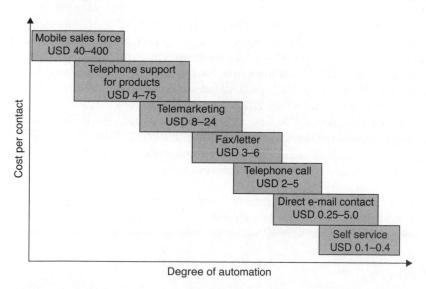

EXHIBIT 2.3 Self-service Makes Possible Unprecedentedly Low Costs for Customer Interaction

and secure. However, it is also true for much communication that machines cannot replace personal contact between the supplier and customer.

Fraport, operator of Frankfurt Airport and other airports, has outsourced the job of servicing the fire shutters to specialized maintenance firms. Until recently, Fraport was struggling to control the expenses associated with this solution and also needed to improve safety. At that point, Fraport wanted a better maintenance process. It fitted all 30,000 fire shutters with short-range RFID chips and equipped the service technicians with mobile measuring devices. The service technicians now have to go within a 10 cm range of the fire shutters to read the shutter number with their mobile device and update the last inspection date. This ensures the technicians actually check the fire shutters close up and also reduces the costs for entering data. After implementing the new procedure, Fraport noticed that it had been receiving invoices for maintenance work on shutters that had not been accessible for years owing to structural changes.

> The customer chooses the most convenient way to communicate with suppliers.

Realizing the Vision

The concept of the customer process is simple. As we have seen from numerous workshops, the most diverse participants are very quick to outline innovative customer processes on paper. So why is it that some companies manage to translate a customer process into success while others draw no competitive advantage? Having a vision of a customer process is the easy part; realizing it is the actual challenge.

Experience teaches us that a company is only as customer-oriented as its CEO. If the CEO does not live out the principles of customer orientation or secure them in strategies and performance measurement, they will only be paid lip service by the rest of the company.

> The business strategy begins with the customer process.

Barriers

The vision of a comprehensive electronic process assistant for customers is still far off—recall that shopping agents were predicted long ago and have yet to materialize at a broad scale. Anyone doubting how rooted we remain in paper processes would do well to attempt to use Internet tools to follow the process of a homeowner building a house. The greatest barriers are:

- *Bad experience.* The euphoria surrounding the Internet did much to discredit the potential of electronic collaboration between businesses. Start-ups with little knowledge of an industry or business frequently marketed solutions without understanding the customers' actual problems. The potential users have already lost so much time and money through the poor quality of most Internet portals that they now shy at any new experience.
- *Inexplicit customer value.* No solution can be successful unless the customer and supplier both have a clear image of its potential value. Many suppliers are not familiar with the customer's real problems, which they could address to win the business. Customers are wary of changing from a known pricing model to an unknown and potentially problematic one.
- *Inadequate networking capabilities on the customer side.* A portal for e-banking can only be successful with customers who have a smart-phone or PC and feel comfortable with IT. Even today, electronic collaboration continues to be limited mainly to large enterprises because only they have sufficient personnel and technology and high quantities of transactions.
- *Customer retention and independence.* The more involved a supplier becomes in its customer's process, the more dependent the customer becomes. The manufacturer of a machine is more likely to get the maintenance prices it wants for its products (say, machine tools) if its products become an essential part of the customer's process. In all cases, suppliers are attempting to retain customers with "worry-free" solutions, while customers are trying to retain their independence in spite of the solution's high value.
- *Insufficient knowledge about the customer and its processes.* Many suppliers have insufficient knowledge about the customer process. The sales team claims to know the customer, yet cannot state the problems facing the customer in its process. In certain industries, it has become standard practice for customers and suppliers to team up to develop new solutions. But most enterprises still find it difficult to sit down with the customer and design products, services, and ultimately, the customer process together. For their part, product-oriented sales forces typically struggle to sell services or solutions.
- *Silo organization.* Often, many companies fail to treat their customers as a whole. For instance, they find it hard to link a delivery to a plant in Lyon with the headquarters in Chicago. This is only partly due to an insufficient IT infrastructure. Unless the CEO promotes an integral view,

the employees are bound to concentrate on their own location, department, or position, regardless of the technical possibilities. Product-oriented sales and service forces frequently lack a broad sense of the customer business apart from the procurement organization.

- *Scaling the solution.* An order-processing solution for Volkswagen and the transmission supplier ZF Friedrichshafen, which has to process hundreds of thousands of orders each year, must be different from an order-processing solution used by Airbus Industries and the turbine supplier Rolls Royce, involving a few hundred custom engines per year.
- *Lack of standards.* The problem with many portals is that the customer has to enter data by hand, say an order, and then type it into or copy it from the in-house system. Having to enter data twice is a sign of insufficient integration resulting from a lack of standardization, since otherwise machine-machine communication could take care of the task. In both online commerce and elsewhere, data quality remains a major stumbling block for both in-company and inter-enterprise commerce.
- *Premature IT.* For many applications, the size, flexibility, robustness, and performance of IT are not yet adequate. Mobile access to portals, for instance, is often still too slow, too unreliable, and too expensive. Again, a lack of standardization forces customers to familiarize themselves with the various user guides and processes used by different suppliers.
- *Long-term payback.* One of the biggest hurdles when realizing solutions for customer processes is probably the fact that there is no inflow of cash in the short term. The managing bodies of every company must ask themselves which of the factors depicted in Exhibit 2.1 justify, or even demand, investment in the customer process.

Enablers

A competitive company is always looking to improve. Where new technological, regulatory, or other enablers are not available to remove inefficiencies, there will be very few starting points for innovation in the customer process. But where new enablers are available, the company's management must understand the impact of the technology well enough to recognize the potential for change.

- *Service-oriented architectures.* Effective support for customer processes usually becomes a possibility only when all the necessary information about articles, customers, orders, and so forth is accessible and connectable. Integration is therefore much more critical to the customer process than flashy Web sites. Many companies have already laid the foundations for customer-process solutions with their ERP systems, but SOA allows more process flexibility while preserving the cost efficiencies from ERP implementation. Also in contrast to the enterprise focus of ERP, SOA allows organizations to compose applications from diverse services originating both inside and outside the enterprise.

The customer need not sense the blend of in-house and outsourced sub-processes, which should appear seamless when performed correctly. Thus services oriented architectures become essential to a networked economy, facilitating cost-effective integration of extended enterprises. The degree of organizational and technical difficulty, however, should not be underestimated: the complexity of SOA implementations usually involves painful trade-offs among cost, performance, scalability, and future flexibility.

■ *Analytical tools.* In contrast to extended enterprises, analytics delivers a benefit of services oriented architecture readiness inside the organization. Data warehouses and related technologies help to evaluate information about customers and their behavior for developing and controlling customer processes. Tools for exploratory search are emerging from research labs into commercialization and address a fundamental problem: how does a person look for something he cannot name?[7] In contrast to older technologies that required pre-built queries, custom-created data sets, and long run-times, in-memory data exploration is more flexible and faster for the user. Tools for predictive analytics are improving in their ability to extract meaning from vast quantities of data. In all these areas, improved analytic tools help data support better decisions.

■ *Embedded systems and mobility.* For the first time, mobile telephony, handhelds, and sensors and actuators in machines (such as cars) have made customer processes that are not limited to a fixed work place accessible to computer support. Many new technologies and applications will shape the next decade, from extensive, cheap advertising media through cars and electronic homes to consumer electronics and "wearable" devices. New, creative uses for RFID, telematics, building-control, and cell phone–based sensors will continue to multiply, though typically in niche rather than sector-wide applications. Automation that reaches deeper into processes and structures helps drive efficiency, while mobility can both improve efficiency and enhance collaboration and creativity by extending workers' data-rich environments.

■ *Social software.* In the past few years, corporate blogs, project wikis, and social networking sites such as LinkedIn have provided improved visibility of customers' organizations and processes. Integration of such *ad hoc* tools with enterprise systems still represents a challenge; however, improved efficiency in finding answers and improved mobilization of human capital can make the investment pay off handsomely.

■ *Content management.* Content-management systems are tools for storing, maintaining, and quickly locating information in electronic documents. They give customers access to any data that has been documented electronically for products, services, contracts, instruction manuals, and much more. Although our CEOs display a gut instinct for the tremendous significance of electronic knowledge, these instincts have not correlated with investment.

In the final analysis, man, not machine, is the crucial element in the customer process. Apart from a few fully automated processes, the customer process is sustained by people and merely supported by machines. IT frees many services from the constraints of individuals, time, and place. It can also make them work more cost-efficiently. The new solutions demand more discipline from employees and a greater ability to abstract topics. Skills upgrades may be necessary. In some cases, new processes also raise justified concerns about job losses. The successful implementation of new solutions relies heavily on the people involved.

Checklist

☐ Does your business know the key customer processes? Does your business model cover the needs of these customer processes?

☐ Which customers use your products and services in similar customer processes?

☐ Which customer processes hold the greatest potential for your company?

☐ What is most important to your customers in a solution (for instance, quality, price, convenience, speed, service availability)?

☐ Which group of products and services does the customer process need? Which of these can your company offer?

☐ Who in your industry brings the most additional value to the customer process through electronic services?

☐ Which of your company's services generate the highest degree of customer retention (and thus the highest costs for moving to a different provider)?

☐ Which services will consumer demand force you to provide electronically in three years time?

☐ Do your electronic channels strengthen your market presence?

☐ When did you last check whether your integrated solutions contain products and services that the customer never uses?

☐ In which aspects are your competitors better at solving the customers' problems?

☐ Which services must your company provide to stay in business?

CHAPTER 3

More Customers and More for the Customer

Management Summary

If enterprise value derives closely from how well a supplier can enhance a customer's processes, it follows that enterprises need to know who their customers are, what they need, and how much they will pay. Despite the logic of this approach, many organizations focus substantially more energy inward than outward. Nevertheless, it is inescapable that reaching more customers and selling them more helps exploit market potential.

Three business concepts support business model transformation based on the twin concepts of reaching more customers and deriving more revenue per customer:

1. *Customer knowledge.* Who are our customers, not only as individuals (Sandra Jones) but also functional locations (VP, western region) and of course enterprises (XYZ Corp)? How do customers' processes utilize our products and services? Who are our potential customers?
2. *Integrated customer care.* How many points of contact does Ms. Jones have in our company? How well do we understand the sum of our interactions with XYZ Corp?
3. *Innovative price structures.* Whether as products, services, or integrated solutions, how does our pricing compare to that of our competition? How does pricing relate to our true cost base for delivering what the customer requires? How quickly and accurately can we adjust pricing?

Achieving integrated and timely market knowledge has proved to be problematic for many firms. Citigroup's vision of increased "share of customer"—as banking clients would seek investment advice, carry charge cards, and buy insurance from Citi units—collapsed between the dual forces of too much internal overhead and too little value delivered. Loyalty programs at many retailers have failed to fulfill the promise of closer relationships and higher spend: many successful firms such as Wal-Mart, well regarded for its use of data, have resisted the trend toward shopper cards. Other retailers remain confident in the concept: Tesco invested £150 million in 2009 to revamp its loyalty card program in the face of competitive pressures in the UK grocery market.[1]

Finally, poor data quality has weakened the conclusions derived from many analytical efforts. In a particular database, are I.B.M., IBM, IBM Global Services, and International Business Machines four companies, one company, or some number in between? Until the data is cleansed, analyzing such metrics as share of customer, total spend, and channel flow-through is impossible.

As large organizations have met with mixed success in their management of customer-related processes in the past 15 years, customers have changed dramatically in many regards. First, transparency has increased: pricing for pharmaceuticals varies considerably by national market, for example, and customers in high-price markets such as the United States are putting pressure on drug companies based in part on the extreme variability of their pricing programs. Comparison-shopping engines are a routine fact of life in many industries.

Second, large areas of the developing world have increased their demand for consumer goods: in short, markets are expanding globally. Mobile telephony is a case in point: as Clay Shirky points out, credible world leaders such as Bill Gates, Kofi Annan, AOL's Steve Case, and others could [falsely] state as late as 2001 that "half the world has never made a phone call."[2] Less than 10 years later, with nearly 4 billion mobile phones on a planet of fewer than 7 billion people, not only has half the world's population made a phone call, billions can make one any time and nearly anywhere.

Third, customers continue to feel more and more empowered. Especially in a recession, when "cash is king," customers in industries from automotive to real estate are negotiating favorable terms. In addition, customers are gaining power from groups. Whether online, through personal and professional social networks, or offline (coordinated via mobile devices), word of mouth spreads faster than ever. In business-to-business markets, blogs and other online sources are shifting information asymmetry, which traditionally has favored sellers, more in the direction of customers.

In the face of these changes, more effective customer-facing processes have become essential for business success. Among their benefits are faster reaction in response to both opportunities and risks, better tailoring of value propositions to customer need, and improved short-term and long-term

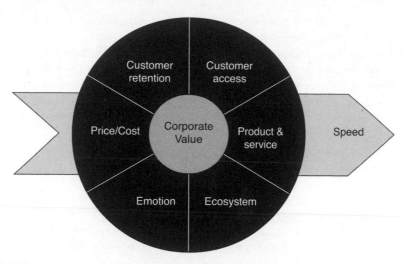

EXHIBIT 3.1   Better Customer Access Affects the Entire Relationship Lifecycle

profitability (from improved pricing and loyalty, respectively). A holistic view of the customer process can be seen in Exhibit 3.1.

- *Product and service.* Creating personalized, innovative services and eliminating redundant ones often demands detailed knowledge about customers and their requirements.
- *Customer access.* IT is a particularly effective means of leveraging new sales channels to target new customer segments and regions and reduce sales costs. All customer contact, from marketing to after-sales, makes customers more accessible, generating information about them and, more importantly, their needs. This makes it possible to address customers on a more personal level and creates opportunities for cross-selling and up-selling.
- *Customer retention.* Knowledge about customers and their processes is one of the strongest reasons for customer loyalty. A customer will not pass on information to a company unless she trusts the company to protect the data against misuse and loss.
- *Ecosystem.* Members of many ecosystems are competing with partner companies to acquire customer data and forge customer relationships.
- *Emotion.* The better an enterprise knows its customers, the more effectively it can target their needs and inspire customer satisfaction and confidence through convenient services.
- *Price/cost.* The price is determined by how valuable a product or service is to a customer and what alternatives are available. Strategic pricing

(that supports segmentation, retention, or other objectives) is a core element of the business model.

- *Speed.* Observations from CRM projects show employee attitudes to customers to be more important than the software. Thus the project must focus on empowering people to solve problems and identify opportunities more quickly than before. Since competitors also invest in new solutions for market and customer development, market share can be captured only from those market players who fail to satisfy rising customer expectations.

Vision

Every enterprise seeks to exploit the market for its products and services. In an ideal case, an organization knows its prospective clients, whether corporate or consumer, and understands their particular needs. It uses this knowledge to gain access to customers, to acquire the biggest possible share of each customer's spend, to secure customer loyalty, and to generate a healthy profit margin from each customer.

A company draws customer knowledge from many sources. Externally, market research, customer surveys, and third-party information services (such as weather data in retail) can set context. Operational data from sales and billing processes can be extremely revealing, while service encounters provide input to R&D, finance, and potentially sales leads. Customer behavior, whether clicking through Web pages, entering search terms, e-mailing queries or complaints, or calling the help desk can enhance knowledge of pricing, product design, and employee performance. Sensor data from machines on customer premises, conveying measurements such as runtime or vibration levels, can illuminate usage patterns.

Data warehouses combine and consolidate this knowledge, enabling analytical tools to support a more personalized approach to customers, to facilitate access to new client bases (in new regions, for instance) and sales channels tailored to specific customer segments, and to reduce costs. Customer and product databases, access to numerous internal and external sources of information, improved training and coaching, and standardized sales processes can support these practices. Because data tools rely on clean, consistent data, many efforts are focused on harmonizing information from different sources. Data warehouses are becoming "smarter" about treating what is put into them by using semantic technologies that advance the state of the art for information handling. This trend does not imply total consistency, however: when data sources disagree, it can indicate fraud, broken processes, or incorrect planning assumptions, all of which are important to identify and address.

New techniques for exploratory search allow analysts to navigate large bodies of data without having to specify a query; trends can emerge from the data while preserving quick response times. Electronic services are available both inside enterprise systems and from external vendors to profile customer behavior, enabling customization of those customers' experience.

> The company that systematically exploits untapped knowledge about markets and customers wins new customers and gets the most from existing ones.

Turning Employees and Customers into Fans

As wireline telephony has given way to rapid growth in wireless services, communications companies around the world have had to change essential elements of both their business model and day-to-day operations. One carrier confronted this challenge with a particularly bold plan.

Telefónica

Headquartered in Spain, Telefónica is one of the largest and most valuable telephone companies in the world. With operations in 25 countries, including most of the Spanish-speaking world along with the United Kingdom, it reported revenues of roughly 58 billion Euros in 2008. Telefónica has more than 250,000 employees and delivers both fixed-line and mobile services to over 250 million people in its various markets.

After its acquisition by the Spanish parent, the O2 brand was noted by Telefónica management as having the highest customer satisfaction in the UK telecommunications market. A global program was launched in 2007, focused on the customer experience and designed to spread lessons from O2 across the company. Early research from 2006 found that customers' expectations were set by their least favorable impressions, potentially undoing a multitude of things done right:

> *The most important thing that we have learnt is that the customer's general satisfaction with his/her consumption experience will be equivalent to his/her worst experiences. Therefore, to guarantee a great customer experience it is necessary that all areas involved in the company-customer relationship must be perfectly coordinated and aligned in order to turn our customers into fans.*[3]

Focusing attention on call center representatives, the project team found that poor information at the point of customer interaction impeded the representatives' ability to solve customers' problems. Mobile data services, for example, required complex solutions for which most representatives lacked expertise. In light of these gaps, the project benefitted from top management's attention. In addition to reviewing systems and processes, the project invested considerable effort in improving employees' training, job mobility, and sense of belonging. A major motivation for the corporate initiative to "turn employees into fans" of the company was driven by the goal of improving the customer experience.

In his letter to shareholders in the 2007 annual report, Executive Chairman César Alierta was direct. Four major priorities would be the focus of the next several years, the first of which was

> *to provide our customers with the best service experience, transforming the company into an organization where customers not only are, but are made to feel that they are, the center of attention. This will be achieved by improving customer support and service, along with enhancing our understanding of customer expectations in order to meet their needs with segmented offerings that deliver added value.*[4]

Thus far the results illustrate how difficult it is to change both employee and customer behaviors. Extra attention was paid to first-call problem resolution, for example, as well as upgrading the availability of online self-service channels. Of the nearly 21 million complaints recorded in 2007, roughly a third related to billing. Both internal processes and external communications were redesigned, and ISO and Six Sigma certifications were achieved.[5]

Four Innovators from the Chemical Industry

The shift in focus from product-oriented to customer-centric also has an impact on pricing. Many enterprises are striving to replace product prices with solution prices. In the extreme example of an outsourced model, a supplier assumes responsibility for operating a packaging machine, for instance, and charges for services rendered, such as the number of candy bars wrapped. Third-party logistics providers will take over most any supply-chain process. Four examples from the chemicals industry suggest the breadth of pricing options in business model innovation:

1. Products manufactured by the Australian technology group Orica Ltd. include explosives for the mining industry. The company used to sell explosives by the kilo. Knowing that the success of a blast—the quantity of extractable rock—depends on more than 20 different parameters, Orica began collecting data about blasts. It uses the information to

determine the right explosive and right technique for every blast. Nowadays, Orica does not just sell explosives, but broken rock (the amount of rock exposed). This pricing method has proved so popular with customers that many other competitors have been forced to adopt Orica's model.[6]

2. "We sell our customers an effect," said Alfred Oberholz, formerly an executive board member at Degussa (now part of Evonik), describing the pricing strategy adopted by his chemicals company. Titanium dioxide is an important element in heat shield glazing, where small quantities can achieve significant energy savings. Other applications include street markings, colored printing ink, and wallpaper, where the same quantity of titanium dioxide generates *less* value for the customer. Thus Degussa's profit-driven pricing model means that the company does not sell chemicals, but square meters of heat shield glazing or kilometers of lane marking. The customers who profit most from the solutions are the ones that contribute most to funding the development costs.

3. Another innovative pricing practice in the chemical industry comes from Eastman. Because of the volatility of feedstocks due to global oil price swings, and because the prices of many transactions are negotiated and "on delivery" rather than off of a price list, Eastman account representatives need a powerful pricing tool to maintain both competitiveness and profitability. Combining modeling and analytic tools with cost and availability data from back-end systems, the pricing environment also integrates workflow so that negotiations can be monitored in timely fashion: account representatives are not left hanging waiting for headquarters approval at the same time that so-called maverick sales are reduced.

4. Dow Corning, a global leader in the silicone manufacturing industry, found that conventional channels left it unable to deliver competitively priced services for the buyers of its commodity products. With Xiameter, Dow Corning now offers a cost-effective, Internet-based standard process for ordering commodity silicones—allowing it to grant customers discounts of 15 percent. Frequently comparing and negotiating prices is a costly business for buyers and hampers their processes. Many customers using the Xiameter chemicals portal opt for six-month basic agreements instead of buying at different prices on different days, because doing so simplifies their purchasing process.[7]

Concepts of Market and Customer Development

As the Economist studies and our CEO survey testify, tomorrow's companies will place greater importance on exploiting the potential of existing customers than on generating revenues from new products and services.

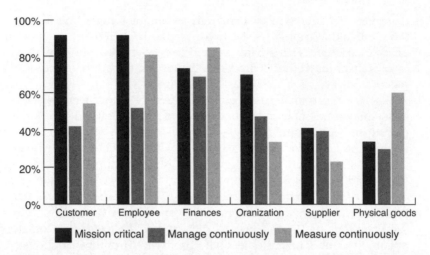

EXHIBIT 3.2 Customer Focus, While Viewed as Mission Critical, Is Seldom Measured or Controlled

For example, in the 2009 Gartner Executive Programs survey, the highest percentage of CIOs (54%) listed customer intimacy as the top goal of their IT and process projects.[8] The main objectives of market and customer development—of marketing, sales, and after-sales processes—are primarily to address all prospective customers and secondly to generate higher revenues from each individual customer.

In a survey of more than 400 CEOs, 94 percent cited the customer as the most influential success factor. Yet fewer than half of the companies had implemented systematic processes to control market and customer development (see Exhibit 3.2).[9]

By the early 2000s the term "customer relationship management" was partially discredited following the failure of a large proportion of projects intended to put the customer at the center of sales and marketing activities. In many cases, however, the focus was on the technology rather than the employee, or the customer for that matter—many companies launched projects entitled "Implementing a CRM tool" rather than "Redesigning sales and marketing processes." A CRM tool does not constitute a process. The division of labor between the IS organization and sales management, for example, could often be improved as the balance between tool selection/implementation and process change is often unclear. Given that even today, CRM is often wrongly reduced to the implementation of systems, we will speak instead in terms of "market and customer development" to underscore the business perspective.

The intelligence for market and customer development is embedded across the enterprise in a variety of customer-facing processes, from campaign management and customer retention management to complaints management and after-market service. IT has enabled many business concepts for exploiting market potential: a call center can access all electronically available information in real time; a customer retention program can use a loyalty card to link all of a customer's transactions; tools for calculating customer financial impact can differentiate profitable and unprofitable customers. The companies we surveyed have high expectations for three business concepts:

1. *Customer knowledge.* Knowledge about potential and existing customers and their requirements is the basis for most market and customer development processes.
2. *Integrated customer care.* Sales management sees the customer as a whole, regardless of whether its information comes from customer-specific product development, marketing, sales, servicing, or accounting.
3. *Innovative price structures.* Fixed prices, quantity-based payments, and services as added extras for products have been consigned to history in increasing numbers of industrial sectors; particularly now, the emphasis is on solutions, not products.

Customer Knowledge

Knowing customers and their needs is vital for measuring marketing and sales performance, and serves as the starting point for developing products and services. Particularly in global, volatile markets, accurate information about local customer demand drives many facets of profitability. Fortunately, IT can contribute to cost savings and competitive advantages in the gathering and management of customer information. Enterprise systems generate multiple sources of customer data that can be used for process improvement, margin enhancement, and other objectives:

- Customer Web sites
- E-mail correspondence with customers
- Customer click behavior on supplier Web sites
- Company notifications (such as product upgrade announcements) sent electronically
- Scanned customer business cards
- Sensor data, such as from customer premise equipment or from medical devices
- Servicing documentation
- Online databases, such as credit reporting
- Electronic transactions, such as order history or configuration information

Since the costs for automatically capturing data are very low, a company can gather larger bodies of more detailed information than before, such as all the items a customer has ever bought with a customer card. Assuming clean and consistent data, databases and data warehouses can consolidate customer data to provide a comprehensive view of a customer:

- Customer profitability
- Preferred communications channels
- Changes in payment behavior
- Changes in ordering behavior
- Privacy settings and preferences
- Behavior in reaction to marketing efforts such as promotions, price changes, and new product announcements

Consolidating all this information creates an integrated view of customers, a vital resource for workers such as marketing analysts. At the same time, the risk of overloading service and sales representatives with too much and extraneous information remains a danger. Customer knowledge can support account management with judicious application of the following types of information:

- Potential customers
- Customer's customers
- Customer's collaboration partners
- Customer's suppliers
- Tasks the customer performs in its customers' processes
- Customer's information requirements
- Customer's business issues
- Decision makers
- Decision influencers
- Buyers
- Users
- Installed devices and their parameters
- Renewal requirements
- Supplementary requirements
- Servicing requirements
- Customer complaints
- Customer suggestions
- Customer-specific pricing and discount schedule
- Contracts and updates
- Company notifications
- Facility and billing addresses
- Creditworthiness and credit history
- Projects and budgets
- Purchase history

For example, Computer Sciences Corporation is a $15 billion professional and technology services firm managing systems integration and outsourcing contracts. Because of the long lead time for large, complex transactions, pipeline visibility was essential for resource allocation and relationship management efforts, but information was scattered across Lotus Notes databases, personal contact managers, and Microsoft desktop applications. Unifying the sales-related data into a single global instance not only improved sales productivity but also exposed additional lead streams as well as up-sell and cross-sell opportunities.

Capital One Financial was a pioneer in the analytical credit card industry, so customer knowledge has always been central to the firm's identity. Nevertheless, by 2007 it had to revisit its customer contact practices. Given that Capital One had expanded via acquisition from credit cards into traditional banking and other lines of business, customers were faced with multiple Web sites to manage different services. At the same time, those customers were receiving e-mail information and promotions of differing content, volume, and intensity from various entities within the firm. The answer lay in the creation of what CIO Robert Alexander called "a single point of truth," created by linking each business's data warehouse into a unified central entity.[10]

The information a business needs to gather depends on its intended use. The more details a company collects about its customers, the greater the danger of incomplete or outdated knowledge and the more difficult it becomes to extract useful information from the growing volume of data. In practice, asking sales people to keep three metrics accurate with timely checks is typically more useful than creating a laundry list of fields that get ignored or polluted by sloppy updating. Particularly in marketing and sales, the culture and processes used for market and customer development, and not tools and data, turn customer knowledge into competitive advantage.

> It is not collecting but applying information that creates value for a company.

Given new mobile capabilities, getting knowledge to decision-makers near the point of customer contact can create significant advantages. The global brewer InBev (now Anheuser-Busch InBev) linked promotional effectiveness, the field sales force, and back-office processes. This integrated knowledge, in turn, supported interactions on customer premises, the retail stores, pubs, and hotels where its products were purchased at wholesale. Mobile handheld devices keep account executives updated on sales effectiveness, promotional budgets, and their individual targets. The initiative also tightened the connection between the firm's various brand promotions and the points of sale to improve supply chain efficiencies: if a big holiday promotion is coming up, sourcing can plan accordingly.

For accounting firm KPMG, understanding the international relationships of its audit clients is mission critical. In compliance with the Sarbanes-Oxley Act, the U.S. SEC does not approve external auditors that have or pursue other business relationships with any enterprises associated with the client. As a result, visibility of customer information at the global level has become a matter of necessity: if the Brazilian KPMG office is delivering tax advice to a given multinational, the U.S. firm cannot bid for the audit.

Information about the market and customers can form high barriers to competitive entry. The Swiss company Creditreform has many years of experience providing credit ratings for and about its clients. In the 1980s, the CEO, Willy Egeli, considered transforming the manual approach to calculating ratings into an online service based on a comprehensive database. This was around the same time as American and European business intelligence services were penetrating the Swiss market. Egeli faced a dilemma that would determine the survival of the company: sell the company along with its already well-maintained wealth of information to one of the much larger competitors, or go it alone in the world of real-time credit ratings and take on the Goliaths?

Egeli decided to go it alone, founded a subsidiary to provide electronic credit ratings, and set about consolidating knowledge of the companies his organization already had on file. The foreign information providers were unable to build up information about Swiss companies fast enough, especially not with sufficient detail or accuracy. Companies continued to request credit information from Creditreform Switzerland, despite its higher prices.

> Business intelligence in the form of customer databases, and the customer-facing processes that use this data, require high initial investments and often demand stamina over many years.

Integrated Customer Care

Whatever a customer's primary process, she often wants a choice of communication channels, but just one well-informed contact person, a single face. These two requirements are so important that we explore them here against the background of customer knowledge.

Multichannel management has become a compulsory element of every company's agenda. If we apply the concept of the customer process consistently, it does not end with a sale but must encompass all activities that are part of the customer process. In practice, the main challenge is moving away from a way of thinking that separates internal departments like sales, production, logistics, service, and financials and, at a later stage, external partners, into "silos."

IT opens up new channels and access media that create new possibilities for account management. Even more important than the channel or access medium, however, is having the same information throughout all of the company's organizational units and regions. This requires standardized processes, applications, and data (for details, see Chapter 8). Only then will the price information obtained on a laptop in the Shanghai branch or in the Danish Internet portal square with the details given by a representative visiting company headquarters in Atlanta.

Lennox International is a $3 billion supplier of climate control equipment. As the customer base grew, traditional sales and relationship maintenance channels did not scale and customers noticed a lack of consistency and personalization across channels. Integrating sources of customer information with the call center application was an important first step in supporting service representatives with guided scripts and an electronic product catalog to increase one-call resolution rates.

Electronic channels can enhance personal customer relationships when activities focus on obtaining information and conducting operational business efficiently. At the same time, they boost customer loyalty by enabling new services.

If a customer cannot get a response about an invoice item without an excessive amount of effort—without being connected to a series of sometimes unenthusiastic administrators—the repercussions for an otherwise good sales experience can be serious. Of course, the same is true of servicing and product information, even of services delivered by a supplier's business partners. Treating the customer consistently across all customer-facing processes requires integrated sales solutions that start by enabling information to flow freely between processes. Further, they extend to automatically recording cross-process, cross-functional measured variables.

When several companies team up to form a close-knit ecosystem, contact with a customer is spread among multiple enterprises. If the organizations involved want to provide high-quality customer service, they must share what they know about the customer. This pushes the limits of trust and data protection, and raises concerns about customer defection and security breaches. Access to customer data is one of the main barriers to segmented value chains in banking, for example, since outsourcing processes would mean allowing data to leave the bank.

The value created for a customer through its relationship with a supplier is the result of multiple contacts between the two parties. For the supplier, the challenge lies in breaking down "silo" structures and possibly even including partners from its ecosystem (see Chapter 7) when considering the customer process. Mergers and acquisitions have left many companies grappling with various sales and service teams, different sales cultures and processes, and diverse article and customer data from heterogeneous systems. The road to integrated sales solutions is difficult in itself, and grows longer with every acquisition and divestiture.

> The company that breaks down silos and shares knowledge provides better customer service (i.e., convenience, problem-solving) and exploits sales opportunities (i.e., cross-selling, up-selling).

Innovative Pricing Models

Customer value and competition dictate a given price. The range of services, emotion, ecosystem, community, and costs involved in moving to a different supplier dictate what a company's products and services are worth to a customer. In most sectors, the days when pricing meant merely marking up the cost base are long gone. Every company wants to achieve the highest, sustainable price possible. Many of our interview partners see pricing as a central part of the business model.

The importance of innovative pricing extends to the public sector, where it can be used as an allocation mechanism, as traffic alleviation programs have shown. Many cities in Europe look increasingly likely to deploy congestion pricing strategies as a means of controlling traffic. A motorist could then decide whether a particular route or parking space was worth its price at a given point in time. San Francisco is also experimenting with dynamic pricing for parking spaces in an effort to deter driving and encourage the use of mass transit.[11] The use of auctions for airplane landing fees as a traffic control mechanism remains controversial.[12]

IT brings many companies the possibility of innovative new pricing structures, which might include incentives in the form of immediate discounts, globally uniform prices and discounts for all of a group's international and domestic subsidiaries, or prices based on current capacity. IT has the potential to cut pricing and settlement expenses, so much so that pricing strategies can give rise to new business models. One widely anticipated business concept is the micropayment system, where a buyer might pay a relatively small amount to download something like a newspaper article. Apple's iTunes store is currently one of the world's largest micropayment environments.

Moving from the world of commodities and products into information goods, while some electronic services can entail considerable fixed costs for infrastructure, their marginal costs often approach zero. As such industries as newspapers and music have discovered, these low marginal costs encourage a perception on the market that "free" is a viable price point. At the same time, such electronic services as credit ratings, software licenses, and Internet and cellular access have successfully maintained profitability.

> Particularly for information goods, prices reflect the customer value rather than the manufacturing costs.

On the other hand, enterprises struggle to put a price on complementary electronic services. The vast majority of banks still do not charge for e-banking, for instance, despite the fact that such services involve massive investment and operating costs. Even though the services create value for the customer, the refusal to charge reflects strategic positioning; if competitors do not charge for the services, being the first mover can be risky.

Airlines, telecommunications providers, and some banks and insurers have opted for a different pricing variety, which, owing to its high complexity, has only become possible with advancements in IT. Their pricing models comprise so many components and rules that the customer is hard pressed to compare different options. Many enterprises and sectors such as the hotel industry have switched to a flexible pricing model. They sell surplus capacity at low prices in order to generate at least some revenue from resources that would otherwise be wasted. The Hotwire and Lastminute.com travel portals are prime examples of dedicated channels for discounting time-sensitive inventory.

Looking after customer-specific agreements is labor intensive; personalized price structures require order-processing systems that can manage them efficiently. Some enterprises have therefore started segmenting services into freely combinable standard modules as well. This approach would, for instance, give a commercial cleaning company the flexibility to offer customers the services they actually need (cleaning intervals for offices, sanitary facilities, and glass facades; different cleaning methods for schools, operating theaters, and workshops; surcharges for special security requirements in banks, law firms, and barracks), while at the same time being easy to manage and simple to price. The individual steps in creating an innovative price structure of this kind are segmentation of the service offering; configuration of the modules to create custom solutions; and pricing based on the service modules actually used by the customer.

> The price is dictated by the value created for the customer and the available alternatives.

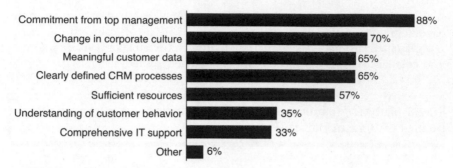

Commitment from top management	88%
Change in corporate culture	70%
Meaningful customer data	65%
Clearly defined CRM processes	65%
Sufficient resources	57%
Understanding of customer behavior	35%
Comprehensive IT support	33%
Other	6%

EXHIBIT 3.3   The Critical Success Factors for Market and Customer Development Are Enterprise-wide and Begin at the Top

Realizing the Vision

Growing customer expectations, diminishing customer loyalty, and the creativity of competitors have made market and customer development even more important. Services such as online banking, which until recently were differentiating criteria, are becoming basic commodities without which a supplier will often struggle to gain a foothold.

Participants in a study by the Institute of Information Management at the University of St. Gallen, summarized in Exhibit 3.3, cited support from top management and a change in the corporate culture as the factors most critical to the success of transformation projects relating to market and customer development.[13] Other scholarship has reached the same conclusion: success starts at the top, and in belief systems.[14]

> Often, the biggest obstacles to customer orientation are not the IT applications but the company's way of thinking, poor examples set by management and ineffective incentives for employees.

Barriers

IT has created a wealth of new opportunities for market and customer development, whose potential has not been fully exploited by any means:

- *Inadequate electronic access channels.* Inadequate electronic access channels restrict business times and locations. Most administrative contact between patients and doctors, hospitals, and insurance companies, for instance, is still limited to five hours a day, five days a week and is

almost exclusively paper based. Accordingly, the processes are inefficient for all involved.

- *Insufficient customer knowledge.* Information about prospective and existing customers is often inaccurate, incomplete, outdated, inaccessible, stand-alone, and often leaves the company when an employee leaves.
- *Insufficient use of knowledge.* The sales team does not use the information consistently. More specifically, it does not pursue contacts with (potential) new customers systematically, is not alert to the needs of existing customers, and misses opportunities for cross-selling and up-selling.
- *Lack of incentives for sharing knowledge.* Many market and customer development concepts rely on the individual's knowledge becoming corporate knowledge, in other words, available to all employees equally. This presupposes a willingness to share information. Conventional incentive schemes that promise rewards only when revenue targets are met oppose this culture. The consequences are silo-like structures and a reluctance to disclose information.
- *Inefficient sales processes.* In many cases, sales processes remain too expensive. Some information has to be recorded more than once. The sales team often does the work of computers, for instance by providing customers with information that they could easily call up themselves. Their sales efforts frequently target the wrong customers. Cultural barriers slow the adoption of solution rather than product selling.
- *Trust, data security, and data protection.* From the customer's point of view, an enhanced, personalized service with more convenient processing conflicts with concerns about protecting privacy and business secrets. Customers who do not trust the security of the Internet or the competence of a particular sales representative will not pursue business relationships with the company through these channels, even if they suffer financially as a result.
- *Neglected pricing methods.* Pricing is often seen as a marginal activity rather than a key element of the business model.
- *Constant change.* Restructuring, globalization, and mergers and acquisitions require the sales process to be reworked time and again. Since competitors employ the same tools, the issue becomes one of gaining a temporary edge and keeping up with the pack, rather than one of building up a sustainable competitive advantage.

Enablers

"The best customer service is simply friendly" was the straightforward conclusion reached recently by a German marketing magazine following a study of customer expectations when interacting with enterprises. While IT cannot replace friendly staff members, it can reinforce their human skills by taking care of routine tasks.

- *Integrated customer databases.* The driving force behind any concept for market and customer development is an integrated database. To present one face to the customer, all employees involved in customer-facing activities need immediate access to the same customer data. In the past 15 years, many companies have sown the seeds for customer databases in their ERP systems and developed them into resources such as CRM systems. Data warehouses offer the opportunity of concentrating data from all kinds of applications in one, common dataset.
- *Analytical tools.* Business intelligence (BI) systems help to analyze large datasets efficiently. Companies with heavily used portals, such as Amazon, examine surfing behavior to better understand visitors' interests and behavior. The search engine optimization (SEO) industry is built on distinguishing the advertising power of words: "guinea pig" and "guinea pigs" reach markedly different audiences. As it turns out, the former term is used predominantly by people who already own pets, while the latter attaches to shoppers getting informed.
- *Multimode access.* Electronic access channels, be they stationary Internet points or mobile connections, are empowering enterprises to serve the customer process everywhere and anytime. Mobile solutions are expected to experience a wave of innovation, given that a minority of enterprises currently uses mobile CRM solutions.
- *Capturing data with embedded systems and mobile communication.* RFID (labels on consumer goods), customer cards (at grocery stores), and inbuilt intelligence in machines (onboard electronics in aircraft engines) can generate customer data that is accurate and up to date in previously unknown dimensions and, in many cases, automatically in a way that requires no human input.
- *Electronic services.* External information services can complement a company's customer knowledge. Such sources as credit ratings, government-issued permits and reports, and industry databases can supplement in-house data.
- *Knowledge management.* Reference solutions, instruction manuals, software, music, and videos either become products in their own right or enable new services that were not economically viable with previous technology. Correspondence, business reports, enterprise portals, and press releases enhance the sales approach.

Checklist

☐ Do you know your potential customers? By segment, by name, with their requirements?

☐ Do you know your customers' budget?

☐ What are you doing to increase your share of your customers' wallets?

☐ Which data are you lacking for account management?

☐ Where do your main competitors have the edge when it comes to customer knowledge?

☐ What data do you lose when key customer account representatives leave the company?

☐ Which changes in customer buying behavior have you detected from your databases in the past 12 months?

☐ Do you use incentives to steer customers toward cost-effective channels? (Does the customer profit from ordering online rather than in store?)

☐ Would a different price structure increase your revenues or profitability?

☐ Does your company present one face to the customer?

☐ Do you provide customers with one central point of contact for all services, including after-sales?

CHAPTER 4

Innovation and Personalization Trump Commoditization

Management Summary

Today's integrated global economy amplifies opportunities, risks, and competition. The recession notwithstanding, the global economy doubled in less than a decade, growing from $31 trillion in 1999 to $62 trillion in 2008.[1] This growth is not explained by established companies in the developed world. Instead, the economies of such countries as South Korea and Brazil are growing at double-digit rates. In such circumstances, competitive differentiation becomes essential: lower-wage countries are joining the mainstream every year, meaning that new low-cost producers will continue to proliferate. Rather than attempt to compete with them, many successful enterprises are instead focusing on margin preservation through innovation and personalization.

In particular, four business concepts have proven essential:

1. The "Internet of things," utilizing cheap sensors and ubiquitous networking to add value via improved awareness of users' contexts and objectives
2. Electronic services, which can scale much more readily than their human-powered counterparts
3. Personalized solutions, which enhance the customer experience both during the transaction (as at Amazon or Dell's customized portals) and during use, as with custom-blended agricultural fertilizers
4. Parallelized development, in which a sequential model culminating in a high-risk "big-bang" launch is replaced by iterative interactions with customers and partners, simultaneously rather than serially addressing field service and logistics issues, for example.

While many companies devote rhetoric to innovation in mission statements, marketing literature, and other documents, truly innovative companies are rare.[2] Managing the innovation process with tools proven to work in other operational domains frequently fails, as does turning loose smart and creative people without adequate guidance or expectations. The skills, compensation, workflow, and economic assessment related to new products, services, and processes will vary from those associated with established practice.

Classic models of innovation, such as the large labs at such organizations as Kodak, AT&T, or pharmaceutical firms, are being cut dramatically. At the same time, innovation in nontraditional organizations, such as the open-source software community or the Apple developer network, has proven to challenge many assumptions (such as the role of stage gates and focus groups) about new product and service development. The "grand challenge" model, in which prizes are offered for the achievement of "stretch" goals, is also proving effective: the U.S. DARPA (Defense Advanced Research Projects Agency) has spurred advancements in autonomous vehicles, Netflix improved its preference-matching algorithm, and an X-prize was awarded for a reusable space vehicle.

Finally, the technology landscape is creating innovation in innovation: Wikipedia is not a company, or a nonprofit, or a club that uses technology to achieve its goals. Rather, Wikipedia and such tools as Amazon Mechanical Turk[3] are themselves the economic entity. People's contributions are collected in a lightweight environment, minimizing overhead and facilitating collaboration, so the technology platform makes possible new kinds of effort and organizations. In part because the barrier to collaboration is low and the editing process is robust, people will donate many hours of labor to these entities without pay.

Because creating a culture and appropriate metrics for innovation is so difficult, and because competitive pressure on margin and markets is so intense, using innovative business concepts as shown in Exhibit 4.1 to drive innovation becomes a lower-risk, higher-probability path for managers.

> Tomorrow's business models will be shaped by customer engagement and, above all, innovative products and services.

- *Product and service.* As we have noted, a few enterprises revolutionize their markets with new enabling technologies. Mostly, however, managers pursue differentiation through functionally advanced products and services for the customer process. Intelligent products and the services that go with them are taking on an ever bigger share of

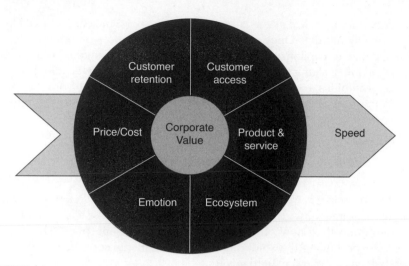

EXHIBIT 4.1   The Impact of Innovation and Personalization Reaches Across All Areas of the Enterprise

the customer's tasks or providing some form of additional value. Modularization, configurators, and new information technologies (such as ubiquitous computing), together with in-depth knowledge of the customer, are enabling a greater degree of personalization.

- *Customer access*. Electronic services are not bound by time or location and consequently can cost-effectively reach new customer groups, particularly in emerging markets.
- *Customer retention*. Personalized products and electronic services are becoming an integral part of customer processes and consequently boost customer loyalty.
- *Ecosystem*. Collaboration with partners makes for lower risk, shorter innovation cycles, and a wider range of services.
- *Emotion*. Beyond a baseline level of quality that is the price of entry, a track record of innovation has a significant impact on the way customers perceive a company.
- *Price/cost*. Parallel development processes reduce the time-to-volume, resulting in a higher price and market share. Building-block systems cut development and production costs. With low marginal costs, electronic services are making new services feasible and affordable to customer groups for whom nonelectronic services were too expensive and too complex to manage.
- *Speed*. Being first to market allows for premium pricing, while "me-too" offers usually face stiff competition from the incumbent. In fashion-driven segments such as apparel or cell phones, precise execution of a

new offer is critical as the launch window may be measured in weeks or possibly months. Once launched, products compete on time to volume in a race to capitalize on economies of scale. This stage is so important for market share that many companies have sacrificed initial margin opportunities and instead implemented volume pricing from the outset in the pursuit of extreme market share: an example is KDDI's Internet connection via fiber optic to the premise in Japan.

Vision

The first objective is to deliver products and services that create more value for the customer than those offered by competitors. A seller can do this by both innovating new offers and customizing existing ones. The second is to start producing the solutions in high volume as soon as possible and thereby achieve market share advantages.

Additional intelligence, as found in cars with electronic following-distance control, can win over potential buyers just as much as attractive body lines or a large range of options do. At Endress+Hauser, which is discussed next, a flow meter's accuracy and resistance to acid contribute as much to the customer process as 24/7 service availability, extensively documented operating experiences, and an efficient secondary market for selling used equipment. The same is true of financial service providers, who try to differentiate their core products by offering increasingly convenient supplementary services.

From Single Standardized Product to Personalized Service Package: Endress+Hauser

Based in Switzerland, the Endress+Hauser Group has 86 subsidiaries in 40 countries and is a leading supplier for the industrial process-engineering industry. Endress+Hauser produces measuring instruments and control units that form the basis for automation solutions, an area in which the company commands a 67 percent share of the European market.

Endress+Hauser's range of measuring equipment includes thermometers. But the thermometers from Endress+Hauser bear little resemblance to the conventional thermometers we might find in refrigerators, where temperature is measured by the expansion of a liquid and users are left to act upon the information. Endress+Hauser's Thermophant T temperature switch not only displays the current temperature inside a technical installation; its integrated electronics allow on-site or remote (PC) configuration

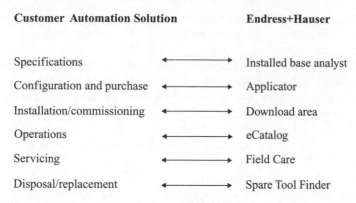

Customer Automation Solution		Endress+Hauser
Specifications	←——→	Installed base analyst
Configuration and purchase	←——→	Applicator
Installation/commissioning	←——→	Download area
Operations	←——→	eCatalog
Servicing	←——→	Field Care
Disposal/replacement	←——→	Spare Tool Finder

EXHIBIT 4.2 Endress+Hauser Provides a Wide Range of Electronic Services

and enable electronic communication with other measuring devices and control units.

Endress+Hauser uses its service portal, W@M, to let customers access existing services more quickly and cheaply and to generate new services for managing their automation solutions. The electronic information simplifies the processes involved in operating a plant, for instance, by providing up-to-date information on all measurement instruments currently deployed, in one place at the push of a button. Endress+Hauser registers 370,000 downloads of technical documents annually, 95 percent by customers. Exhibit 4.2 provides an overview of the services available on W@M.

The automation solutions deployed by Endress+Hauser customers are intelligent combinations of the company's measuring devices, control units, and services. Endress+Hauser's customers represent many industries, including machine and plant engineering, electrical engineering, chemicals and pharmaceuticals, food manufacturing, and energy production. The measuring devices and control units they operate in their automation solutions therefore differ widely in scope, purpose, type, and configuration. By providing modular products that the customer can combine as required, Endress+Hauser helps the customer design and operate customized equipment. It provides real-time information concerning the customer's installed base of devices. The customer gets extra value from operating the equipment and is more likely to remain loyal to the company.

When designing products and services, Endress+Hauser is guided by the life cycle of a customer's industrial plant. Its range of services spans all the life-cycle phases: planning the plant with the supplier; selecting and purchasing the required devices; installation; commissioning and operating the devices; maintenance; procuring spare parts and replacement devices. That lifecycle generally plays out in the following sequence:

- The customer uses the Endress+Hauser Web site to find out about the company and its services and arrives at the enterprise portal W@M.
- Using the "Applicator," a service in the W@M portal, the customer selects the appropriate measuring devices.
- The customer orders these products, along with spare parts, consumable materials, and services from the electronic product catalog in the online shop.
- The "Order Status" function lets the customer track the order.
- "FieldCare" is an electronic tool for calibrating the measuring devices and assists the customer during the commissioning stage.
- The customer can use the "Installed Base Analyst" to manage the devices they have in place, including third-party products, and store the data in the "Common Equipment Record" in the W@M portal.
- The download area contains all the latest versions of product manuals, operating instructions, and other documentation and software.
- The "Spare Finder Tool" works out which spare parts the customer requires.
- "Product Status List" shows whether Endress+Hauser devices are still produced and whether spare parts are still available.

Procter & Gamble (Innovation)

Cincinnati-based Procter & Gamble (P&G) has been doing business for more than 170 years. Operating in more than 180 countries, P&G defines the multinational corporation. With dominant products in many consumer packaged goods categories, it is home to many of the world's most powerful brands: Bounty, Tide, Crest, Gillette, and Pampers, just to name a few. As of 2008, 23 brands were billion-dollar sellers, including the Fusion shaver, which attained the stature only two years after launch.

As of the late 1990s, however, the company had stagnated. New product introductions were slow and often ineffectual. Competitors gained traction in key market segments, as when Colgate launched a new antibacterial toothpaste that helped it gain six points of market share over P&G's Crest brand in only two years. The company's stock price lagged market indices during the broad run-up in market capitalization, and in June 2000, A.G. Lafley was named to replace a CEO who had been in the position only 18 months.

Under Lafley's management, the first decade of the 2000s represented a dramatic turnaround. As the 2008 Annual Report was titled "P&G: Designed to Innovate" Lafley led a number of key initiatives that transformed both the cultural and process dimensions of new product and service introductions. Under his leadership, the company achieved a new level of brand and product introductions, such as the Spinbrush toothbrush, the Swiffer floor cleaning system, Crest White Strips tooth brighteners, and the Febreze odor eliminator.

The key concepts of P&G's new approach were collected under a banner called "Connect+Develop." Whereas in 2002 only 15 percent of the company's new products came from outside P&G's worldwide network of labs, in 2008 more than half did so. At the same time, internal investment in R&D remained atop the industry, at $2 billion annually, in part because of an increase in sales-per-employee productivity of more than 6 percent per year. A key factor in freeing cash for investment is a shared-services model in which common operations are centralized to gain savings in volume purchasing and lower administrative expenses, responsible for more than $600 million in cumulative cost savings.

The innovation process is also regularized and managed, addressing the dimensions of rewarding talent, assessing new product fit within the brand, testing the concept, and rolling out the innovation to the appropriate markets at the right price with the right timing. Innovations are themselves categorized, according to the 2008 annual report:

- Disruptive innovation creates new categories, new segments, or entirely new sources of consumer consumption. These are innovations that address consumer needs no other brand or product has met. Virtually all of P&G's billion-dollar brands were created with disruptive innovations.
- Sustaining innovation is what we focus on most. These are extensions or improvements of existing products: big initiatives that meet consumer needs by filling gaps, eliminating consumer trade-offs, or providing new benefits. Examples include Pampers Caterpillar-Flex, which improved the fit and comfort of baby diapers, and Crest Pro-Health Rinse, the Crest brand's entry into the mouth-rinse category adjacent to toothpastes.
- Commercial innovation generates trial on existing products without a product or package change. Examples include the Gillette Champions and Pampers Unicef programs, marketing efforts that give consumers new reasons to be interested in and loyal to a P&G brand.[4]

This combination of inside and outside resources has proven its worth. P&G actively courts potential partners in all phases of product development and launch, from basic chemistry to packaging (see Exhibit 4.3). By aggressively attacking the NIH (not invented here) syndrome, P&G has multiplied its potential sources of insight and solutions. It makes selected

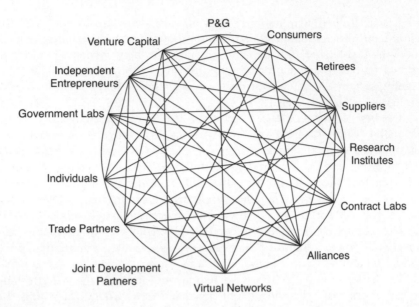

EXHIBIT 4.3 Procter & Gamble's Connect+Develop Initiative Connects Internal and External Innovation

resources available to the community, but also listens intently for signals of emerging consumer needs in such online forums as Vocalpoint (for mothers) or Tremor teens, a word-of-mouth tool. P&G instruments and measures those 350,000 moms and 200,000 teens to provide marketing support to other companies targeting those same markets, taking an in-house capability and turning it into a revenue generator.

IT supports the Connect+Develop program in several ways:

- An Internet-based coordination mechanism enables outreach and partnering activities that would not be feasible in a paper-based process.
- The complexity of relationships and efforts requires sophisticated reporting and tracking capabilities.
- The New Product Development process is highly regularized and automated with an easy-to-use toolset.
- Market intelligence is widely sourced and widely available.

The financial results of Connect+Develop are impressive: annual earnings-per-share growth for 2001–2008 were targeted at 10 percent and averaged 13 percent. The retooled innovation strategy drove seven consecutive years of organic sales growth ahead of targets, in the 6 percent range every year. From June 1, 2000, when Lafley took over, until January 1, 2009, P&G stock appreciated 88 percent while the S&P declined 32 percent.[5]

Pioneering Co-creation: LEGO Group

Perhaps no toy is as well known around the world as the LEGO® brick, which was patented in 1958. The privately held company embodies the ideals of its Danish homeland, particularly good design, high quality, and a respect for childhood, at the same time that it helps children of all ages from many countries explore their creativity.

Beginning in the late 1990s, the company embarked on a program aimed at expanding its reach by partnering with industry leaders in most every phase of the business: manufacturing, distribution, and design. LEGO thus could achieve greater scale without adding infrastructure and changing the core culture. In addition, the company surveyed its customers and found unprecedented levels of loyalty and affinity: the small company is regularly voted the most admired corporate brand in Germany, for example. To mobilize that base of users, LEGO reached out before the launch of the MINDSTORMS® robot kit, asking four leading users, also known as master builders, to help design the product. Later in development, 100 more users were invited to assist, and shortly before launch, over 100,000 people signed up to test the kit.[6]

The product turned out to be quite successful, both because of user involvement and because the word of mouth was so vibrant among the loyal community. Robot competitions continue to engage children, teenagers, and grownups alike, and also serve as a constant source of both customer needs and innovative ideas. FIRST (For Inspiration and Recognition of Science and Technology) LEGO League was founded by Dean Kamen, who also invented the Segway. The organization conducts competitions in 30 countries, and in 2008 more than 137,000 children entered.

Later, users of the standard brick set were given the ability to download LEGO's software design tool (see Exhibit 4.4). They can build virtual designs and submit the proposals to LEGO, which often makes them available to the public. LEGO pays no royalties, but the satisfaction and peer reputation are sufficient compensation among hard-core fans. Those fans can congregate on a rich variety of social networking sites for LEGO users, which the company does not sponsor but actively tracks. The line between inside and outside continues to blur, presenting a series of management challenges involving intellectual property, liability, and other issues, but probably no company has so successfully involved its customers in the design process: its 120 internal designers now have the power of 120,000 invested customers to draw upon.

EXHIBIT 4.4 LEGO Digital Designer Allows Users to Build and Share Designs in Software

Source: The LEGO Group, "LEGO Digital Designer," http://www.lego.com/eng/create/digitaldesigner/. LEGO and MINDSTORMS are trademarks of the LEGO Group.

At a private event for other executives, CEO Jørgen vig Knudstorp explained the unique dynamic of "Free" as a price point in the labor market. "These people don't get paid and they don't want to get paid," he stated. "They work for free and they literally work hundreds of hours for free. [Instead,] you give them something else, some other reward than a financial reward which is typically more things like recognition. So we now actually launch products where we say, this product was built by Fan so-and-so. You can go to his Web site and see all the things he has done." Among the LEGO community, reputation is a sufficiently powerful currency to motivate extensive contribution.

The Tata Nano: A Case of Disruptive Innovation?

Who will be the Henry Ford of India, bringing personal mobility to the masses? Fifty years from now, it may be clear that the answer is Ratan Tata. The head of the powerful group bearing his family name that includes everything from IT services to tea to steel at global scale, Tata is seeking to reinvent the automobile, claiming the mantle of "the people's car" from Volkswagen and Ford. In doing so, he is being forced to reinvent an established business model by rethinking everything from design to distribution.

Tata reports that he was inspired to build a radically affordable car by the number of Indian families he saw getting wet on their motorcycles. The project began in 2003 and utilizes several breakthrough principles to enable it to be sold at a little over 1,000 rupees, or $2,500, its target price. First, vendors are utilized in new ways, assuming responsibility for design and parts at unprecedented levels: 85 percent of the components will be outsourced to a group of vendors 60 percent smaller than the industry standard.[7] For example, many parts, including the engine, are being made by Bosch.

Second, the design of the car strikes a new balance between cost-effectiveness and durability. Tata himself removed a front windshield wiper from the specification, while the storage area in the rear of the automobile is accessed from the inside, saving on hinges and body construction costs. Each wheel has three rather the conventional four lug nuts. While power steering is not available, air conditioning is and has proved to be more popular in initial orders than the base model.

Finally, Tata is looking ahead to truly mass production, in part by addressing some side-effects of conventional automobiles. The two-cylinder engine generates 33 horsepower, but possibly in response to pollution concerns, Tata has two engines in development that would reduce environmental impact: one runs on compressed air, the other on electricity and possibly solar panels. In a county with 90,000 traffic-related deaths a year, the Nano is reported to have already surpassed crashworthiness standards.

IT is essential to the business model, which is not surprising given Tata Motors' sister company, a global provider of outsourcing and other services. A parts and service network is being established to assist existing independent mechanics to be able to repair the vehicles; the more familiar dealership model will not apply. Initial applications to purchase, and their status updates, were managed via the Internet, rather than in showrooms.

Plans are already taking shape for the car, which has a waiting list of more than 100,000 full deposits beyond first-year production, to go on sale in Europe and in the United States a year later. If the Nano is successful, Tata's greatest innovation will be the commoditization of a formerly expensive product, the *down-engineering* of the automobile.

Concepts of Product and Service Development

Many executives aspire to develop exclusive, market-leading products and services. While new *product* development is challenging, as we have seen, finding innovative *services* that afford extra customer value is frequently even more difficult. Comparing sales contributions from new products against competitors gives an indication of how well an enterprise is tapping its development potential. 3M's historic norm in this regard, for instance, was that each division generate 25 percent of its revenues from products launched in the past five years.

How well a company succeeds in developing products and services is closely related to the quality of its market and customer development efforts; pure R&D spend does not drive market growth without attention to distribution, channel, customer service, marketing, and other issues. By collaborating with many different customers, an enterprise can acquire specialized knowledge about aspects of its customers' business that even they do not possess.[8]

Understanding customers in this way opens opportunities for new services with added value. In particular, we focus on four business concepts in more detail:

- *The "Internet of Things."* As everything from Geiger counters to thermostats to webcams is connected to a common network, businesses have many opportunities to involve themselves in customer processes, and to allow digital intelligence to improve product performance.
- *Electronic services.* Customers can access electronic services at low cost, unrestricted by time or location. The marginal costs incurred by the provider often approach zero, as we saw with Hilti's tool fleet portal (see Chapter 3).
- *Personalized solutions.* Personalized products and services create packages of services for specific customer problems. Personal fitness trainers, executive education programs, and many industrial process outsourcing models operate on this basis.
- *Parallelizing development.* In many market segments, the necessary time-to-volume cannot be achieved unless the customer and supplier design new products together in real time. Amazon's collaboration with book publishers on the Kindle e-reader platform is an example of parallelized development with a partner ecosystem.

The "Internet of Things"

By providing a standard mechanism for connecting devices, people, and sensors, the Internet is being transformed from a computer network into a shared backbone for many facets of modern life. By performing tasks for the customer, connected and/or intelligent products and services make the customer's process less complex and less costly. Examples can be as small as a telephone that saves dialed numbers or finds the optimum wireless network, or as large as locomotive that utilizes sensors, computing capability, and sophisticated algorithms to optimize fuel economy, power output, and environmental emissions. In an ideal case, the product performs its part of the customer process without requiring any input from the customer.

INTELLIGENT PRODUCTS   In several markets, according to the Boston Consulting Group, more than half (52 percent) of a product's competitive advantages already come from its "intelligence."[9] Miniaturization, digitization, wireless networks, and embedded software are improving the functions and usability of a wide range of products. These might be stand-alone, as in a video camera with image stabilization software, or connected, as in a remotely accessible building management system.

A compressor is in many people's minds nothing more than a simple device for compressing air, the successor to the conventional air pump. A wide variety of enterprises—from brewers and chipmakers through paint shops and carpenters, as well as dentists and hospitals—need compressed air in varying quality. Every year, Europe alone consumes around 80 billion kilowatt hours of electrical energy creating compressed air; in the United States, the Department of Energy estimates that compressed air accounts for 10 percent of electric use in the manufacturing sector.[10]

State-of-the-art compressors, including those manufactured by Germany's Kaeser Kompressoren, do more than produce compressed air. Their intelligent control units allow compressed air systems to be operated efficiently in variable conditions (such as changed requirements or fluctuating demand). "On average, the energy consumption of a compressed air system could be reduced by 30 percent. To enable our customers to realize this potential, we offer more than just intelligent control units for individual compressors. All our compressors can also communicate by means of a bus system with a master compressed-air management system, which is capable of controlling operations to ensure energy efficiency and safety in entire plants with multiple compressors," says CEO Thomas Kaeser, stressing the importance of IT in his company's products.

Automobiles feature a number of electronic aids that actively control the vehicle to protect occupants, ranging from antilock brake systems (ABS) and active traction control to fuel injection control units and electronic brake boosters. Surprisingly to an outsider, today more processor chips find their way into cars than computers.

THE WIDE RANGE OF INTELLIGENT, CONNECTED PRODUCTS   The "electronifica-
tion" of everyday objects (also referred to as ubiquitous computing, perva-
sive computing, or ambient intelligence) is a new source of customer value,
particularly for consumers, expanding in areas including home automation,
entertainment, telematics, and care for the sick and elderly:

- Sensatex has incorporated sensors into t-shirts to constantly record
  physiological information for high-risk patients. While the prototype,
  developed at Georgia Tech for the U.S. military, has not entered production, Zephyr (a New Zealand firm) has developed a range of bio-
  metric monitoring devices. Its BioHarness, for example, measures pulse,
  respiration rate, body temperature, exertion level, and posture information, then transmits this data via Bluetooth to a range of devices and, if
  appropriate, the Internet via mobile phone. For example, a sports team
  coach or fire department captain can monitor the state of players' or
  firefighters' physical performance on a laptop screen.
- In 2005, adidas developed what it claimed was the world's first intelligent shoe, the adidas 1. Thanks to a small computer under the heel,
  the shoe could adapt the cushioning level in real time to conditions
  underfoot as well as the wearer's weight and pace. A year later, Nike
  introduced a system that connected sensors in the shoe to the runner's
  iPod to record run time, distance, and conditions.
- Otto Bock, a leading manufacturer of orthopedic technology, produces
  a microprocessor-controlled artificial leg called the C-Leg. The C-Leg enables leg amputees to move naturally even in extreme conditions, taking 50 readings per second and dynamically adjusting to fit the wearer's
  needs, which can include running.
- Products with embedded intelligence help businesses and consumers to
  combat brand and product piracy. In the field of medicine, for example,
  studies by the World Health Organization (WHO) suggest that around
  10 percent of the world's medicines are either counterfeit, not licensed,
  or of poor quality (often by being out of date). The U.S. Food and Drug
  Administration (FDA) has recommended the use of RFID technology to
  identify and track drugs between the manufacturer and patient, in large
  part to address counterfeiting.[11]
- As global carbon dioxide levels come under closer scrutiny and energy
  prices remain unstable, building automation systems promise to combine occupant comfort, lower costs, and better environmental performance. Adjusting lighting, heating, humidification, and cooling levels to
  occupancy, sunlight, ambient temperature, and other parameters holds
  the potential to lower greenhouse gases, save money, and maintain
  comfort and productivity.

Intelligent products must present intuitive controls and user interfaces if users are to benefit easily and conveniently from their capabilities. Endress+Hauser offers control software for its automation solutions, which formats complex information graphically in a way that enables process engineers to monitor equipment without difficulty. The requirements of the user interface for Otto Bock's C-Leg are even greater: the artificial leg must interface with the body in a way that recognizes and makes different movements without the wearer having to intervene.

TECHNOLOGY INNOVATION AND BUSINESS MODEL CHANGE   New product technologies are transforming consumer behavior and creating scope for new business models. To take one example, the digital camera made its first slow steps toward superseding conventional cameras in 1980 and has been gathering pace ever since. Digital photography is changing the way users capture the world, allowing them to take more pictures because they can delete them easily later. Exchanging digital photos is also simpler and quicker through Facebook, Flickr, and similar electronic services.

The combination of optics and electronics led to a new business model that has enabled electronics manufacturers in particular, such as Sony, Kyocera, and Hewlett Packard (HP), to force conventional providers into niches or out of the market completely, a fate that befell AgfaPhoto. Kodak is concentrating on professional image processing (in medical technology, for instance) with mixed success. Traditional manufacturers like Zeiss and Leica supply the electronics companies with lenses and brand names for their products and expand into services related to optics and photography.

The victory over film cameras was short-lived, as stand-alone digital cameras were in turn challenged by cameraphones, shifting the balance of power from the likes of Nikon, Minolta, and Canon, and now including Nokia, Samsung, and other new entrants to the photography market. According to the Wireless Business Owners Consortium, cell phones will outsell digital cameras by 12:1 by 2010. For retailers, the profit margin on a cell phone sale is roughly five to ten times the profit on a camera sale: approximately $15 on a $200 or greater camera as opposed to $150–$250 average gross profit margin on a cell phone.[12]

> The potential of intelligent products is comparable to that of the Internet.

Electronic Services

When customers want more than a stand-alone product, they may need a more complete solution for their problem or requirement. While intelligent products provide enhanced functions, electronic services support an entire solution. They are available around the clock, from any location (presuming power and bandwidth), and on a variety of devices. Once developed, their marginal costs are minimal when compared with nonelectronic services such as call centers, so they can scale extremely cost-effectively.

Supported by advances in networking and portal technology, enterprises are increasingly choosing to deliver their solutions expertise through electronic media. This means that customers can use a supplier's intelligence in various forms (see Chapter 2):

- Transactions (orders, payments, renewals, and terminations)
- Marketing information and user documentation about products, services, customer processes (price lists, installation dimensions and instructions, troubleshooting guides)
- Training and education in print, animations, via audio podcast, or on video
- Advice (application design, product configurators, shared experiences of other customers)
- Product delivery (digital information goods include software and music downloads, as well as news of many kinds)
- Maintenance (downloads of firmware and related updates, spare parts search, calibration, asset tracking)

Endress+Hauser, for example, provides up-to-date documents at low cost, checks and advises on the availability of products in real time, and reduces process costs and lead times with electronic orders. Without IT, it would be hard to imagine a feature like "Condition Monitoring," which notifies the user as soon as malfunctions are detected in a machine. Other examples of widely used services include those deployed by many logistics companies for tracking and tracing shipments, electronic auctions like eBay, online payment systems, and the many options for downloading digital entertainment, both legally and illegally.

A study by Mercer Management Consulting of 200 German mechanical equipment manufacturers shows that these companies generate a profit margin of 2.3 percent from machine sales, compared with approximately 10 percent from services. The study concludes that while the German machine industry as a whole could and should generate up to 50 percent of revenues from services, this figure stood at less than 20 percent in 70 percent of companies. The potential is illustrated by ABB Turbo (see Chapter 2), which generates more than half of its revenues from servicing turbochargers. The same opportunity applies to many other enterprises whose approach has traditionally been product-centric.

The entrepreneurial appeal of electronic services lies in the revenue model. While these services can be very expensive to develop and run, a company that can distribute fixed costs across the highest number of transactions soon takes up a unique selling position. Relatively high fixed costs and low marginal costs for electronic services mean that each additional customer represents ever-higher profit potential: ABB Turbo Systems can allocate the costs for developing and running its services across more turbochargers than any other competitor.

In addition to exhibiting these cost characteristics, electronic services also frequently exhibit network effects. Much like flu shots, personal computer software, fax machines, or even the English language in business, the more people who adopt a platform, the better off the existing users of the platform become. If customers believe a given service will shape the standard, they will base their investments on them and thus bolster the strongest provider.

> Electronic services offer huge potential for unique selling positions.

Providers can replace expensive, nonelectronic services with electronic ones. The customer can use electronic services without the help of a salesperson or consultant and regardless of time and place: Amazon's toll-free telephone number is extremely difficult to find, forcing customers to utilize self-service. Google offers no help desk for its software applications. In return for better availability, customers complete certain parts of the process themselves. They print online tickets from amusement parks and concert halls; they update their address details regarding magazine subscriptions and financial providers; they use automatic check-in kiosks at the airport; they use online configurators to design customized computers, vacations, financial products, or industrial equipment. Exhibit 4.5 shows which kind of self services are in highest demand.[13]

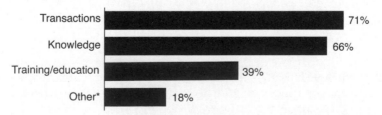

* Retrieval of documentation, product development, employee self services

EXHIBIT 4.5   Self-service Reaches across Multiple Application Areas

The easier it is for a customer to interact with an enterprise using some kind of device—Internet, mobile phone, machine, telephone with recorded message—the more likely the customer is to actually use the electronic services on offer. Critical success factors for electronic services are therefore availability, response time, and usability. Self service does not necessarily mean less convenience, as testified by the popularity of options such as checking out of a hotel using the TV's remote control or drawing money from a cash machine.

If electronic services support the customer process from start to finish, they create significantly more customer value than discrete products and services.

> Electronic services can reduce personnel costs, boost customer loyalty through additional value, and generate revenue over the long term.

Personalized Solutions

A company that knows its customers well and creates effective internal process may be able to provide tailor-made packages of products and services. This approach creates more value for the customer than separate standard services that customers have to combine to solve their particular problems.

IT allows services to be personalized. It makes it simpler to create standard modules, to configure them for the customer problem, and, finally, to manage the custom configuration.

CEO Thomas Kaeser describes the vision of custom solutions at Kaeser Kompressoren: "Our customers want compressed air for the specific applications in their business—not just compressors." As discussed above, customers can choose to outsource all their compressed air needs to Kaeser and pay for the amount of and types of compressed air they consume as a recurring expense, as opposed to purchasing capital equipment.

Other companies on the landscape also see personalization as the way forward:

- At Endress+Hauser, personalization involves combining numerous of the company's measuring devices and control units to create an automation solution (for a brewery, for instance). Services include the "Installed Base" for maintaining configuration data and facilities for logging device-specific calibration settings. It creates additional value for the customer by tailoring products and services to the customer's exact production process.

- ABB Turbo Systems' 3.5 million theoretical variants for each turbocharger size enable it to provide a made-to-measure solution for every one of its customers' application areas.
- Adidas, Nike, and Timberland allow customers to create customized footwear and equipment. The "mi adidas" scheme allows them to measure their feet and design their own, made-to-measure shoe from a selection of colors, soles, and other elements. They can even have their name emblazoned on the finished design, or order two shoes of different sizes. Nike's equivalent service is called Nike ID; Timberland allows customers to design personalized versions of many shoes and boots. The custom price typically represents a 20 to 50 percent increase over retail, which represents an even higher premium to the manufacturer because they do not share the final selling price with a retailer.
- Whether on Google News, the BBC, or any number of aggregators, readers can customize the news they see, the stock quotes presented, or the sports scores that are highlighted.
- Airlines that buy GE aircraft engines have the option to structure customized maintenance, financing, and risk management agreements with GE's OnPoint solutions. Payments can line up with credit availability, cash flow cycles, or other constraints. The balance between capital and operational expenditures can be adjusted to meet market conditions. Engine availability can be managed for long life, depreciation, or other objectives, and operational data is used to forecast future needs and opportunities.

Personalized solutions create customer value, which may have the unintended consequence of limiting the customer's options for resale or integration with standard products. These solutions also increase complexity on both sides of the transaction because the seller has to manage multiple variants side by side for products, services, and processes. This means that a company cannot accept greater complexity unless the customer is willing to pay for it. Modularization and IT allow mass customization—personalization for a large customer base—by making processes less complex and easier to control.[14] Customers can have a personalized product, like a car in a specific color with a particular engine power and other features, but manufacturers can quickly create production and supply chain problems if the complexity is not managed appropriately. At most automakers, each model is available only with particular features, often offered in bundles, rather than fully a la carte.

> Nature itself provides an interesting example of this type of modularization. According to the latest research, the human blueprint—the genome—is made up of around 25,000 genes. This means that a human being has fewer genes than the common wall cress, a weed with 27,000 genes. It is not the number of genes that makes each human unique, but the way the genetic information is linked.

CAD and ERP systems set off the first wave of personalization. They facilitate variant management, but more importantly, they enable companies to control all aspects of customer-specific configurations, from specification to servicing. Embedded systems are currently unleashing a second wave. In clothing, devices, and even people, embedded sensors and actuators supply an endless stream of data about the "customer" and its context, permitting changes to be made at any time. Since they do not require active intervention from the person concerned, they allow for much more intensive interaction between the individual and the network.

Some luxury-class cars automatically adjust the mirrors, seat position, transmission settings, and steering wheel to suit the present driver, making the whole driving experience more enjoyable. Besides increased convenience, vehicle manufacturers are also working on personalized passenger-protection systems.

Parallelizing Development

Traditionally, product and service development has comprised four consecutive steps:

1. Assess customer requirements
2. Design solution
3. Produce solution
4. Deliver solution to customer

This rigid sequence applied to both consumer and capital goods.

Advancements in IT and organizational behavior mean that many of these activities can run in parallel. Interdepartmental and even inter-enterprise activities can become faster and more cost effective. Integrated activities of this kind drastically reduce the time it takes to satisfy consumer demand. Parallel development may not be a luxury: Some personalized solutions may call for collaborative engineering, for supplier and consumer to work together to assess requirements and develop suitable products and services.

It is now standard practice when buying a fitted kitchen for customer and sales advisor to plan the kitchen together on a laptop. It is easier for the customer to visualize the result and the sales advisor can explain ideas better.

Software vendors often work with pilot customers to create new applications. The ability to draw on customer experiences is a real plus when developing solutions that are ready for the market. And while customers may have to accept longer implementation cycles, collaborating with the vendor is appealing because the final solution is tuned to their individual requirements. They also benefit from the solution before their competitors.

3M's lead-user method directly involves key customers in brainstorming and product development activities. So far, the company has succeeded in creating a new, main product line from every lead-user project. Five years after the project, these products are generating around $146 million annually, eight times as much as products developed over the same period with no customer involvement.[15] Another objective of collaborative engineering is to reduce the total cost of ownership through in-depth knowledge of the customer process.

Parallelization means more than customer and supplier working together on development projects; it also requires the supplying company to synchronize internal processes. The speed with which a company develops services (time-to-market) and makes them available in large quantities (time-to-volume) determines market success and profit margins.

New products must be ready for series production quickly. Over the past fifteen years, vehicle manufacturers have more than halved the development cycle by synchronizing and sometimes outsourcing development activities with suppliers. In the tech sector, similar coordination is required between customers and suppliers. With a 69-percent market share, Merck KGaA, known primarily for its pharmaceutical activities, is the leading manufacturer of liquid crystals, which are used in products such as computer screens. For Merck KGaA to allow its customers to get new products ready for series production within three months, it must be able to develop and produce sufficient quantities of new liquid crystal compounds within a few days.

Close partnerships throughout the entire life cycle promote customer loyalty and create long-term sales opportunities: The company that works with the customer beginning with the development stage has the best chance of selling the customer services for operations and servicing.

The company that synchronizes development activities reduces the time-to-market and can boost customer loyalty.

Realizing the Vision

Enterprises in high-wage countries offset the high pressure on product prices by extending the service business and ultimately by offering complete solutions, to the extent of running a complete solution for the customer. Our CEO interviews revealed a clear focus on services, in some cases coupled with an emphasis on providing complete systems and solutions.

Barriers

In spite of considerable potential, there is still a huge discrepancy between vision and reality when it comes to product and service development. This is due to:

- *Increasing complexity.* Personalization often leads to uncontrollable complexity. Customers and suppliers struggle to understand, manage, produce, and service all the variants, keep sales and service forces trained, and keep spare parts in stock. Inter-enterprise processes also drive complexity, especially when every business partner has proprietary processes. Consequently, many companies fail to combine product and customer data across the entire life cycle. In addition, the "long tails" characteristic of information and Internet-related landscapes can generate very customer large data sets with little apparent pattern.
- *Lack of trust.* Customer and supplier are afraid of losing business expertise. Measures to protect information against misuse are expensive, time-consuming, and often ineffective.
- *The use of conventional metrics for new markets.* As Clayton Christensen notes in *The Innovator's Dilemma,* "markets that don't exist can't be analyzed."[16] In a consumer products company accustomed to global brands delivering sales of $100 million and up, getting the attention of product managers to support a product that might (1) divert resources from existing lines or (2) steal market share from those brands is difficult—particularly if the new product's prospects cannot be established with conventional market research.
- *Long payback cycles.* Innovative enabling technologies like mobile networks and solutions like sensors for monitoring physiological information are dropping in price. Even so, customers are used to free services and are reluctant to pay for (expensive) "added-extra" services, so pricing and positioning new product-service bundles can be difficult.
- *Premature IT.* Many IT solutions are not yet fully functional. RFID technology, for instance, remains unsuitable for many environments. Sending or receiving large e-mails by cell phone is not only expensive, but can also be very slow and prone to error.

- *Lack of standards.* Many new solutions would be technically feasible and affordable but lack standards that would allow the sensors, devices, control units, and networks to be combined (for instance, in telematics, building automation, and consumer electronics). For every USB or Bluetooth success story, multiple proprietary standards slow market development.
- *Inadequate networking capabilities.* Small business partners in particular may lack the infrastructure and know-how required for collaborative solutions. Large enterprises may be difficult to work with because of organizational multiplicity and complexity.

Enablers

Designing new, value-adding products and services calls for creative developers and, above all, in-depth knowledge of customers and their needs. This is the basis on which a small number of IT developments has enabled new products and services:

- *Service-oriented architectures.* With standardized, modular services, companies can combine capabilities embedded in both structured and unstructured process steps. The process thus is able to flex while allowing the underlying platform to remain stable, a principle known as loose-coupling.
- *Configurators.* When products and services are personalized, the number of variants increases. Configurators allow the customer to enter a small number of relevant, value-adding parameters to specify a solution.
- *Knowledge management.* The development process produces a lot of unstructured information like appraisals, printed patent specifications, and presentations. Content management systems (including product data management systems) can be used during the development phase to keep track of documents with different versions and dependencies. Many knowledge management solutions, including enterprise search, still fail to deliver the speed and functionality required by modern business ecosystems. Semantic tools for enhancing the metadata layer in data warehouses are vital for machine-to-machine interactions, but where people are in the loop, such tools as tagging and social networks can deliver excellent results.
- *Communication standards.* Communication standards such as the Internet protocols and numerous other protocols for wireless communication allow intelligent products to connect to one another without the need for a human interface. Further-reaching semantic standards, say for exchanging collision alerts between vehicles, require the providers to acquire a critical market power and will therefore be longer in the making.

- *Electronic services.* If a customer has to understand three different online solutions at three different banks in order to make an international transfer, or three different processes at three different couriers in order to send a parcel, the electronic services will not be readily accepted. However, if all business partners use the same standard software or the same online service, they will be accepted sooner. PayPal is an excellent example.
- *Embedded systems and mobility.* Intelligence is being incorporated into everyday items thanks to miniaturization, huge advancements in enabling technologies, and price erosion caused by mass production. Mobile communication networks these smart things and frees them from the restrictions of location.
- *Workflow management.* When several designers from one or more companies work together on a solution, they can encounter coordination problems when it comes to time management and change management. Computer-based workflow management (process management) organizes inter-enterprise processes. It makes processes transparent, reduces waiting times, checks whether deadlines are met, and allows performance figures to be measured.

Checklist

- ☐ What percentages of your revenues and profit come from services?
- ☐ Which services do you invoice to customers?
- ☐ Which company is the leading service provider in your sector?
- ☐ What percentage of total costs do service costs represent? How much of this could you eliminate through automation?
- ☐ Which three services do your customers need most urgently for your product? Who will provide them first?
- ☐ What support do customers need most urgently to plan and develop their solutions? Who offers such support?
- ☐ What can you offer to do for your customers to help them run and dispose of a solution?
- ☐ Could you modularize your products further (components, patterns, services)?
- ☐ How much does it cost customers to run your solution in comparison to rival solutions (total cost of ownership)?
- ☐ Can you adapt your products and services to customer requirements faster and more cheaply than the competition?
- ☐ Are your innovation cycles shorter than your competitors' (number of new products and services per year)?

CHAPTER 5

Silent Commerce

Management Summary

For all the attention to the Internet, intangible companies such as Google or Microsoft, and enormous social networks including MySpace and Facebook, we still live in a physical world. Everything from necessities such as food and fuel, to luxuries like out-of-season produce or imported wine, needs to move through supply chains.

While it does not receive the public attention of celebrities, bank failures, or technological gadgets, supply chain management is similarly critical for business success, and faces some critical challenges.

- *Complexity.* As more countries enter the global economy, raw materials and manufactured goods take on more variations and have to move greater distances. More parties can be involved in a given transaction, potentially including credit agencies, lenders on all sides, customs and security officials, freight forwarders, brokers, various shippers, outsourcers, and others.
- *Security.* With so-called asymmetric warfare becoming a reality on every inhabited continent, the safety of goods in transit can no longer be assumed. One need look no farther than the coasts of Somalia or Indonesia for compelling evidence of this issue.[1]
- *Customer expectations.* With speed becoming the watchword of electronic interactions, customers extend their expectations to delivery of physical goods when, where, and how they desire. Ever-tougher competition for customer business intensifies this tendency, which is also an artifact of superior execution by such companies as DHL, FedEx, and UPS.
- *Environmental sustainability.* With both financial and political pressure on companies' environmental footprints, the fuel consumption and exhaust, bilge, and other emissions of a global trade system are coming under increased scrutiny. Workplace health and safety issues

vary considerably around the world, and exposure to potential toxins and other risks complicates supply-chain management in some settings.

Just as fulfillment was at the heart of the drive to redesign internal processes, it will also be the driving force for collaborative processes that span company boundaries. Enterprise portals, electronic data exchange, collaborative electronic services, as well as sensor and actuator technologies are freeing many procedures from integration gaps and manual interaction. At the same time, they can introduce additional complexity that must be managed.

As business managers consider business model innovation involving the supply chain, three business concepts can serve as building blocks:

1. *Flow of information, not goods.* Sometimes phrased as trading "information for inventory," this concept builds on the insight, exploited powerfully in commodity exchanges and overnight-delivery companies, that information about things is often more valuable than the things themselves.
2. *Automation.* For a wide variety of reasons, ranging from health care costs to error rates to hazardous-materials exposure, automation can deliver significant advantages in the supply chain, and the potential far outweighs the results to date.
3. *Postponement.* Delaying certain processes in final assembly, custom configuration, or deployment in a bundled solution essentially buys a firm increased option value, with hard financial paybacks and discernible competitive benefits.

For any of these business concepts to be realized, the data for orders, articles, suppliers, and customers must agree and be accurate across the ecosystem. Establishing a standardized data basis remains a challenging task for a single firm, as any veteran of such a project can attest. Ensuring timely, synchronized data across a network of firms is even more difficult for technical, political, cultural, and economic reasons, but the competitive impact of doing so is rewarding.

Data quality is essential as supply chains are tuned to various criteria. When fuel costs spiked in 2008, trucking mileage, in particular, came under scrutiny. When credit is tight, firms manage inventory with an eye toward preserving working capital. In epidemics, shipments that can avoid quarantine at ports of entry rise in value. Outsourcing and the use of third-party logistics providers (3PLs) have had ebbs and flows of market enthusiasm. Labor markets, both in wage scales and skills availability, vary considerably by geography. Each of these considerations affects how supply chains are managed.

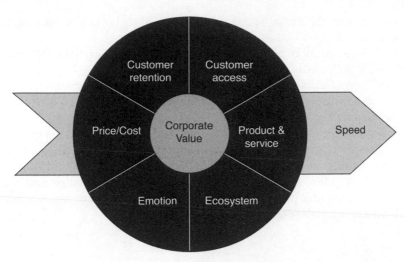

EXHIBIT 5.1   The Implications of Silent Commerce Affect All Facets of Enterprise
Value

In the early 2000s, a wave of seemingly annual disruptions—hurricanes
and tsunamis, terror attacks, the SARS virus, and port strikes—challenged
many notions of supply-chain optimization that assumed stable oil prices
and smooth flows of money and goods on a global scale. In the wake of
these events, the concept of robustness, or resistance to disruption, gained
in popularity, sometimes at the expense of pure cost-centric optimization.[2]
What we are calling "silent commerce"—differentiated supply chain
management—is not isolated to a single function, but has implications for
all phases of the customer lifecycle, as Exhibit 5.1 suggests:

- *Product and service.* Customers have come to expect high-quality products and services along with reliable, personalized order processing as
  a matter of course. The more flexibility customers have in the order
  process, the more they value the supplier.
- *Customer access.* IT, in the form of both the Internet and mobile devices,
  is enabling the fulfillment process to cover more customer segments and
  regions.
- *Customer retention.* The more involved in the customer process a supplier becomes, the more costly it becomes for the customer to switch
  suppliers.
- *Ecosystem.* The greatest potential lies in the area where least progress
  has been made: in collaborative order management, which involves coordinating enterprises along the supply chain. The customer does not
  usually perceive the performance of individual companies, but puts

one face on the entire supply chain with all its suppliers and logistics partners.

- *Emotion*. The more silently a supplier fulfills an order, the more attractive the supplier is to the customer.
- *Price/cost*. Transparency can result in lower inventory levels and transportation costs. By enhancing its planning procedures with requirements data from other business partners, a manufacturer can also realize lower production costs. Modularization, globalization, and the principle of postponing assembly are introducing economies of scale to component manufacturing.
- *Speed*. Very few enterprises start to scrutinize the timeliness and quality of their order-processing techniques until they have already fallen behind their competitors.

Vision

Customers can concentrate on their processes, obtaining their personalized products and services exactly when and where they need them. There is no waiting, and customers use the communication channel of their choice. With silent commerce, customers are unaware of all the activities the supplier coordinates behind the scenes. To achieve this, suppliers need access to rich information about the customer's requirements:

- An industrial facility receives cleaning and maintenance services on its equipment automatically. The transaction is structured essentially to buy uptime, energy efficiency, or some other outcome related to the customer's business performance, rather than supplies and service calls after equipment failures or reductions in performance.
- A retailer is sent cosmetics on the basis of current shop-floor stock and sales forecasts, without having to submit an order. A few deliveries a month, covering the entire product range, mean the retailer has less administration for goods receipts.
- A repair shop uses a single portal to order spare parts and accessories and receives the articles from the nearest warehouse or directly from the manufacturer, depending on their urgency.

In short, the vision is of the customer and suppliers, as well as *their* suppliers, working together like one, integrated company. This presupposes a high level of organizational intelligence:

- All involved have a common understanding of the fulfillment process.
- All parties have real-time access to relevant information, such as customer sales forecasts, production plans, actual sales, and all master data.

Inflexible "silo" structures will lose ground to collaborative order management. Delays and multiple data entry steps due to integration gaps will disappear in the face of real-time data exchange.

Seamless Fulfillment, Silent Commerce

Two examples from different corners of the textile industry illustrate how supply chain and related processes can create differentiation, aid in market expansion, and create tighter relationships with customers.

Li Ning

Founded in 1990, Li Ning is China's most popular brand of athletic wear. Named for its founder, an Olympic gymnast, it was one of the country's first publicly traded companies. 2008 revenues equated to $979 million. Li Ning is breaking new ground in many facets of the Chinese apparel market, often outmaneuvering Western brands. Strategy, branding, and supply chain efforts have proven to be synergistic.

Li Ning began as a manufacturer addressing the Chinese market. It now outsources some low-value-added manufacturing tasks to third parties, focusing instead on branding and distribution. In so doing, the company has moved from being a supplier of retailers to a customer of an external supply network. It has worked with DuPont on raw materials, and attempted "open innovation"[3] efforts by recruiting architects and other visually talented professionals to try their hand at product design. In 2005, Li Ning also signed a 50-year agreement to be the exclusive distributor of products from the French AIGLE brand.

In 2006, product launches were doubled from twice a year to four times, providing Li Ning with more credibility as a fashion leader. The product line has broadened to include 2,000 varieties of products within 30 categories aimed generally at mid-market, rather than the high end targeted by foreign competitors. Such breadth and positioning help Li Ning compete with Nike and Adidas. The company also sponsors a range of foreign teams and athletes, including the American basketball player Shaquille O'Neal, who was signed on the basis of his appeal in China: his endorsement is not active in the United States. In 2008, Li Ning also opened a design center in Oregon—Nike's home state—to expose its product developers to western trends.

Li Ning distributes its products to a network of retail stores, numbering more than 6,200 as of the beginning of 2009. The vast majority of these are franchises, though the company owns more than 300 directly managed locations. The company monitors production and quality levels in its network of factories, allowing rapid order fulfillment without the expense of high inventories. Even though most major sportswear brands manufacture in China, Li Ning enjoys a "home field" advantage owing to its faster cycle times and shorter supply chains: after concerted effort to deploy new systems and processes, inventory has been reduced from 84 days to 61, while shipment times to stores dropped from two months to two weeks.[4]

CWS-boco International

With 18 branch offices in Europe and China, CWS-boco is one of the world's leading one-stop suppliers for professional washroom hygiene solutions and textile services, employing 8,000 employees worldwide. With annual turnover of 779 million Euro, CWS-boco is a subsidiary of the Haniel Group. The firm's innovative form of fulfillment can serve as model for a service business: CWS-boco furnishes all types of work wear, tailored to the specific needs of particular trades and industries. CWS-boco's services include supplying, caring for, and storing work wear: it launders 80 million articles of clothing per year. The customer no longer has to stock a range of common sizes for new employees or replacements for worn articles. Instead, CWS-boco outfits every one of its customers' employees with a personal set of clothing, taking account of such aspects as labor turnover and changes in clothing size. It also addresses customers' specific requirements, for example legal and security implications.

The company relies on two innovations to process orders efficiently: identification technologies and a modular service offering. The modular clothing service allows CWS-boco to configure service contracts easily and, more importantly, manage them efficiently so that its solutions remain competitive.

Identifying each article means that service contracts can be linked to individual pieces of clothing. RFID chips and 2D bar codes link each garment to detailed information about the clothing, its wearer, and its care requirements. This enables CWS-boco to deliver the agreed services for every article, using a mainly automated fulfillment process (see Exhibit 5.2). The firm's IT systems let the company manage numerous different contracts efficiently by breaking down the individual contracts into separate standard services for order processing. During the entire process of maintaining the clothing, CWS-boco collects real-time, customer-specific performance parameters such as delivery reliability or replacement quota. The IT systems are focused on process ownership by lines of business, with an eye toward global deployment through extensive re-use.

Additionally, CWS-boco delivered an innovation on an apparent commodity item: washroom soap and paper towel dispensers. The company's ParadiseLine dispensers' front panels can be customized to match any

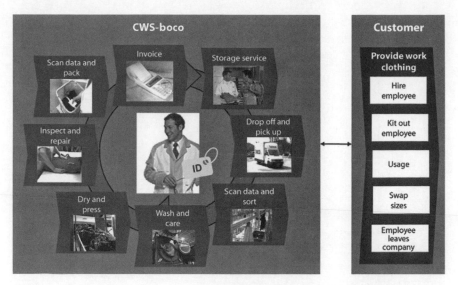

EXHIBIT 5.2   CWS-boco's Clothing Rental Service Includes Online Fulfillment
Processes

architectural or design concept, convey branding or social awareness messages (concerning hand-washing in flu epidemics, for example), or even be
fitted with a flat screen monitor (see Chapter 4 for more on innovation).

Concepts of Fulfillment

Assuming that business in the 2010s will be driven by the customer process,
the primary consideration for managers is knowing customers and their
needs (the customer process) and then offering them high-value products
and services. Almost all the executive managers we surveyed cited these
priorities. By contrast, the ability to fulfill orders flawlessly from production
through delivery was seen as a matter of course, even though the state of
execution lags this standard.

When consultants and analysts speak of "operational excellence,"
they refer to the balancing of two targets: flexibility and efficiency (see
Exhibit 5.3). High flexibility and low process costs are rival targets. Highly
standardized fulfillment processes, which can be unattractive to customers,
are particularly cost effective; processes with high flexibility traditionally
came at the cost of high overhead, buffer stock, and/or labor-intensive
workarounds. Modular services, by contrast, give companies the flexibility to configure customer-specific solutions and simultaneously maintain

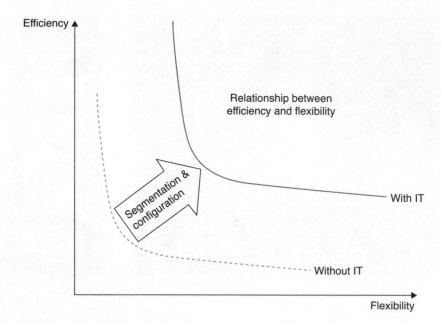

EXHIBIT 5.3 IT Increases both Efficiency and Flexibility, Improving Operational Excellence

manufacturing efficiency because the standard modules (product components or service modules) can be produced cost-effectively.

> IT enables companies to take control of the complexities that multiple variants bring to the fulfillment process, to automate many of the steps involved in creating standard modules, and to assemble them into personalized solutions.[5]

The concept of computer-integrated manufacturing (CIM) was born in the 1970s and aimed at eliminating integration gaps in the manufacturing information flow. In other words, the goal was to integrate all the IT applications involved in the production process in real time. Its objective was to reduce lead times, process costs, and inventory levels while increasing flexibility.

Today, we realize that academia and industry alike radically underestimated the complexity and cost of integration, harboring inflated expectations of the time it would take to implement solutions and the potential benefits. Many of the ideas of CIM have eventually become a reality, even a matter of course. Today's business concepts expand on many facets of the original CIM vision:

- *Flow of information not goods.* More knowledge—about inventory, requirements, and events—shared among involved parties translates to fewer shipments, lower inventory levels, and less overproduction.
- *Automation.* New technologies mean that automating process steps still holds great potential for reducing process costs and lead times while increasing flexibility, profitability, and customer satisfaction.
- *Postponement.* A customer-focused method for order management starts relevant subprocesses as late as possible in order to restrict warehouse stock, as far as possible, to multipurpose components.

Flow of Information Not Goods

As the various companies in a value chain introduce higher levels of informatization and sensor technology for capturing data automatically, their view of the fulfillment process can become clearer and more timely. Ideally, the result is complete transparency into factors such as inventory levels, production capacities, and exceptions in the fulfillment process. Compared with humans, sensors capture more detailed data faster and more economically. Measuring devices from Endress+Hauser, for instance, use radio technology to transmit real-time information about storage-tank levels back to the business process software.

Numerous entities are using RFID technology to monitor transportation assets. Deployments involving brewery kegs, industrial gas cylinders, and shipping pallets have all generated positive return on investment as their visibility increases in closed-loop supply chains: the assets need to find their way back to their owner after being used at a customer location.

At a larger scale of transportation asset, DB Cargo developed a telematics system to monitor the 13,000 freight cars it currently uses for railway transportation in Europe. The mobile stations attached to the freight cars not only communicate their current location, but also check measurements such as the refrigeration temperature and report unauthorized access to freight cars as well as severe impacts caused by careless shunting maneuvers. The system automatically alerts the parties involved to deviances from the planned transport schedule.

Dow Chemical and the American Chemistry Council teamed to utilize satellite communications, global positioning systems, RFID, and other sensors to monitor the status of hazardous materials in transit. If a material that poses a threat to humans is being transported by rail, determining the substance and appropriate precautionary measures can take valuable time in the event of an incident. Sensors monitor the chemical tankers for tampering, leaks, and temperature and pressure changes. The system will include mapping capabilities and automated e-mail or cell phone notifications to relevant parties if irregularities are detected with a shipment. The railcars already had RFID tags, facilitating a key piece of item-level identification for the project.[6]

Intel Corporation is a $38 billion manufacturer and marketer of microprocessors. The production process occurs in extremely expensive fabrication facilities, frequently under clean-room conditions. Industrial gases are considered "factory-critical" in that only 36 hours' inventory is held on site and a shortage could necessitate a plant shutdown. Because the cylinders and other vendor-owned containers had no tracking mechanism, factory managers had no visibility into potential disruptions. RFID tags were applied to the canisters and tracked through the supply chain, from fill through transport to consumption and return. Savings include decreased scrapping of product, valued in the millions of dollars. Risk is reduced both through inventory visibility and the ability to quarantine all items in a lot suspected of contamination or out-of-spec performance.

Retailers utilize a variety of methods for automatic replenishment of sold items. Point of sale systems can generate order requests at certain numbers of units scanned, for example. A more complex approach uses a time basis, which can factor in seasonality by comparing to past years' performance. Algorithmic modeling can factor in promotions, weather, seasonality, and economic health, and other variables to generate sophisticated automated forecasts and orders. More complex still are multi-echelon systems that monitor various actors in the supply chain, tracking inventory levels, shipment size and frequency, and consumer behavior.[7]

Transparency into requirements and stocks throughout the entire supply chain can avert the "bullwhip effect." The term refers to a troublesome pattern of behaviors in which fluctuations in demand at the end of the supply chain, instead of leveling out, increase in amplitude as they travel up to previous stages. If suppliers do not have information about a customer's stock levels and requirements, their only way of determining requirements is from the customer's order. Random events can be interpreted as trends, so actors across the chain often overcorrect inventory levels. Various parties adapt their sales forecasts and inventories, consequently submitting disproportionately high orders to their suppliers. The consequences are excessively high inventories and surplus capacity.[8]

Intercompany transparency in the fulfillment process reduces the costs for transportation, storage, and production, and requires less administration, assuming a relatively small number of actors that need to align.

Automation

The ideal fulfillment process requires minimal human interaction unless the order management system is unable to make a decision or automation is not a viable option. Business process software, machine control, and sensor and actuator technologies are taking on many tasks that were previously completed manually. Humans are needed, for instance, if in-flight order changes or cancellations need to be addressed. Highly automated processes incur fewer costs and, above all, prevent indecision, delays, and errors caused by integration gaps.

Examples such as NikeID (see Chapter 4) and NuImage's Build Your Own Awning (see Exhibit 5.4)[9] show that personalization and automation need not be polar opposites: on the contrary, automation is the key to

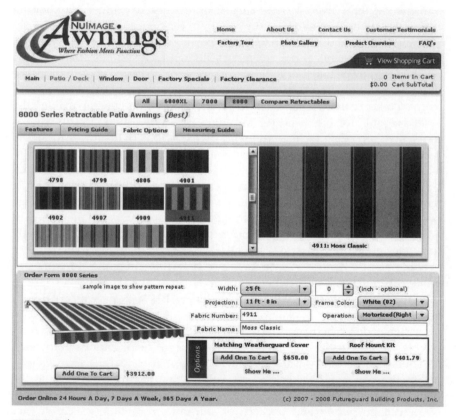

EXHIBIT 5.4 Automated Self-Service Customization Is within the Reach of Any Size Business

Source: © 2007–2008 Futureguard Building Products, Inc.

making personalization affordable. The initial outlay for automation may be high, but the results are low marginal costs for individual products.

> The role of people in the fulfillment process is changing progressively from processor to process monitor and enhancer.

Certain services, like personalized product documentation and certificates of analysis, lend themselves well to automation. Electronic order documents are frequently an integral part of deliveries. With global trade on the increase, automated processing of customs and security documentation is being facilitated by a new generation of tools. The automated notifications frequently inform the customer that he need do nothing, but the transparency of a given process step at an ecosystem partner may help in planning, risk management, or supply chain processes.

Automating and modularizing services is often described as "industrializing" the way services are created. Building-block systems enable media producers to piece together different components to create contributions for different channels. The BBC, CNN, and other news organizations can package video for broadcast, for Web distribution, and for archiving, making the asset available for future needs. Metadata issues are often critical: what is the source recording technology, who owns various rights for distribution, when has the asset been used, what is the edit history, etc.

Zappos is a popular U.S.-based online retailer that was recently acquired by Amazon. It competes by delivering extremely high levels of service that have helped the company develop a loyal following, even though the price points are only minimally discounted. Satisfied customers tell their friends: 43 percent of new customers come to the site based on word of mouth. Revenues grew from $1.6 million in 2000 to over $1 billion in 2008. In 2009, *Fortune* named Zappos #23 on its list of best 100 companies to work for, while *BusinessWeek* named the company #7 on its Top 25 Customer Service Champs—ahead of such established leaders as BMW, Four Seasons Hotels, and Nordstrom.[10]

After it diversified into apparel and accessories, which are not compatible with the racks on which boxed shoes are held, Zappos automated its Louisville, Kentucky warehouse with industrial robots that bring shelving sections to stock picker/packers rather than making people go to the items. Productivity has increased, error rates are extremely low, and an order can be picked and packed for shipping in as little as 12 minutes after receipt. In addition, shrinkage is reduced because employees are excluded from the shelving area. Robots do not need light or air conditioning, so power consumption is lower than for conveyor systems that typically run continuously whether or not items are on the belts. Finally, workplace quality is improved for the employees: injury rates are lower, workers do less walking, and they can speak conversationally in the absence of typical warehouse noise levels.

Office Depot sells office supplies around the world. Its new distribution center in Leicester, England, combines a variety of automated solutions, given that its large SKU (stock-keeping unit) count includes many different demand patterns. The 450 most frequently ordered products are picked automatically, while a pick-to-light system allows employees to identify and select fast-selling items without paper order. Finally, a pick-to-tote area supports employee ergonomics for medium and slow-selling items. The facility won several awards for environmental sustainability: shipping boxes are custom-cut to height for each order, reducing wasted shipping volume and cardboard use, and the conveyor automatically shuts down during periods of slow order activity. The new facility supports same-day delivery while doubling the throughput of the previous system.[11]

Automated fulfillment processes are already eliminating many potential sources of quality defects. They also supply detailed, up-to-date quality information for detecting and preventing errors early, as approaches like total quality management (TQM), Six Sigma, and ISO 9000 aspire to achieve.

> Automation and modularization enable personalized services with high fixed costs but very low variable costs.

Postponement

Sometimes called delayed differentiation, postponement is the process of a supplier delaying various decisions and activities as late as possible to preserve option value, lower inventory levels, and respond more precisely to demand. While the key concepts date from 1950, with key refinements in 1965, the practice of postponement is still far from universal.[12] It represents a shift from make-to-stock to make-to-order production, with many challenges to prevailing financial, labor, marketing, and other processes.

Postponement has four primary forms:

1. Purchasing postponement, which delays procurement of raw material inputs, particularly those that are expensive or have special handling requirements
2. Manufacturing postponement, in which work-in-process inventory is held until orders specify the particular facets of final assembly

3. Logistics postponement involves the movement of semi-finished goods to facilities close to customer delivery points for final completion
4. Time postponement, a practice of maintaining finished goods in a central location for rapid dispatch to customers in response to custom orders

An extreme case of postponement is the lobster. Because it must be kept alive until cooking, the shipping requirements are stringent. Clearwater Seafoods of Canada ships lobsters by the truckload 1,600 miles inland, from Nova Scotia to Louisville, Kentucky, avoiding the potential delays of processing multiple small orders through customs. Once in Louisville, the crustaceans are transferred to saltwater holding tanks to recover from the 30-hour ride. After being rejuvenated, they are shipped in special containers through UPS's Worldport hub to destinations around the world. 30,000 pounds of lobster per week moved through the distribution center as of 2006.[13] (In another IT innovation, Clearwater also uses a Google Earth widget to map the current location of its fishing vessels on its Web site.)

IKEA has taken the concept of manufacturing postponement to an extremely high level: final assembly of many furniture items occurs in people's houses. The company (see Chapter 7) works closely with its suppliers to source and design attractive furniture than can be location-neutral and flat-packed whenever possible, making its products acceptable in many countries while keeping transportation and warehousing costs low.

Benetton and HP's postponement solutions became classic examples. Benetton manufactured white T-shirts to begin with, dying them only later once there was a more exact indication of customer demand. The company could always deliver, but did not have to stock large quantities of every color before fashion trends emerged.[14] As far back as the early nineties, HP began shifting the final process of assembling printers and other computer hardware to plants located as close as possible to the customer—to the major sales centers.[15]

After a manufacturing facility burned down, Milliken, a privately held textile manufacturer based in South Carolina, rebuilt it along radical new lines. Using a proprietary ink-injection technology called Millitron, the new factory could produce carpets and mats with customized patterns, standard colors, or both. The current generation of the Millitron is being selectively licensed around the world and features over 13,000 micro-injectors that dye the carpet yarns from top to bottom, with 400 individually addressable dots per square inch. Just as Benetton only manufactured white T-shirts, Milliken postpones coloration until demand is known.

Different companies associate different solutions with the concept of postponement. Sharp, a global electronics manufacturer, produces components in low-wage countries and processes them into consumables close to the customer. Forty percent of Sharp's production activities take place in Japan, 60 percent overseas. Postponement is relatively common in electronics markets, as different line voltages, license details, language requirements, and partner agreements require that a game console, for instance, will be slightly different from country to country.

From the customer's perspective, postponement means being able to specify requirements as late as possible. Vehicle manufacturers are particularly well known for this practice. "For some years now, BMW customers have been able to modify their personalized vehicle up to five days before assembly begins. The plant, in turn, has to defer production until the specifications have been finalized. And in turn, a gearbox or seat supplier has to defer production until the precise requirements are known. This process is already possible for 90 percent of all orders, thanks to close electronic links between dealers and the BMW Group, but also between the BMW Group and its suppliers, and ultimately, between suppliers and their suppliers," explained Jürgen Maidl in 2004, who was at that time CIO of the BMW Group.

The automotive industry associates postponement with just-in-time (the time of assembly) and just-in-sequence (the assembly sequence) delivery, concepts that have all but eliminated the need for storage in the production process.[16] But such efforts have also eliminated inventory buffers, with the result that delivery problems can bring production to a halt in the space of a few hours.

While the costs in money and change efforts are significant, postponement's benefits are clear:

- Lower inventory costs for finished goods but also potentially raw materials and work in process
- Lower transportation costs
- Lower risk of product obsolescence
- Lower demand variability, simpler forecasting, and greater responsiveness to market trends
- Customized products can deliver competitive advantages such as time to market, as well as command a price premium

---

If a company shifts final assembly to a time and location close to the customer in time or space, it can supply more personalized solutions and avoid make-to-stock production, while still realizing economies of scale.

Realizing the Vision

If we compare the status of intercompany order management with the internal processes commonly found today, we can discern a wide gulf. Even the automotive industry, a pioneer in networking customers and suppliers, is still far from achieving seamless processes between OEMs and suppliers; in fact, the overall health of the relationship between OEMs such as Ford and tier1 suppliers, like Johnson Controls or Bosch, is extremely unclear as bankruptcies are unfolding on both sides. New forms of fulfillment require management to demonstrate new business models and a readiness to cooperate.

Barriers

The main barriers to efficient order management are:

- *Lack of information due to inaccurate data entry.* Tracking and analyzing deliveries in detail will remain too expensive, as long as data has to be entered manually: Billions of dollars annually are spent across the globe rekeying data. Stock levels, delivery status, and order error messages are not accurate or up to date. Exceptions, such as an imminent break in the cold chain for foodstuffs, cannot be detected in enough time to implement corrective action.
- *Data islands.* Information about stock, requirements, and exceptions as well as master data for products and business partners is kept locally (often in spreadsheets or point-solution systems) in individual companies. However, it is not accessible either to other units in the same company or to partners in the chain.
- *Lack of standards.* Catering perfectly to a customer process means processing orders across company boundaries while appearing to deliver them from one source. This requires standards for processes (planning procedures), applications (BOM management), data (article master data), and information technology (radio frequencies for RFID). Such perfection will still be a distant dream throughout the 2010s, but slow progress will continue to be made.
- *Process islands.* Even within one company, it often proves impossible to implement a single, standard process for order management. Given that the majority of all companies currently use multiple systems in parallel for entering and managing orders, it is obvious that vast amounts of data are being transferred manually between systems.
- *Increasing complexity.* Businesses have been striving for internal process integration for more than 20 years. Intercompany cooperation is

far more complicated. Personalized products and services, coupled with increased automation, add to the complexity.

- *Insecure basis for partnering.* New forms of order fulfillment depend largely on business partners, customers, and suppliers pulling together. Two key issues are the critical mass and an acceptable (fair) distribution of costs and benefits.
- *Power shifts.* Cooperation is an obstacle because it involves ceding independence and threatens to weaken the market position.

Enablers

A wide variety of tools are becoming available to enable enhanced fulfillment processes:

- *Service-oriented architectures.* Building on the data standardization and cost efficiencies of traditional ERP, SOA enables better inter-company collaboration, allowing business processes to span organizational boundaries. A business ecosystem can define end-to-end processes, supported by a variety of corporate entities, sharing data and lowering processing costs while maintaining consistency and security.
- *Enterprise software.* IT accommodates new solutions for order management in many ways. The most significant enabler remains the classic ERP system, which has morphed into a suite of components that better support process modularity and flexibility through standardized interfaces to other systems. Software vendors have also enhanced the functions of ERP systems with process software for fulfilling orders (supply chain management) as well as increased analytic capacity, which can enhance the planning process.
- *Internet.* In the 1980s, high costs and rigid processes prohibited the widespread use of Electronic Data Interchange (EDI). Only between 2 and 8 percent of companies, usually large enterprises, use EDI. Additionally, those that do deploy it on average with less than one third of trading partners and for very few processes. Cheaper and more flexible Internet technology has helped electronic collaboration between companies.
- *Electronic services.* Internet-based services for creating customs forms, tracking deliveries, processing credit cards, and authenticating business partners fulfill coordination tasks in the order-management process and achieve economies of scale for subprocesses needed in many enterprises. Their binding semantics bring companies one step closer to a standardized fulfillment process.
- *Embedded systems and mobility.* Widely available low-cost sensors heralded a quantum leap in data collection techniques. They allow the flow

of goods to be recorded in detail and in real time at a reasonable price. Actuators can execute measures (withdraw stock, for example) without manual interim steps. Mobile technologies are freeing sensors and actuators from the restrictions of location, say for monitoring cold chains or marking spoiled goods automatically. The 2-D bar code, able to be read by any smartphone, has moved beyond the supply chain and into public usage for advertising, direction-finding, and other applications.

■ *Content management.* Content management systems organize unstructured electronic documents like e-mail correspondence and shipping documents, as well as software downloads and assembly instructions.

Checklist

□ What degree of delivery precision do you achieve—do you fulfill orders to a high quality, on time, and in the right location? What degree of precision does the customer expect?

□ How many orders have your customers rejected in the past year due to quality defects? How does this figure compare to your competitors?

□ What are your administrative costs for order processing?

□ In which areas are your order lead times too long?

□ Which standards will you need to comply with for order processing in 2010? Which organizations are determining the standards?

□ Which enterprise in your value chain will dictate the fulfillment process in the future?

□ What percentage of revenues do your logistics costs represent? How does this figure compare to your competitors?

□ Can you and your partners track the status of an order through the supply chain beyond your own company boundaries?

□ What will be the next projects for reducing costs and increasing flexibility in your fulfillment process?

CHAPTER 6

Strategy-Compliant Management

Management Summary

Executive management performs two major roles: The first is to direct current operations, while the second is to transform the organization's business model. Management always remains the preserve of people, but IT can provide additional tools, particularly to enhance the quality and visibility of information related to both facets of top management's remit.

The first set of activities, operative management, *translates* the business strategy into action in day-to-day activities, *monitors* results, *assesses* results against predefined targets, and, where necessary, *initiates* corrective measures. It guides the company toward the realization of its strategic objectives. Many managerial tasks often relate to recurring, routine processes such as budgeting, incentive setting, evaluating, and reporting.

The second, transformational element encompasses a range of activities: strategy development, continuous adaptation of the business model and organization, and transformation projects. The goal of business model transformation is to move the company away from its current situation and toward long-term competitive objectives such as margin growth, maintenance of market share, or geographic expansion.

A core body of data that integrates internal and external sources can provide an accurate picture of the company's activities to support both facets of leadership's task; many firms aspire to have this body of information serve as a "single source of truth." Companywide standardization can make it possible to compare organizational units, address customer needs more seamlessly, and allocate resources. In the pursuit of this standardization, new technical tools help to curb complexity, provide insight, and cope with information overload.

The business concepts related to strategy-compliant management include many of the essential tools at an executive's disposal:

- *Environment analysis*. In a volatile, complex world, knowing what is happening in the relevant contexts is essential.
- *Management process*. The objectives, how they will be achieved, and how they will be measured are often surprisingly difficult to discern in an organization.
- *Standardization*. Uniform metrics, management processes, and incentive policies anchor the strategy within the organization.
- *Focusing*. Employee performance can often be evaluated on a few key figures derived from the critical success factors in the business strategy.
- *Cascading*. Cascading the business strategy consistently shares the corporate goals among business units, departments, and individual employees.
- *Management by exception*. Management by exception is an old principle that has acquired new significance thanks to the depth and breadth of integrated enterprise data, and a high degree of business process automation.
- *Corporate governance*. Issues related to executive pay, corporate social responsibility, and regulatory compliance, not to mention basic viability and profitability in the downturn, have focused a spotlight on board-level activity.

If the seven factors in Exhibit 6.1 determine enterprise value, it follows that they must also shape managerial approaches:

1. *Product and service*. Quantitative and qualitative analyses—of products, markets, budgeting, and governance—contribute to the success of the firm's offerings.
2. *Customer access*. Sales management sheds light on market potential and exploitation.
3. *Customer retention*. Difficult to express in figures, partner effectiveness and customer retention are becoming increasingly important metrics.
4. *Ecosystem*. Coordinating the ecosystem occupies a wide variety of often redundant resources and sometimes subtly influences enterprise priorities.
5. *Emotion*. Brand value, customer satisfaction, employee loyalty, and investor confidence are difficult to quantify, but IT can help measure and track relevant indicators.
6. *Price/cost*. The accounting requirements dictated by international regulations cannot be fulfilled without an integrated base of information

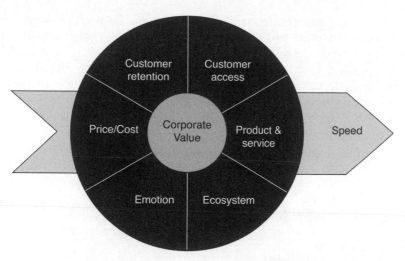

EXHIBIT 6.1   Management That Increases Enterprise Value Must Be Consistent and Align with Strategy

combined with consistent managerial processes. Internal resource allocation is similarly impossible without sound data.

7. *Speed.* Cascading targets makes it easier to implement strategic objectives faster across all management levels. Thanks to internal and external information sources, changes can be recognized and implemented quickly and assessed sooner. It becomes possible to respond faster to "background noise."

Vision

Executive managers face tremendously high expectations. They should exhibit strong leadership skills, boost stock price and dividends, understand the business yet think out of the box, drive the company's transformation, and act as role models.

The information available to management is better than ever before. Enterprise software records every business transaction; mobile devices and sensors capture data automatically; e-mail keeps track of exchanged messages; the Internet provides a gateway to external sources of information; and digitization makes every piece of information usable.

We are entering an age in which every piece of information ever created will essentially become available within seconds, anywhere in the world—but only if one knows what to ask for.

The management dashboard—an integrated data platform with a uniform, enterprise-wide structure and shared semantics (meaning)—will become the single source of truth for objectives, monitoring, and analysis. Search engines, visualization and analysis tools, and other aids distill and deliver the relevant data to people in specific roles. They reduce the deluge of information by conducting intelligent searches, selecting data, and reducing the dataset to exceptions, for example, if critical patterns arise or threshold values are exceeded.

External reporting also reflects management's speed and ability to provide information. Management is able to publish quarterly and annual financial statements efficiently and ahead of the competition. Mergers, acquisitions, and ecosystem partner interactions benefit from superior operational and strategic information.

From Reporting to Strategy Implementation

While initial implementations of ERP systems considerably improved reporting accuracy with standardized inputs and outputs, more recent generations of these systems have stressed integration with and instrumentation of strategic management processes. Three companies from different countries, industries, and cultures illustrate how this transition is being carried out.

Management by Key Figures at SAP AG

With a market share of 41 percent[1] and peer group share of 60 percent, SAP AG, based in Walldorf, Germany, is the world's leading supplier of enterprise application software.

To implement the strategy, management guides the company using clearly defined key figures that are communicated throughout the company, divided into three categories. First, there are key figures that are published externally and flow directly into the financial markets' valuation of the company. They include operating margin, sales figures, and market share. Then there are key figures that are communicated externally but need further explanation, such as investment in research and development. Finally, there are figures that are purely internal, such as customer and employee satisfaction.

Most key figures are calculated, presented, and compared on the basis of four rolling quarters. Every quarter, the comparison period moves forward one quarter. This ensures that the key figures are up to date and relevant for decision making. SAP executives compare the figures from the current period (four quarters) with the results from the previous period and with the budget.

SAP compares all its key figures with the actual values from the previous year, the previous forecast, the defined goals and objectives, and, where applicable, competition figures and market expectations. It assesses and remunerates all employees on the basis of personal development and the key figures relevant to their respective areas. Management thereby ensures that the strategy is implemented directly and that the whole organization focuses on a small number of corporate-level critical success factors.

The value-based key figures for operational activities aim at sustainable, profitable growth. In the case of sales growth, the major concern is increased license sales, since new license sales generate additional revenue from servicing, consulting, and education. SAP breaks down business area profitability into regions, product groups, and industry sectors and balances the figures with market surveys.

SAP regards customer satisfaction and customer penetration as critical success factors. In addition to market share by region, product, and industry, SAP's share of key customers' IT budgets (share of wallet) plays a decisive role.

Every year, SAP measures satisfaction levels among its 86,000-plus customers[2] and commissions an external, neutral partner to compile the results. Customer satisfaction is considered when employee objectives are set and reviewed. The "net promote score" is a key control mechanism, indicating the number of customers willing to recommend SAP to other companies. In addition, the company monitors the value of the SAP brand name. In 2001, it rose from position 96 to 44 in *BusinessWeek's* rankings, climbing to position 34 in 2004 and 31 in 2008.

Another aspect of management is improving the portfolio of solutions and products. Key figures for the quality of products and services can be used as indicators to formulate and implement the strategy. Once the achievable market has been defined, it is possible to quote the market share for each solution, product, and region. In the case of new products, the momentum of the product launch and market penetration is of particular interest. In research and development, the most revealing key figures are utilization (number of production installations) and the number and weighting of patents.

Employees and partners must keep developing in line with customer requirements, market trends, and technological innovations. SAP continuously assesses the quality delivered by partners as well as its employees' qualifications and profiles. To measure employee satisfaction, SAP conducts an annual employee survey, the results of which are used in manager appraisals. Indicators of successful partner management include the number of certified partners and the percentage of their portfolio made up by SAP products.

SAP's approach to management pursues two basic principles: clarity and unity. This means standardized key figures across the company—understandable to everyone. SAP does not manipulate the data for different target groups or purposes; instead, it ensures that all parties work with the same figures, basing decisions on and being measured against the same facts.

A management portal summarizes the main key figures from different applications for different roles, ranging from the supervisory and executive boards down to secretarial level. (See Exhibits 6.2 and 6.3.)

The portal contains structured and unstructured information. Structured information such as transaction data flows directly into the portal from the internal transactional systems or external data sources. It consequently portrays a realistic image of the company and prevents redundancy, inconsistency, and "embellishment."

Approximately 50 percent of the managerial information in the portal is unstructured, consisting of data such as customer feedback, audit details, and project and analyst reports. A search engine makes it easy to locate information.

Managing Scale at Saudi Aramco

Owned by the Saudi Arabian Government, Saudi Aramco is a fully-integrated, global petroleum enterprise and a world leader in exploration and producing, refining, distribution, shipping, and marketing. The company manages the largest proven reserves of conventional crude oil, 260 billion barrels, and manages the fourth-largest gas reserves in the world, 263 trillion cubic feet. Saudi Aramco, through its affiliate, Vela Marine International Ltd, owns and operates the world's second largest tanker fleet to help transport its crude oil production, which amounted to 1.7 million barrels per day in 2008. In addition to its headquarters in Dhahran, Saudi Arabia, Saudi Aramco, through its affiliates, has joint ventures and subsidiary offices in China, Japan, the Netherlands, the Republic of Korea, Malaysia, Singapore, the United Arab Emirates, the United Kingdom, and the United States. Saudi Aramco also refines and distributes oil products throughout the Kingdom of Saudi Arabia to meet domestic daily energy demands.

Nearly everything about Saudi Aramco is big or unique. From its volume (by itself, the company produces an eighth of the planet's oil) to the terrain of its wells, where temperatures routinely exceed 140 degrees Fahrenheit and specially designed trucks cope with the soft, impassable sand, to its governance structure, Saudi Aramco faces unusual management challenges.[3]

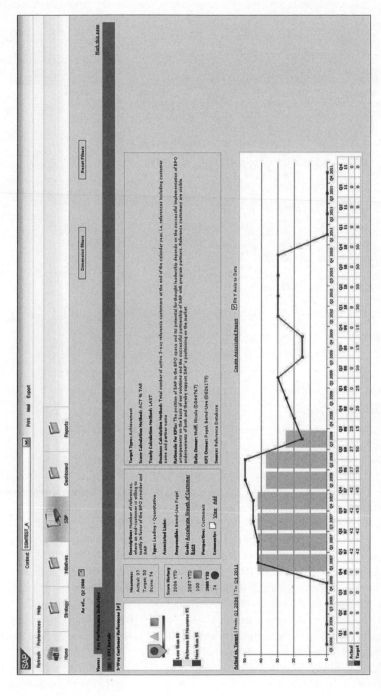

EXHIBIT 6.2 SAP Corporate Portal—Key Performance Indicators (excerpt)

Source: Courtesy of SAP.

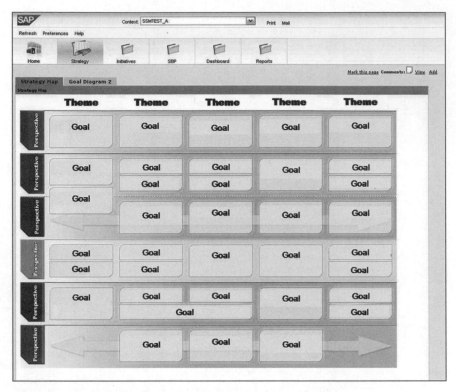

EXHIBIT 6.3   Goals and Objectives in the SAP Corporate Portal (extract)

Source: Courtesy of SAP.

Saudi Aramco began as an oil concession granted by the one-year-old nation of Saudi Arabia to Standard Oil of California, now Chevron, in 1933. The first commercial oil field was discovered five years later, and such infrastructure as refineries, pipelines, and ports were built thereafter. Gas field development and shipping capacity were added later. In the 1970s and 1980s, the Saudi government acquired the company's assets, and Saudi Aramco was established in 1988. It now operates worldwide.

Saudi Aramco publishes an annual review with extensive nonfinancial data, in some cases (with regard to reserves, for example) more complete than that released by investor-owned companies. The board of directors includes both Saudis and three former top executives from western businesses.

Human resources challenges abound. The company's home land of Saudi Arabia is an Islamic kingdom, but about 5,000, or 10 percent, of the company's employees are expatriates come from 66 different countries. Reducing this reliance on outsiders has led to a concerted effort to encourage contractors to increase their employment of Saudis. At the same time, formal knowledge management efforts are in place to map the competencies of retiring professionals. Saudi Aramco also provides medical care (over one million patient visits per year), sometimes through company-owned clinics and hospitals, and in some instances the company has built the whole city.

Material assets also require management attention. With drilling, refining, and other operations across the world, knowing what equipment is where, not to mention spare parts availability, can have a measurable effect on output. Assets can range from drilling equipment to helicopters to pipeline supplies; the materials system catalogue includes 570,000 SKUs. Project management operates on a massive scale: the Shaybah site, for example, could not begin construction until 50 million man-hours were expended moving vast amounts of sand.

All these processes support the main effort: extraction and sale of petroleum and gas products. In 2008, Saudi Aramco produced 3.25 billion barrels of crude oil. While Saudi Aramco is primarily an oil company, it also owns housing, hospitals, various communications networks, and fleets of tankers and aircraft. It employs more than 50,000 people in many time zones, who speak multiple languages with various degrees of fluency. It must manage huge oil reserves, growing global demand, profitability, and long-term planning, as well as social and economic development objectives. In short, while the company is one of the biggest in the world, it may also be the most complex.[4]

Coping with Hypergrowth at Vestas

In the midst of a global economic downturn, how many companies' shares gained 25 percent in the first half of 2009? The company was neither a biotech startup nor a Silicon Valley tech firm, but rather a heavy manufacturer headquartered in Denmark. Vestas, the world's leading producer of wind turbines, seeks to put wind power on a par with oil and gas. Addressing this bold vision, the 30-year-old company is experiencing intense interest from both customers and investors. Such success has doomed many previous companies that were ill-equipped to cope with the many dimensions of hypergrowth, but the picture at Vestas looks promising in part because of the management processes already in place in this unique firm of 20,000 people.

Revenue increased from 3.8 billion Euros in 2006 to just over 6 billion Euros in 2008. The company has delivered strong results in a highly uncertain market, in part because of a strong organizational culture and in part because of disciplined management practices. The division of labor in corporate governance between what we called transformational and operational management is crystal clear, in part because of Danish law. According to the company's Web site,

> *The Board takes care of the general management of the company such as:*
>
> > *Appointing the Executive Management*
> > *Ensuring responsible organization of the company's business*
> > *Defining the company's strategy*
> > *Assessing the adequacy of the company's capital contingency programme*
>
> *The Executive Management takes care of the day-to-day running of the company, observing the guidelines and recommendations laid down by the Board.*[5]

The company maintains a long-term view, and there is then smooth continuity between long- and short-term objectives. The firm's strategy, vision, and mission are precisely defined:

No. 1 in Modern Energy

Wind power is modern energy because it is financially competitive, predictable, independent, fast and clean. Based on its No. 1 in Modern Energy strategy, Vestas intends to build the world's strongest energy brand.

Wind, Oil and Gas

The Wind, Oil and Gas vision expresses Vestas' ambition of assuming leadership in the efforts to make wind an energy source on a par with fossil fuels. Modern energy currently accounts for less than 2 per cent of the world's electricity production.

Failure Is Not an Option

The Vestas mission 'Failure is not an option' expresses the organisation's commitment to optimising its work processes, to safety and products and to a structured follow-up on all errors.'[6]

The firm acknowledges the place of emotion and human capability in its statement of culture: Vestas is driven forward by its employees, whose willpower, imagination and ability to constantly develop the technology and the organisation have made Vestas the industry leader.... Vestas seeks to promote a culture characterised by independent initiatives and collaboration across professional and organisational boundaries and in which the dynamics and sense of responsibility that usually characterise a small company are retained.[7]

From such a systematic framing of objectives and resources, setting operational goals is a short step. For 2009, three straightforward numbers informed investment, sales plans, inventory levels, procurement practices, hiring, and other activities:

1. Achieve an EBIT margin of 11–13 percent
2. Ensure net working capital represents a maximum of 10 percent of annual revenue by the end of 2009
3. Achieve revenue of 7.2 billion Euros

Given the nature of the industry, in which service calls can occur 390 feet in the air, employee health and safety receive close attention, both as operating targets (15 employee injuries per 1 million working hours) and as strategic initiatives. The following model (see Exhibit 6.4) shows a plan for cascading workplace safety objectives and programs.

The firm emphasizes communication and transparency. Both in-house and customer-facing company magazines are available to the public on the Web site. Quarterly and annual results are published in six languages, and the company's order book is open.

Given so much market uncertainty in alternative energy, Vestas benefits from the stability of a solid, easily conveyed, long-term vision as it translates into day-to-day actions on the part of both the management team and the workforce. Especially with a global client base, a rapidly changing landscape of regulations and subsidies, intellectual property challenges, and a variety of other challenges related to its unique market and technology, management clarity is paramount. The effort put into precise definitions and relationships between the company's long- and short-term goals, advantages, and challenges will almost certainly deliver tangible benefits in today's energy market.

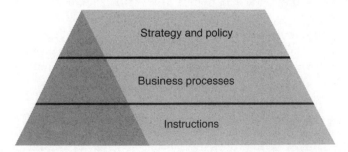

EXHIBIT 6.4 Strategy at Vestas Cascades to Processes and Individual Task Instructions

Concepts of Operative Management

Many companies have good strategies that are poorly implemented. Missed targets often result from deficiencies in the way the business strategy is conveyed and measured within the organization: insufficient resources, poor communication, lack of defined responsibilities, and inadequate instruments to monitor realization.

IT has enabled a range of business concepts related to management that until recently have been difficult to deploy at scale. Even with technology's assistance, however, these concepts still require appropriate executive attention:

- *Environment analysis.* External information, especially from specialized information providers, can deliver early warnings with regard to changes in customer and competitor behavior (trends, critical patterns) and enable business managers to respond in good time.
- *Management process.* The management process sets the targets, defines the key figures, monitors performance, and implements the measures.
- *Standardization.* Uniform metrics, management processes, and incentive policies make it easier to anchor the strategy within the organization and communicate its objectives.
- *Focusing.* Employee performance measurements and the incentives for their attainment are based on a few, meaningful key figures derived from the critical success factors in the business strategy.
- *Cascading.* Cascading the business strategy consistently shares the corporate goals among business units, departments, and individual employees.
- *Management by exception.* Management by exception is an established principle that has acquired new significance thanks to the depth and breadth of integrated data associated with enterprise software and the user-friendly presentation of information in portals and analysis tools. The sheer volume of data often forces management to concentrate on exceptions.
- *Corporate governance.* Increasing demands for transparent management from stakeholders and particularly legislators are prompting many companies to improve and harmonize internal and external reporting systems.

Environment Analysis

An agile company scours diverse external sources for information about customers, competitors, products, technologies, regions and many other issues. Companies are drawing on electronic information from analysts and news agencies, as well as from company Web sites, magazines, e-shops, and patent databases. Blogs and other social media such as Facebook and Twitter have assumed an important position alongside search engines, albeit at the cost of extreme "noise."

In their book *Fast Strategy*, Yves Doz of Insead and Mikko Kosonen of Nokia list five sources of knowledge exchange with the outside world:

1. Leading customers
2. Noncustomers
3. End-users
4. Partners and complementors
5. Substance experts and think tanks[8]

Some of these will be unfamiliar to certain types of managers, particularly when the emphasis is on exchange, but the list is a useful one.

Environment analysis combines contextual information with internal knowledge (content management) and applies it to detect opportunities and risks early and respond before competitors. If a sporting goods manufacturer wants to stay ahead, it must be quick to recognize fashion trends and launch its own product at the right time, since the high profit margins are usually achieved while a trend is still new. Companies are battling for access to information and, more importantly, to use the information for business decisions.

In certain situations, the algorithmic sense-making available in common analytical tools is useful in uncovering and providing relevant information, wherever it may have originated. The cost and availability of such information are improving: in oil and gas, for example, IT has helped drop the cost of a 3-D seismic map of the subsurface from $8 million per square kilometer in 1980 to $1 million in 1990 to $90,000 in 2005. But even the best analytics cannot replace the human intelligence needed to draw the right conclusions from the information.

Market intelligence is never perfect. People's purchase intent measurements rarely track with subsequent market share or profitability measures. Two indications can be inconsistent for many reasons: different methodologies, different sample populations, or different analytical objectives. As they track housing starts, for example, lumber companies, mortgage lenders, and municipal authorities have diverging agendas and do very different things with the same numbers. Thus, even when much is known about the future, interpretation and action never follow a straight line.

The changes enforced by market and competitive conditions leave companies torn between agility and continuity. Employees must accept and be able to cope with market and process change if the company is to retain its momentum and flexibility. Controlling these conflicting objectives is a key managerial task.

> For many companies, introducing managers to the use of both external and internal information represents a huge shift in policy.

Management Process

The closed-loop management principle is one of the oldest: Define targets—implement targets—measure performance—derive measures. It is simple and logical. Most every manager claims to follow this principle—but if the managers among us are honest, how many of us would have to admit to still having large areas of white on our "management maps"? Robert Kaplan and David Norton of Harvard Business School have revised the classic model, updating it and including more connections to both strategy on one end of the cycle and execution on the other (see Exhibit 6.5).[9]

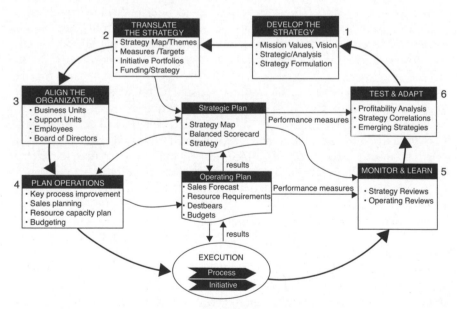

EXHIBIT 6.5   Revised Time-Proven Management Loop: More Nuances and Aligning More Completely to Strategy

Source: Reprinted with permission from *Execution Premium: Linking Strategy to Operations for Competitive Advantage* by Robert S. Kaplan and David P. Norton. Copyright © 2008 by Harvard Business Publishing Corporation; all rights reserved.

Implementing a rigorous closed management loop is a substantial undertaking, in part because a manager's many constituencies and objectives may operate on different "clock speeds": in retail, conceiving the fall merchandising program must occur long before the holiday selling season so the feedback loop is essentially annual, but labor turnover can become an issue in a matter of weeks, while credit shortages or interest rates move on yet another time scale. Integrated business software can supply accurate data that cannot be brushed aside easily, and business-intelligence tools make it simpler to evaluate this data in routine comparisons of target and actual values.

> The principle is old, but the complete life cycle of closed-loop management can now be completely supported by IT.

Standardization

In certain organizations, all units pursue the same goals regardless of country, culture, size, and other attributes. They can thus be assessed against the same criteria. Consumer package goods companies might be a useful example here. In other companies, the diversity of markets and particularities of business processes drive a greater need for local differentiation by geography, product line, or sales process. At General Electric, the jet engine division has very different management processes compared to the broadcast unit, so standardization would be a poor use of resources. In large banks, credit card operations, business lending, and high-net-worth services ("private banking") share little in the way of clients, processes, or performance metrics. Overcentralization can also impede merger and divestiture efforts in dynamic firms with high turnover among operating units.

Global companies have to find a balance between centralized, strategic approaches and local requirements. The international subsidiaries of global organizations are often relatively autonomous. Nonetheless, the organization may need to be able to effect complete attitude changes worldwide and implement global values, standards, and strategic decisions at all levels of the company.

Standardizing key figures and rules aligns strategy, business processes, employees, and systems throughout a company, potentially at the cost of flexibility. When standardization makes sense and a firm commits to implementation thereof, the following rules must be observed:

- *Consistency.* All parties use the same concepts to mean the same thing. Standardization is not primarily an issue for information systems; people must come to agreement on the whys and hows of defining which measures to derive, using which rules. Language differences, cultural issues, and regulatory circumstances often come into play. The quest for consistency also encompasses the subprocesses in the management process, such as performance feedback and cascading.

■ *Single source of truth.* All parties use the same data platform to prevent distortion, such as "embellished" reports. Of course, every person sees only the data that is relevant to his role. Managing the roles and authorizations (planning, management, and control) is becoming an increasingly complex task in global companies that are based on central information systems. Although essentially an HR task, access definition and control frequently falls to the IT department, in part because of the security and regulatory/audit implications.

■ *Uniformity counts above up-to-dateness.* The information used by all employees involved in a decision should be up to date, but it is even more important that the fact base be consistent to maintain organizational coherence.

> Common targets call for a standardized management process.

Cascading

A company anchors its strategic goals across the board by setting targets at all levels, from business units and departments down to individual employees.

SAP follows a clearly defined process to cascade corporate goals across the different areas of responsibility (see Exhibit 6.6). Once the corporate mission and business strategy have been developed and the target figures defined, the individual members of the executive board derive goals for their own organizational units and define strategies for achieving them. The proposals are discussed with the CEO and signed off by the executive board.

From this point on, the task of translating the strategy into action lies in the hands of individual board members. They use the same procedure to finalize the goals for their own areas. The process continues in this way until the goals have been firmly fixed at employee level through performance feedback meetings and clearly defined goals and objectives.

Harmonizing corporate and employee goals by setting personal goals and objectives, collecting performance feedback, and offering incentives provides management with an important control variable for implementing the business strategy. In general, only things that are measured as targets and passed on as defined goals and objectives are actually implemented.

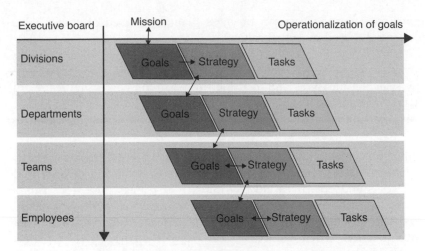

EXHIBIT 6.6 Cascading the Business Strategy at SAP

Source: Courtesy of SAP.

SAP conducts an annual performance feedback meeting with every employee. Participants compare actual achievements with planned targets and set goals for the coming year.

The cascading process breaks down corporate goals into separate modules that contain goals and strategies for the divisions, areas, and teams. The financial accounting, accounting, and controlling departments face the challenge of consolidating the results from these modules into consistent reports for the different organizational levels.

> Business process software and business intelligence allow data to be cascaded in various dimensions. However, very few companies actually use the possibilities consistently.

Focusing

Management must understand and communicate the "bare essentials." Consequently, managing also means translating the business strategy into a few, measurable key figures. This reduces complexity and keeps the company pointing in one direction.

Over the years, academics and practitioners have designed and tested a multitude of key-figure systems. Examples include balanced scorecards, Economic Value Added (EVA), and activity-based management.[10] Key figures are often the basis for business planning (based on target values) and control (based on actual values).

> By selecting measures and focusing on a handful of key figures, management sends clear signals to the organization.

Employees recognize the relevancy of the corporate goals expressed by the key figures and dedicate more energy to achieving them. The defined goals and objectives hide all but the key areas. SAP, for example, presents its managers all the measures in a portal that addresses different roles. The key figures give management a quick diagnosis of the company's situation. When necessary, more detailed analyses can be retrieved for individual areas. Balancing individual incentives, set annually, with the unfolding realities of daily business life remains one of the most difficult tasks of management. Motivating people both to do the right thing (choose the highest and best uses of their time) and to do the thing right (knowing when to follow established practice, and when to innovate) is no simple matter.

> Management means focusing the company on the bare essentials. The basis has to be on the combination of real-time, trustworthy data from the transactional IT applications with well-communicated strategic vision so everyone knows both what is to be done and how well it is being accomplished.

As Albert Einstein famously said, "Make everything as simple as possible, but no simpler." It is possible to err on the side of complexity, particularly in matrixed management where lines of authority are unclear. Tracking product integration, regional distribution, and sales organization all at once inevitably results in awkward processes, frequent meetings, and unclear responsibilities. At the same time, oversimplification is a danger as well, potentially blinding an organization to fundamental shifts in its competitive position.

Management by Exception

Management automates routine managerial tasks and concentrates on exceptions. Integrated management systems free up managerial resources while business activities are in sync with the defined goals and objectives. In the event of an exception (new sales trends, for example), management intervenes.

At KPMG, for example, management is based on key figures such as profit-sales ratio, profitability, and return on equity. All key figures are prepared monthly and presented to management in standardized reports. In addition to these periodic reports, KPMG compiles exception reports that describe any irregularities and provide extra, in-depth analyses of the affected areas.

> Management by exception relieves managers of routine tasks and reduces complexity at management level.

If a company uses standardized key figures based on the transactional systems, exceptions can be identified and escalated automatically. The crucial factors here are (1) the ability to escalate exceptions consistently and (2) a historical perspective to understand normal operating bands for key measures.

Corporate Governance

While it means many things to many people, transparency is a fact of life in executive management. Many countries have passed laws and regulations aimed at curbing the increasing number of corporate scandals, restoring investor and public confidence, and maintaining visibility of taxable entities and events. Financial metrics represent only one aspect of a company and are usually based on historical data. More attention is being paid to such issues as corporate social responsibility, onshore versus offshore labor practices, environmental sustainability, and intangibles such as brand equity, employee loyalty, and innovativeness.

According to a study by the Brooking Institution, between 50 percent and 85 percent of the assets held by U.S. firms do not appear in the financial reports of the companies surveyed.[11] New reporting guidelines from the IFRS require (or at least enable) intangible assets like brand value, client base, and human capital, irrespective of actual financial transactions, to be recognized separately as assets in the balance sheet; GAAP standards can vary considerably from IFRS rules. In order to manage intangible assets such as process quality, customer retention, and patents, companies need to find a way of assessing such assets accurately, presenting them in comparable dimensions, and summarizing them as binding goals and objectives.

IT plays a surprising role in corporate governance, specifically in the realm of regulatory compliance. If the company's compliance software suite is complete, auditors can attest that a known supplier is documenting business processes in a standard, concrete way because they have seen the same software in related companies and processes. In addition, software from a supplier that guarantees that it is up to date on legal standards worldwide can provide further confidence to investors, auditors, and regulators alike. All told, enterprise software can be a tool for increasing transparency of business processes both internally and externally.

Customers and investors have been sensitized by accounting scandals like those that gripped Enron and WorldCom in the United States, Parmalat in Europe, and Satyam in India. Governments, stock markets, customers, and suppliers are penalizing companies for opaque bookkeeping. Stakeholders are demanding information about companies' long-term health. In response, many organizations are not only improving their reporting systems but also focusing their management methods on key figures like customer satisfaction and employee quality, as well as introducing performance-related pay for managers.

One of the benchmarks against which the quality of management is measured is the speed with which external reports are published and their ability to provide meaningful information. "Fast close" refers to the practice of accelerating the preparation of quarterly or annual financial statements. In particular, companies operating in international capital markets are competing to present investors with audited group accounts in record time. Nineteen of the 30 DAX companies publish consolidated financial statements within 90 days. This is considerably quicker than the publication period of six months stipulated by the German Stock Corporation Act. At the same time, Cisco publicized the benefits of its "virtual close" only months before taking a $2.2 billion inventory write-down in 2002, so speed is not everything.

Fast close needs all areas related to accounting to be optimized, and it especially needs compatible information structures based on standardized group reporting guidelines and integrated software solutions. To satisfy management and legislators better, many finance departments are working to standardize processes and data. They are bundling group resources in shared service centers or outsourcing them to external specialists. To be successful, the management and reporting systems must build on data from transactional processes, rather than be running in parallel isolation.

> Sound corporate governance needs standard financial and reporting processes built on transactional data.

Realizing the Vision

Few areas show as deep a divide between theory and practice as management. Members of the same executive board can have a different understanding of management and put tools to different use. It is difficult to distinguish good and bad styles of leadership objectively: executives who have succeeded at one company frequently falter leading a different one.

Barriers

If we assume that IT helps managers record internal and external business activities faster and more accurately, and to implement companywide measures, then why do managers use IT tools in very different ways?

- *Managerial discipline.* Standardized managerial processes with standardized parameters and tools require a high level of discipline, for instance, to maintain sales forecasts or measure performance. Impulsive managers tend to respond to individual events. Employees frequently pursue personal career goals more fervently than corporate goals.
- *Regulations.* The Sarbanes-Oxley Act, new accounting standards such as the IFRS, and other regulations tie up management resources and investible funds. At Raytheon, a defense contractor, 175 IT people alone were involved in Sarbanes-Oxley documentation, testing, and audits.[12]
- *Challenging ecosystem management.* Planning and performance measurement are no longer restricted to one company, but in the case of supply chain management (SCM), for instance, relate to entire business networks without an overarching management instance. As many companies make the transition from hierarchical organizational structures with simple reporting paths to organizations based on processes, projects, and networks, managers have to face up to new challenges. Clear, hierarchical management processes and decision-making channels may be very efficient within one company but cannot be applied in an ecosystem, which operates more on the basis of persuasion and diplomacy.
- *Data islands.* Given the barriers to new management concepts already mentioned, it is easy to forget that an integrated data platform is the basic condition for end-to-end processes. In many cases, the information for managing a company is stored in heterogeneous IT applications and prepared using hundreds of spreadsheets. This approach runs considerable risk of reports overlapping or becoming inconsistent.
- *Increasing complexity.* Integrated business software produces such detailed data about business activities that it becomes possible to implement global management policies based on multiple dimensions

simultaneously, such as functional area, process, product, project, and region. It is no longer technology that sets the limits, but the degree of complexity that people can handle. The number of necessary coordination meetings alone restricts what is technically feasible: people can only work so many hours or comprehend so much information.

Enablers

Barriers preventing efficient management that are caused by people's behavior call for transformation efforts. Some hurdles, however, can be cleared by new advances in IT. External catalysts like Sarbanes-Oxley and the IFRS can accelerate implementation projects.

- *Service-oriented architectures.* Management visibility into extended enterprises, long supply chains, and outsourced partnerships requires high-quality data and compatibility among multiple information systems. IT heterogeneity is a fact of life in nearly every organization. SOA bridges internal operating units, and in addition, bridges across ecosystem partners. Strategic intent can be conveyed and monitored across enterprise boundaries, better supporting effective action in a networked economy.
- *Enterprise software.* Business process software—ERP systems and their enhancements for customer relationship management (CRM), supplier relationship management (SRM), product lifecycle management (PLM), and supply chain management (SCM)—now form the backbone not only for operational transactions but also for management based on reliable, actual data.
- *Integrated data platform.* Business software can deliver a base of integrated data in a form previously unknown. However, very few enterprises are actually exploiting the potential of such data.
- *Data warehouses.* No organization can get by with software from one vendor alone. Consequently, the company's information is spread across numerous IT applications. Data warehouses bring companies a big step closer to establishing efficient management databases, acting essentially as a reference database to connect all the necessary sources of information.
- *Analytical tools.* Analysis tools (business intelligence systems) are closely related to data warehouses and allow some users to navigate easily through large sets of data. For example, if an exception report highlights an unfavorable development in the profit margin at company level, analysis tools can help find the cause by product group, customer group, or region, The more precise the diagnosis, the more accurate the corrective measures will be.

■ *Knowledge management.* Besides direct communication between people, management is based partly on figures and partly on documents. Meeting minutes, e-mails, contracts, market research reports, product descriptions, and, in particular, Internet resources have fueled the flood of information immensely over the past 10 years. While enterprise search technologies have their place, significant attention is being paid to the role of social networking systems, both formal and informal, in finding answers inside a company or ecosystem.

Checklist

☐ What are the five most important key figures for managing your company? How up-to-date and reliable are these key figures?

☐ What are the critical success factors for your business?

☐ Which trends have you recognized before your competitors in the past (for instance, changes in customer behavior)?

☐ Which trends did you recognize too late? What were the consequences?

☐ How quickly can you launch a product in response to a new trend?

☐ How quickly can you respond to your competitors' marketing campaigns?

☐ Are your management figures based on transactional systems and data?

☐ Do you include forward-looking key figures such as "sales pipeline" in your management strategy?

☐ Do you have key figures for your company's innovativeness?

☐ Which other soft factors do you assess continually and systematically?

☐ How long do you need to produce a forecast for the next three quarters?

☐ What range of coverage do orders have?

☐ What range of coverage do prospective revenues have (how long do you need to process existing orders)?

☐ How closely related are employee goals and corporate goals?

☐ How long do you need for end-of-quarter closing and how does this compare to your competitors?

☐ Which managers are not following your management process and why?

CHAPTER 7

Value Chain Redesign

Management Summary

The business world is in the midst of a massive reorganization that will reshape global networks for research, production, sales, and service. The instruments of this reorganization will be dichotomous: globalization and regulation, specialization and commoditization, outsourcing and insourcing, disintermediation and reintermediation, contract manufacturing and specialized service providers, and mergers and acquisitions. That is to say, successes will be found in many configurations; "best practices" will include contradictory alternatives. Information technology, global trade agreements, deregulation, global logistics, and cultural changes are enabling and driving both collaborations that pay no heed to borders (IKEA is an example) and traditionally organized local champions (such as Tata).

Indeed, one can look in many directions and see evidence that the world is "flat," in the words of Thomas Friedman's bestselling book.[1] Labor, ideas, capital, and markets are emerging for a vast range of goods and services in many parts of the world. On the *Forbes* 2009 list of the world's richest people, Mexico, Sweden, Germany, India, and Spain are represented in the top 10. India and China are poised to become automakers, Russia is profiting from vast mineral wealth, and South Korea's history since 1960 represents an economic miracle driven by industries as varied as shipbuilding and consumer electronics.

At the same time, the world still is home to many forms of local advantage. Silicon Valley has been frequently imitated but never duplicated as a center of innovation. French wines are superior to British ones. Milan is a bad place to drill for oil but a good place for fashion designers. A patent will have very different value depending on whether it is litigated in China, the Netherlands, or South Africa. Creative, idea-driven people, who drive critical sectors of the economy, tend to like to live in hospitable, tolerant environments around similar people. The nature of their economic contribution means that they can live nearly anywhere, connected via broadband and cellular technologies to the necessary resources.

Thus the economic world is home to both flat and differentiated tendencies. Local advantage might consist of traditional advantages (rich farmland, beaches and sunshine, or a natural port) or information-age attractors: a cosmopolitan atmosphere, good universities, astute bankers, cultural amenities such as orchestras or parks. As the rapid rise of Dubai illustrates, cities with such advantages can emerge quickly. At the same time, market opportunities and competitive forces can emerge nearly anywhere. These two factors, in combination, provide the context for value chain redesign, as resources, competitors, and markets operate in ever-changing combinations.

Recent research at top business schools including Harvard, Northwestern, and University of California–Berkeley has identified one family of these combinations, the *business network*. These networks can be complex and relationship-driven, as at Cisco, or volume-driven and oriented toward transactions, as at SWIFT, which handles messaging for wholesale financial institutions worldwide. Collaboration and a focus on the early phases of value creation (such as R&D) are common in the first type, while the coordination function of a volume orientation naturally leads to more emphasis on speed and efficiency. More recently, companies such as Nokia must participate in both collaborative and coordinating networks. Business Network Transformation takes many concepts associated with business model innovation and extends them across different ecosystems of participants.[2]

The business concepts associated with value chain redesign should be familiar to anyone who has watched the last 20 years unfold:

- *Globalization.* Capital flows, trade, politics, and media have connected more and more of the world's nations since 1989, the year that witnessed the fall of the Berlin wall, the confrontation at Tiananmen Square, and the beginning of the cell phone boom: modern globalization has its roots in the events of that year. Firms must address both increased competition and the potential implications of increased economic nationalism such as new tariffs, immigration restrictions, and restrictions on capital flows.
- *Specialization and aggregation.* Increased competitive pressures have raised the bar of execution, making room for specialist firms that excel at one aspect of the value chain. Laws, standards, and technologies have facilitated the specialists' interconnection and recombination.
- *Networkability.* The ability to rapidly forge new partnerships and efficient forms of collaboration—which means electronically as well as contractually—is a source of competitive advantage. Both mobility, in the human domain primarily, and the use of semantics (such as formal ontologies) in system domains can support the objective of increased

networkability. Closely related to these semantic structures are many facets of services-oriented architectures, with formal standards for definition, discovery, auditability, and other task stages.

■ *Servicization.* "Services" operates at a different level here. As opposed to software services such as "create order" in an SOA model, many enterprises are exploring revenue generation using services such as contracted maintenance or monitoring as opposed to, or in combination with, products.[3]

■ *Ecosystem management.* Together with partners, many enterprises are striving to become the leading supplier for a particular customer process—mostly based on a particular information technology (e.g., the iPhone, GPS, or UMTS). When they succeed, these firms can spread development costs across a large number of customers and enjoy other benefits such as faster time to market.

The "LEGO" (or "modular") economy in which companies, processes, and applications can be combined at will is not a vision but an illusion. Similarly, the naïve idea of the large-scale electronic marketplace has flopped. It has given way to the more pragmatic vision of a platform that will leverage standard technology, data, software, processes, and business agreements to enable agile forms of collaboration.

When all is said and done, however, business—not technology—is the driving force behind the value chain. Successful collaboration depends on business models and agreements, well-defined and executed processes, and negotiation skill, rather than technical standards, as Exhibit 7.1 shows.

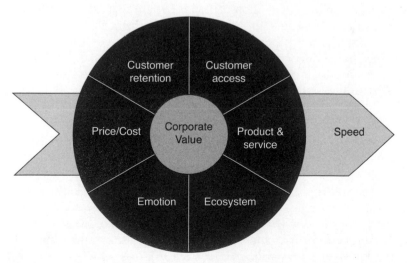

EXHIBIT 7.1   Value Chain Redesign Affects Multiple Facets of Enterprise Value

The main challenges to value chain redesign are:

- *Product and service.* The customer process drives the value chain. A company's business model must dictate which competencies account for its position in the value chain, which products and services it delivers itself, who serves the rest of the customer process, and which companies form part of a given ecosystem.
- *Customer access.* Many customers expect their business partners to have a global presence and market share, implying a guaranteed future. Particularly with new, complex products and services, market share is the critical success factor.
- *Ecosystem.* The customer wants reliable, coordinated services. If one company is unable to offer all the necessary services, the customer needs an ecosystem of capabilities that enhance and complement the products and services of the main partner in the value chain.
- *Customer retention.* The more complex the product and the closer the partnership, the more difficult it is for the customer to switch to a different manufacturer or ecosystem.
- *Emotion.* The relationship between the various brands in a value chain is not well understood. Intangibles such as confidence, familiarity, and a shared customer base can prove decisive in ecosystem negotiations.
- *Price/cost.* Many companies are reaping substantial benefits from having the right ecosystem. Global access to customers helps enterprises achieve economies of scale by sharing the fixed costs for development, assets, and marketing across high volumes. In addition, companies must make use of low-cost locations.
- *Speed.* Customers will choose the ecosystem that achieves the critical mass first. The battle for positions of dominance in value chains is only just beginning. Big-bang approaches as favored by Covisint, which aimed to interlink entire automotive value chains in the blink of an eye, failed due to their complexity and balance-of-power considerations. The more promising strategies still have a vision for the value chain but build on manageable and cost-effective implementation steps.

Vision

Enterprises will apply the laws of the networked economy in their business models. They will concentrate on the partnerships with the highest potential and on those areas where they outperform competitor ecosystems. They will outsource jobs that others can do better. With seamless internal and external processes, they will achieve short response times, a high level of security, and low administration costs. As coordination and transaction costs approach zero, the boundaries between enterprises will often blur.

Process boundaries are changing at least as much as company boundaries. A sales organization in Malaysia advises a customer using the same IT tools, product catalog, and global prices as the sales team at the head office in London. The sales team remains the sole customer contact throughout the fulfillment process. In the background, however, the individual order items are dealt with either by the company's warehouses and plants or by suppliers.

In many cases, the companies involved are coordinated as they were 100 years ago, apart from the fact that documents are now transmitted electronically. Redesigned collaborative processes hold much greater potential than redesigned internal processes because they affect more business units (silos) and, with a few exceptions, little change has been made to date.

> Business must be prepared for value chains to undergo a massive reorganization.

Ultra-efficient collaboration will remain an elusive goal unless enterprises coordinate their products, services, and processes. This applies equally whether the task in question is building a house, running a hospital, or landing and dispatching an aircraft. As a result, companies within individual value chains are beginning to form ecosystems, working hand in hand to serve a particular customer process. Ecosystems historically have grown up around a dominant product or partner (also known as an orchestrator). In the case of a new house, this is often the general contractor, in the case of a hospital, the health system, and in the case of a plane landing, the airport operator. Increasingly, however, we are seeing a shift away from the "800-lb. gorilla" model to include some networks led by more of a coordinator. In some instances, IT is being used to establish shared data and processes to help coordinate the multiple parties, such as electronic medical record systems, or common logistics and trade platforms.

> The result of globalization, specialization, and IT enablement is competing ecosystems.

From Value Chain to Ecosystem: Seven Redesigns

The early twenty-first century has proved to be a time rich in business-model innovation as electronic connections facilitate new modes of collaboration, globalization presents new challenges and opportunities, and product innovation and customer expectations leap-frog each other with stunning speed. Value chain redesign can take many forms, as the following examples suggest.

Lindt & Sprüngli's Chocolate Network

Lindt & Sprüngli is a leading manufacturer of luxury chocolate. In the past, the longtime Swiss chocolatier's sole sales channel was the wholesale sector and its processes were geared to this customer group alone. Its process software consequently managed pralines in delivery units (say, a shipping crate of eight individual boxes) and pallets, rather than individual boxes.

In 2001, Lindt & Sprüngli decided to extend its conventional sales channels and serve end customers directly (see Exhibit 7.2). Similar to flower-delivery services, Lindt & Sprüngli has set its sights on the "gift" customer process. Private individuals can select Lindt & Sprüngli products over the Internet or through a call center and send the gift with a personal greeting. Since the logistical intricacies of this process do not map to Lindt & Sprüngli's main strengths, it decided to draw these skills from yellowworld, a subsidiary of Swiss Post, which acts only as a logistics provider[4] by means of an exchange.

yellowworld commissions the specialist firm Oeschger VPS to manage warehousing and small-scale picking. Swiss Post and its international

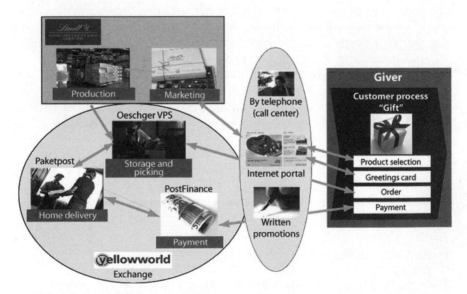

EXHIBIT 7.2   Lindt & Sprüngli's Chocolate Network Spans Multiple Organizations

partners make the physical deliveries. Payments are processed using a platform provided by yellowworld in collaboration with PostFinance, the banking arm of the Swiss post office.

Working with external partners, Lindt & Sprüngli was able to build up the new business area for private customers quickly and at low cost. The customer gets a convenient solution for buying gifts, while low capital outlay and ongoing costs mean the solution presents minor risks to Lindt & Sprüngli.

Virgin Mobile

In the days of wireline voice networks, becoming a telephone company took years or decades to scale. The capital intensiveness of rights of way, poles, wires, and switches was often considerable, particularly when large areas, low population density, and/or hostile terrain were involved. Telecommunications was often treated as a natural monopoly, and such firms were often the largest and most powerful in a given nation.

In the cellular era, competing providers frequently build overlapping physical networks. At a certain point in market saturation, the cost of customer acquisition outpaces the cost of keeping an existing subscriber. Once the buildout is mature, and a carrier cannot market well enough to cover all of its fixed costs with "owned" customers, a service provider may sell bundles of minutes to a Mobile Virtual Network Operator, or MVNO, that competes with the carrier. These companies may or may not run their own billing and customer service operations because these functions can be outsourced to yet another provider: an MVNO can launch with almost entirely virtual infrastructure.

Beginning in 1999, the Virgin Group bought network capacity from T-Mobile in the United Kingdom and launched Virgin Mobile, a wireless phone company with no spectrum or network infrastructure. It became the fastest growing mobile provider ever seen in Britain, reaching its first 1 million customers more than twice as quickly as the next fastest competitor. With more than 200 different extensions of the Virgin brand in the United Kingdom, the company's established expertise in attracting customers for everything from music to train service allowed it to provide differentiated, profitable service while buying commodity minutes, effectively interposing itself between established carriers and expensive "conquest" customers.

In 2006, Virgin acquired broadband, wireline voice, and cable television capability when it bought ntl:Telewest. The newly named Virgin Media (traded on the U.S. Nasdaq) became the first UK provider to offer high-definition programming, and the first UK provider to offer a "quadruple play" bundle of communications services, expanding on the base established by the brand in mobile.

While the Virgin MVNO has not found universal success, in the United States or Singapore for example, it was a pioneer of the MVNO model that now extends to more than 360 companies worldwide, operating over 400 businesses in nations from India to Russia to Chile. Amazon operates as an MVNO, with Sprint providing the unbranded wireless access to its Kindle readers, for example, while Samsung and a team of entrepreneurs are using the model to deliver the Jitterbug phone—a product aimed at senior citizens and featuring a simple interface and convenient form factor.

IKEA

In roughly 50 years, IKEA has risen to prominence in global retailing, becoming the world's largest furniture manufacturer. With approximately $30 billion in revenues and more than 300 stores, it has exported Scandinavian design to four continents and become an icon for both its innovations in flat packaging and the bold color scheme of its retail locations. IKEA also relies heavily on networks of trading partners, building on long-term relationships originating as long ago as the 1960s.[5]

IKEA is a complex organization, with 550 business units in more than 50 countries. These units, in turn, coordinate the activities of 1,300 direct suppliers and 10,000 subsuppliers, ensuring quality and low environmental impact far up the value chain. Several hundred logistics suppliers connect 26 distribution centers in 12 countries. Not surprisingly, one business unit has the role of lead coordinator, working in vertical functions ranging from marketing to supply chain and purchasing. This centralized group stands in contrast to most of IKEA's distributed operations, which rely heavily on local expertise and autonomy.

IKEA is a highly permeable organization as it works in this vast network, codeveloping products and technologies with partners. Such close cooperation necessitates, and builds, high levels of trust among network participants. The perspective focuses on long-term mutual gain, so purchasing does not frequently swap suppliers solely on the basis of low price. The more complex the product, the closer the relationship: upholstered furniture is more likely to be produced by a long-term partner than a rug, for example. IKEA recognizes that network relationships are neither unilateral nor command-and-control: trading partners may defect for a better deal, or take knowledge learned in collaboration with IKEA to new projects.

Much of the network relationship depends on size: such large companies as Maersk (in logistics) and Akzo-Nobel (in coatings) have become key parts of the IKEA network but still do considerable volumes of business elsewhere. Smaller specialty companies will relate differently to IKEA. Geography also plays a part on network formation: proximity to IKEA's dense network of stores in Germany and central Europe will provide suppliers with short supply chains fast responsiveness. Even so, Chinese suppliers rank first among all nations, given the cost advantages; Poland is second.

Thus IKEA utilizes its expertise in network management to great advantage. Its resources and capabilities are often combined with those of a partner: the potential for mutual learning and benefit serves as a decision criterion for some classes of relationship. IKEA also looks for the organizational capability, often demonstrated on past projects, for a trading partner to manage its own goals at the same time it is in a collaboration that demands shared data and other forms of interaction. IKEA actively develops these capabilities in its partners, increasing the level of interaction as it sees proof of organizational traits.

Sharp Corporation

From the time shortly after its founding in 1912 when it marketed the Ever-Ready Sharp Pencil, Sharp Corporation has established a consistent record of innovation that continues to the present day. The firm's roughly $30 billion in revenues come from a variety of leading-edge product lines, including medical devices, office automation, and home appliances. Sharp's investments in LCD display and solar panel fabrication are particularly noteworthy not only for their technological sophistication but for the new organizational models that are being utilized.

A new facility at Sakai, in Osaka, will be a world leader in both LCD and solar panels, in separate but co-located facilities. After providing the initial funding, Sharp will be joined in 2011 by Sony (34 percent) as a co-investor in the $4 billion LCD plant. A giant array of solar panels will power both the solar and LCD facilities, including LED lighting, making the complex a world showcase for "green" technology. Every supplier, most notably a Corning glass works, will be co-located on site, helping make the entire facility run as a virtual company and minimizing transportation expenses and emissions, waste, and coordination costs.

The co-located companies will share physical infrastructure such as a security systems, data networks, and energy supply, but also can work more collaboratively by sharing physical presence. Planning and forecasting, computer-integrated manufacturing, and logistics should all run more smoothly without barriers of distance. In addition, the collaborating companies share a services-oriented IT architecture that reduces redundancy of shared functionality and accelerates deployment through sharing of common components. Based on the reduced redundancies in infrastructure and the shared IT design methodology, cross-organizational processes can converge with benefits in speed, cost, and quality.

Beyond the Sakai complex but continuing the theme of organizational innovation, Sharp partnered with Enel SpA, an Italian power generator, entering the market for solar power on the generation side as well as investing in cell and panel fabrication. Envisioning solar cell factories as the "oil fields of the 21st century," Sharp is aiming "to establish a presence across the entire solar power value chain as a total solutions provider."[6] This means that Sharp seeks to establish presence in the production of solar cell materials, cell manufacturing, systems integrators, and power producers. Enel's partnership with Sharp also helps bring Italy significantly closer to Germany as Europe's leader in solar production.

De Beers

For over a century after its founding in 1888, De Beers focused its efforts on becoming the leading supplier to the world's diamond market. The practice of buying back inventory (ultimately $5 billion worth), however, both hampered cash flows and exposed the company to competition from new diamond discoveries in such countries as Canada and Australia. For a time De Beers stopped doing business in the United States, one of its largest markets.

Starting in 1999, the company radically revised its operations, moving from control on the supply side to become a marketing-driven entity targeted at increasing global demand. The company used its reach and unsurpassed industry knowledge to track stones from origination to sales floor in order to guarantee that they are "conflict free" (to counter charges raised in the movie *Blood Diamond* and elsewhere) and produced without any child labor. Under the new model, De Beers is more profitable, with 40 percent market share than when it held 80 percent share.

IT provided important capabilities in this reinvention. Production is closely matched to individual markets so that cutting and polishing activities connect to demand rather than generic inventory. Optical imaging and yield management systems guide cutting: given the extreme value of rough stones, even incremental improvement can pay significant dividends.[7] Finally, maintaining chain of custody is vital in the twenty-first-century diamond business, creating an opportunity for further advantage from effective IT practices.

The ability to address human rights charges so decisively has turned out to be a competitive advantage for the company, which reported net earnings of $730 million in 2006. Now privately held after having had its ownership intertwined with the Anglo American mining firm, De Beers also increased its investment in the health and well-being of the people in its producer nations, including Botswana, Namibia, South Africa, and Tanzania. It is also working with those nations to increase the amount of finished jewelry produced near origin to increase employment and harvest more value from the ultimate diamond buyer.[8]

Amazon Web Services

After 15 years of confounding various critiques of online retailing, Amazon. com continues to lead the industry and innovate outside it. In 2006, the firm announced it would supply any or all infrastructure elements as services, allowing businesses of any size to buy server disc space (Amazon Simple Storage Service, or Amazon S3), Messaging (Amazon Simple Queue Service or Amazon SQS), or computing capacity, known as Amazon Elastic Compute Cloud, or Amazon EC2. Uptake has been rapid: NASA Jet Propulsion Laboratory is analyzing telemetry images from Saturn in the Amazon's cloud, Netflix is transcoding movies into different formats so that it can streaming them into variety of devices, while ESPN launched its FanPages social network application on the storage and compute services. The New York Times converted 70 years of newspapers (11 million articles, or 4 terabytes of data) from TIFF to PDF format in roughly 24 hours using 100 compute instances.[9] In 2007, roughly a year after launch, Web services bandwidth exceeded the bandwidth utilized by all of Amazon.com's global Web sites combined (see Exhibit 7.3).

While it appears to violate current thinking about focusing on core competencies, Amazon's move from retail to infrastructure makes sense on several levels. First, Amazon is, in its core, a technology company. By

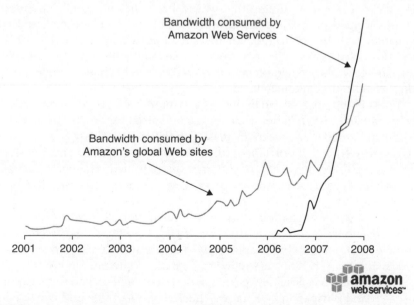

EXHIBIT 7.3 Amazon Quickly Consumed More Bandwidth Delivering Web Services than Running the World's Largest Web Commerce Operation

Source: Amazon.com.

creating a platform of Web services, they can build (and be paid for) sophisticated, scalable applications. Building on its expertise in cost-effective retail customer service, the company now listens as well as anyone in the business to its new customers, software developers. Second, both Google and IBM, two frequently mentioned providers of cloud computing, run businesses with high or relatively high margins. Commodity computing, by definition, cannot be a high-margin business over the long term, so Amazon's experience with low-margin high-volume operations prepares it well. Finally, Amazon has spent billions of dollars to become the Web's leading retailer, and has developed a core competency in operating massive scale technology infrastructure and datacenters. Every lesson the company has learned about power management, asset virtualization, and system robustness is now generating profits independent of book or toy or DVD sales.

Nokia

On March 17, 2000, a fire broke out at a Philips microchip fabrication facility in New Mexico after the plant was struck by lightning. At Nokia headquarters in Helsinki, signals of a potential supply disruption were noted almost immediately. Three days later, Philips told Nokia and Ericsson, another major customer, that cleaning up the plant, including the clean room, would take about a week. Doubting this would be sufficient, Nokia undertook a three-pronged program to address the situation: one team increased coordination with Philips to monitor the situation, which ultimately saw the New Mexico plan closed for six weeks. A second team redesigned certain components so they could be manufactured at other facilities, while a third team began to find alternate vendors.

Ericsson did not respond in the same fashion. Its second-quarter operating loss totaled $200 million, while Nokia's earnings report did not mention the fire and noted a 42 percent increase in profitability. The two companies' fate diverged from that point forward, as Ericsson lost 3 percent market share and eventually teamed with Sony to create a new handset venture. Nokia, meanwhile, eventually earned 40 percent of the global handset market in 2008.[10]

The company's response to its supply disruption illustrates Nokia's superb execution as the coordinator of a business network. In its efforts to compete in the smartphone market against Apple and Research In Motion in particular, however, Nokia is striving to manage a different kind of business network as well. As social networking, video over cellular, and services such as search and navigation become essential elements of its end consumers' experience with mobility, Nokia is managing new kinds of partnerships, innovation, and relationships with the people who carry its devices.

Given the rise of mobile data platforms and networks of increasingly broad bandwidth, Nokia can collect a powerful array of data about its customers' collective habits. With help from a new generation of IT, this data is being used to support two goals. First, learning how people live as digital nomads through direct observation of live data, rather than focus groups or traditional market research, allows Nokia to design new types of customization and other enhancements to user experience. Second, the use of collective data supports prediction. An example of the latter is research being done in collaboration with the University of California, Berkeley and CalTrans in which the signals from cell phones are being used to monitor traffic flows in real time. Eventually, such technology could be used to predict traffic patterns and calculate optimal routing.[11]

As data devices change both customer behavior and the company's relationship with and capabilities relative to those consumers, a variety of business model issues emerge: how does Nokia's relationship with its trade customers evolve in parallel? How does Nokia compete with Apple's earlier-to-market App Store? How does Nokia generate value-added services as a handset manufacturer?

In answer to the last question, Nokia is moving decisively and at scale. Its $8.1 billion purchase of Navteq to increase its presence in mobile mapping (relative to Google in particular) was bold, and other handset manufacturers including Samsung are licensing the service. Nokia's purchase of the Symbian mobile operating system (with 50 percent of the global smartphone market) led to its being open-sourced a short time afterward. Finally, the company's global footprint is allowing it to play in the music distribution business: Dance Fabulous, a mobile game, features songs for sale by Cindy Gomez, who both dances capably and sings in eight languages.[12] Such a content presence is a long way from the supply-chain expertise for which Nokia, until recently, was better known.

Competition in Networks

Information and technology are rewriting the laws of value chains. A succession of dominant companies has emerged, each of whose business model was unthinkable only a generation before. After the turn of the twentieth century, AT&T was followed by IBM. Several decades later, Microsoft emerged, and then Google reinvented the landscape yet again. Three major concepts, in particular, are generating many new competitive dynamics that help explain these companies, among others: network effects, power law distributions, and two-sided markets.

Network Effects

Externalities are a familiar concept in economics, referring to aspects of a transaction unaccounted for by pricing mechanisms. Externalities are often negative: water or air pollution results from industrial processes that do not price environmental impact into the goods' cost. In information contexts, however, externalities are sometimes called *network effects*, and can be positive. Such beneficial network effects occur when the actions of someone else in the network make a given individual better off.

Flu vaccinations are an example: the more people at my workplace who get inoculated, the lower my chances of being infected. Fax machines provide another classic illustration of the concept. Imagine owning the first fax machine on the planet, paying a large sum for the technical innovation, novelty, and unique parts. The worth of the machine, however, relates not to the raw material and intellectual property inputs, but to the utility, which in the case of the first fax machine is zero: nobody can exchange faxes with our privileged customer. Fast forward to 10 years later, when the fax had become widely adopted: every time anybody anywhere in the world installs a fax machine, our customer's device gains in option value as the potential network of connections grow one at a time.[13]

Network effects can be subtle. The more Toyotas or Volkswagens there are on the road, the more completely developed the dealer and spare parts networks will be. Until a new entrant such as the Tata Nano builds a sufficiently large customer base, service will be more expensive for the company to provide than it will be once economies of scale are reached. For a given customer to have access to low-cost, available spare parts for her vehicle, the best thing she can do is encourage her friends and family to buy from the same manufacturer.

Technical and other standards are both a cause and a result of network effects. For any given asset to be valuable, whether it is a shipping container or a cell phone, it needs to be compatible with other devices and a preferably shared infrastructure. Global cellular telephony and the container shipping industry are both fairly standardized, as opposed to written language, which remains diverse. Even so, English has emerged as a *de facto* global standard for many types of international business, and the BBC Web site will have more visitors than *Le Monde* or *Asahi Shimbun,* not necessarily because of quality but because of its readership base. Standards wars, such as VHS-Beta or Blu-ray versus HD-DVD, are common in information industries because the stakes are so high.

Power Law Distributions

Before World War II, a Harvard linguistics professor named George Zipf studied how often various words in the English language were used. Not surprisingly, "the" and "and" were used extremely frequently, while "oxymoron" and "parametric" were uncommon. The plot turned out to have a log-log shape, which looks like the curve in Exhibit 7.4 when mapped on a

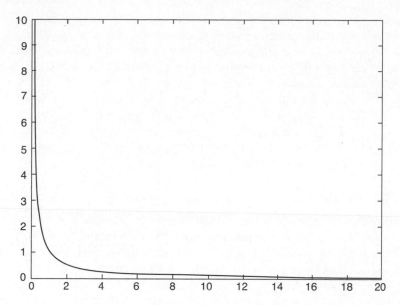

EXHIBIT 7.4 A Power Law Distribution Explains Both "Winner-Take-All" and "Long-Tail" Phenomena

linear rather than log scale. In the search engine era, researchers found that Web site traffic behaved similarly: a small number of sites received the vast proportion of all traffic, while a vast number of sites had nearly zero traffic.

Several insights followed from these observations. First, Zipf distributions turned out to be one of several so-called power laws: the nth position in a list is theoretically $1/n$ as big as the first list member. Earthquakes, for example, follow a power-law distribution: very few earthquakes are extremely powerful, while many, many earthquakes are so small as to be unnoticed except on sophisticated instruments. In social science, Pareto distributions, commonly known as 80/20 rules, also follow similar curves. Second, much attention in the 1990s was focused on the head of the curve: in Web traffic, a very few sites (under 50, initially) accounted for the majority of all traffic. Looking at Google, Microsoft, CNN, and Yahoo!, some observers contended that network scenarios often produced "winner take all" tendencies.[14]

A few years later, Chris Anderson of *Wired* magazine looked at the right side of the graph and coined the term "the long tail" to describe the Internet's tendency to promote extreme market diversity.[15] For every Harry Potter book or Batman movie, there were thousands of YouTube videos or blog postings with audiences measured in single digits. Such merchants as eBay and Amazon capitalized on the long tail in way that traditional retailers, confined by real estate, search costs, and inventory velocity, could not.

One other point about power laws bears mentioning. While a Gaussian (bell-curve) distribution underlies numerous planning assumptions in finance, marketing, and supply chains, in a connected world, the extremes of a power law often do a better job of explaining the world. In a bell curve of human heights, the entire population is accounted for in less than one order of magnitude: nobody is shorter than 1 foot or taller than 10. In risk, wealth, and information landscapes, however, Bill Gates can be tens of millions of times wealthier than another person on the graph. Similarly, leveraged investment risk must be measured in multiples far greater than those in most Gaussian planning models.[16]

Two-Sided Markets

In some networked scenarios, a company must address not one market but two. That is, it is not enough to assemble raw materials and convince customers to buy one's product. The classic case of a two-sided market is a credit card company such as Diner's Club or Visa. The credit card consortium must convince consumers to carry the card, but consumers want a card accepted by many merchants. Thus the credit card must convince merchants to accept the card and install the necessary infrastructure, but merchants want assurance that customers will shop at their establishment and make the investment worthwhile.[17]

More recently, software companies have faced a similar two-sided market. Independent software developers create applications on a given platform, adding value to the platform, but developers want access to monetization paths. Apple's success with the iPhone's App Store, with 1.5 billion downloads in the first year, stands alongside the credit cards as an example of the powerfully self-reinforcing tendencies, much like a mechanical flywheel, that characterize a successful two-sided market. Customers flock to the platform, creating incentives for more providers to join, which in turn attracts more customers and so on.

Concepts of Value Chain Redesign

In accord with these three dynamics, among others, the laws of networking are shaping business models in the information age. The main concepts are:

- *Globalization.* Companies procure, produce, and sell on a global scale and thus achieve great economies of scale. They can also benefit from diversity, learning in one market and bringing innovation to another.
- *Specialization and aggregation.* Companies are concentrating on their core competencies and drawing complementary services from third parties to cover end-to-end customer processes.

- *Networkability*. The ability to forge new partnerships and rapidly implement efficient forms of collaboration can be a source of competitive advantage.
- *Servicization*. Digitization is creating new services that are delivered chiefly through the Internet. In addition, a company's information infrastructure is essential to support the stress that servicization—charging for a product-service hybrid rather a stand-alone product—can place on a product-centric business model.
- *Ecosystem management*. Together with partners, many enterprises are striving to become the leading global supplier for a particular customer process. If they succeed, they will be able to spread development costs across a large number of customers and transactions.

Globalization

Globalization pursues the following goals:

- To serve customers in all their locations and cater to their regional needs
- To increase the sales volume and thereby achieve both revenue growth targets and economies of scale
- To exploit the comparative advantages of different locations (including labor costs, knowledge, raw materials, transport routes) for R&D, procurement, production, and distribution

If the Brazilian subsidiary of a Japanese firm purchases equipment from a European manufacturer, it expects a Portuguese product catalog with current prices and delivery times, a discount based on the total purchase quantity of the Japanese parent company, and a single contact person, even if the components are delivered from Sweden, South Korea, and the United States and assembled for the customer in Brazil.

For many companies in the middle market, globalization is essential for the simple reason that local demand is insufficient to occupy production capacity at scale. A 2009 survey by Canadian Business Online of that country's 100 fastest growing companies showed that 42 had at least 50 percent of their revenues from exports.[18] Elsewhere, a global center of expertise in roller coasters has emerged in Switzerland, based in part on the region's heritage in gondolas and material handling systems. Given an extremely limited domestic market for amusement rides, it is essential for such firms as Intamin and Bolliger & Mabillard to compete on a global scale.

IT is lifting geographical and temporal restrictions. The stock exchange in Tokyo and a Mexican regional bank can become virtual neighbors as the time and effort needed to place an order in Mexico City and Tokyo become comparable. Even an airport operator like Fraport in Frankfurt, originally

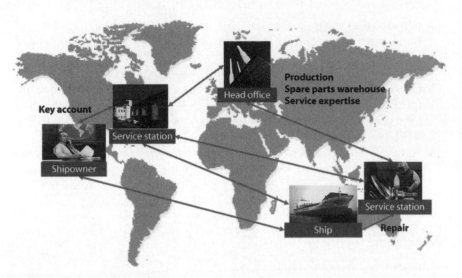

EXHIBIT 7.5 "Virtual" and Physical Proximity Coincide in ABB Turbo Systems' Global Spares Business

with a firm regional focus, now sees its services and associates operating from Shanghai in China to Jacksonville in the United States.

At the point when physical deliveries need to be made or services delivered in person (machine repair, for instance), physical proximity continues to be a decisive factor. This is why ABB Turbo Systems maintains its own service stations in more than 70 key ports worldwide, thus ensuring physical proximity to its customers' ships. But it is the virtual proximity of the service stations to one another and to the head office (see Exhibit 7.5) that actually enables captains and ship owners to enjoy the same high levels of service around the globe as would be provided from the head office.

> With IT, anybody with whom a company can communicate in real time becomes a "virtual neighbor."

Companies as large as GM or DuPont and as specialized as Endress+ Hauser all rely on a global network of production locations to manufacture standard components that are made into local solutions close to the customer. Many companies' strategies include increased emphasis on networking internal plants and sales organizations, and shortening supply chains by keeping production as close as possible to the end customer market.

Specialization and Aggregation

Many companies are combining elements of specialization and aggregation in order to provide a comprehensive service for specific customer processes. *Specialization* results from a focus on serving selected customer processes exceptionally well. After concentrating on particular products and services then establishing an efficient sales and marketing process for the selected customer segments, a company may emerge as a market leader. *Aggregation* entails supporting all aspects of the customer process, providing all the products and services the customer needs from one source.

IT enables companies to be disassembled and reassembled in a way that would have been unthinkable until recently. Three developments in particular have both accelerated and expanded in geographic scope:

1. Enterprises are specializing by selling off divisions and outsourcing non-core competencies.
2. They are securing leading market positions by acquiring competitors.
3. They are rounding out their range of services by buying from complementary providers, or forming loose networks for production, R&D, or sales.

IT makes it easier to integrate companies by supplying a common infrastructure for standard processes and enterprise-wide control. But it also opens increasingly more alternatives to takeovers because it can integrate suppliers and service providers in planning and execution processes as though they were internal departments.

Chemicals groups like Ciba, Hoechst, and Bayer used to focus on product know-how. Over the past 20 years, they have made a radical transition from a product-centric business model to one that revolves around customer processes. Many groups split up into different organizations for pharmaceuticals, nutrition, materials, plant protection, and specialty chemicals. The new organizations, in turn, concentrated on specific segments (Novartis on oncology and ophthalmology, among others).

These chemicals companies became exercises in portfolio optimization, gaining scale and scope through the buying and selling of lines of business: acquisitions and divestitures could be completed more smoothly once the process became a focus of both management and execution. Without the impediment of intertwined IT systems, they could team up with the relevant divisions of other chemicals companies (Ciba Geigy with Sandoz, for example) to gain market force, and bring in skills to complement their coverage of a given segment. At the same time, they began investing in research activities in new-product development projects as opposed to acquiring entire companies. Aggregation across multiple entities thus parallels specialization of new product development in targeted markets.

IBM is a company with vast resources, yet its various groups function in a number of ecosystems. Its R&D, marketing, and services groups all align with customer needs: a lab working on databases might specialize in databases in insurance, or life science, or government clients rather than on databases in a technical sense. Aggregation occurs as solutions from multiple providers must be integrated, whether individual elements are homegrown or not: depending on customer needs, IBM's services organization can just as readily sell and integrate Microsoft SQL Server as its own DB2 database product.

Only at first sight do specialization and aggregation appear contradictory notions. In reality, many companies today specialize in one or a few customer processes and still have the ability to offer a complete solution to a customer's problem. This means focusing on a small number of processes for specific customer segments as well as being able to incorporate products and services from other providers in the value chain.

> Electronic networking enables new ways of dividing labor. Every company must scrutinize the elements of its value chain.

Networkability

Companies want to implement collaborative business models faster and more efficiently than their rivals. They want to integrate a new supplier in their processes easily, replace an existing supplier seamlessly, begin joint development activities with a new customer immediately, outsource noncritical business functions effortlessly, and prove the success of a new acquisition rapidly. Amidst economic uncertainty especially, being able to switch suppliers or identify new customers may become a matter of economic survival. In the event of a credit crisis, for example, or such unfortunate circumstances as plant fires, influenza quarantines, or natural disasters, value chain partners must move quickly to avoid being taken down by difficulties at trading partners.

If L'Oréal sets up a collaborative process with Tesco to supply individual stores, possibly via vendor-managed inventory (VMI), the process initially involves only L'Oréal and Tesco in a 1:1 collaboration. If L'Oréal wants to set up a VMI process with Wal-Mart, it will invariably involve a different process with different contracts, different software, and different data formats. The same would be true for Tesco if it wanted to establish a VMI process with Unilever. This multiplicity drives complexity and costs, and restricts the intensity of collaboration, the goal of which is m:n (any supplier to any customer in a given market). Moving from 1:1, to 1:n, and finally to m:n mappings is the toughest barrier to a company's networking capabilities.

> Enterprises can support m:n processes if they understand one another straight away, that is, if they speak the same business language.

In the example of L'Oréal and Tesco, standardization is limited to the two business partners (1:1). Cisco achieves standardization by imposing its solution on new business units (1:n), at the cost of flexibility and organizational tension. Many standardization committees aim to create m:n capabilities by setting standard collaboration rules for all the members of a value chain. RosettaNet is a standard for the IT industry that has been adopted by over 450 enterprises. It aims to increase the networking capabilities of IT manufacturers and thereby enable new business models to be implemented rapidly.[19]

ELECTRONIC SERVICES Inside of a business organization, tasks or subprocesses that are needed by various departments can be handled in one place, either within the company or externally, and then used by the different departments. Procedures like receivables collection, travel booking, parcel shipping, and payroll are "common components" in the organization, which can be bundled together internally to reduce complexity (in a shared services organization) or bought from specialists (outsourcing or online service providers).

Following the strategic macroperspective of the laws of networking, such seemingly small services could be regarded as a microperspective unworthy of managerial consideration. To boost the efficiency of an ecosystem, however, it needs not vaguely worded alliances but concrete tools, such as electronic services, including those for exchanging credit information.

The first service provision option is to combine common components within the company. Shared service centers are internal service providers for human resources, financials, real estate, tax, purchasing, and other processes that can work more effectively centrally than locally. A manufacturer of communication equipment with revenues of $23 billion was able to reduce the proportion of revenues spent on its financial process from 2 percent to 1 percent by introducing shared services.

An alternative to internal competency is shared services which centralize processes within groups of affiliated companies, while the next step is to share the services among several companies. One prominent example is provided by ADP, an $8 billion company responsible for the payroll for more than 50 million employees from more than 585,000 organizations. From the perspective of ADP customers, this practice is known as business process outsourcing.

An extreme form of specialization involves fully electronic pay services that cover small, isolatable tasks rather than entire processes. Economically, they are particularly attractive because the marginal costs per transaction are next to nothing, permitting economies of scale and, in some cases, economies of networks and standardization as well. From the customer perspective, such services are known as outtasking, examples of which include:

- Electronic Bill Presentment and Payment (EBPP), such as Billtrust (EBPP enabled one U.S. energy supplier to reduce the costs per invoice from $3.20 to $0.50[20])
- Logistics services, including selection of best shipping alternative for specific packages; preparation of customs data; shipping papers; and shipping-independent delivery tracking (One example is Austria's inet-logistics.)
- TradeAbility, an online service from UPS for managing export and import transactions, such as checking embargo guidelines or selecting the correct customs authority tariff codes
- Automatic credit check before acceptance of an order (for example, Convergys)
- Collaborative inventory management for a supply chain, for example for automotive supplies (TradeBeam)
- Hybrid navigation systems to complement CD-based onboard systems with current traffic news (such as PTV)
- Search engines, including specialized vertical industry tools such as VADLO in life sciences
- Travel search engines like kayak.com for finding flights and hotels

Electronic services have the potential to boom because they profit immensely from the laws of networking and are tackling processes that currently hold considerable scope for improvement. Very few companies will find a competitive advantage in payroll, or in building their own credit checking capability. Such activities, particularly when the provider has emerged as a global leader, are economically attractive for both buyer, who can concentrate on differentiating activities, and providers, who benefit from economies of scale that increase with every new account.

In some industry sectors, de facto standards are emerging as a result of many companies' use of the same software package despite the immaturity of industry semantics and similar definitions. That is, because companies that routinely trade with each other use similar software, their vendors effectively define interaction standards for machine-to-machine transactions. The benefit of such an emergent standard, which constitutes a network effect, is simpler value chain coordination as well as easier M&A activity, either in spinning out a business unit or integrating an acquisition.

A business opportunity has also emerged in providing master data to a group of companies. Such companies as Agentrics and NeoData provide data synchronization services for companies in the retail value chain. The International Material Data System (IMDS) is an online service for documenting all the materials used in a vehicle and was developed to assist in the disposal of vehicles. Siperian and other providers provide master data management to a range of industries.

> Master data can bring a position of power even within one company; between different companies, it can bring a strong competitive advantage.

From management's perspective, electronic services hold dual attraction: when the enterprise is a customer, they can boost efficiency and reduce complexity; as a service provider, these services are a means of developing services based on the company's expertise.

EXCHANGES Standards like those described thus far provide a valuable basis for networking within individual industry sectors, but they are far from capable of launching a real-life collaborative process between two enterprises. All they can do is create a framework for concrete business agreements, specific collaborative processes, the IT applications and electronic services actually deployed, and, not unimportantly, universal master data.

Most value chains need an orchestrator to define and enforce the rules of play for an ecosystem. The greatest success to date has been enjoyed by the purchasing platforms (private exchanges) of major players like Siemens, General Electric, Lufthansa, Wal-Mart, and Volkswagen. They helped these large enterprises to standardize processes with their suppliers. But purchasing platforms only enable 1:n relationships. They increase the networking capabilities of the orchestrator, but they do not solve the problem of the suppliers, not least because none of these purchasing platforms have achieved an industry-wide standing, let alone acceptance across the business community as a whole.

One of the most significant exchanges is General Electrics' former purchasing platform, Global eXchange Services (GXS), which now operates as an independent firm and processes over a billion transactions each year involving more than 100,000 trading partners. GXS supports its partners with a wide range of electronic services for the fulfillment process and supply chain management.

Companies need a host of services that may include, among others:

- The development of binding business agreements
- Inter-enterprise product catalogs
- A legally binding record of all electronic business transactions
- Intervention in the event of exceptions
- Interenterprise transparency as regards delivery statuses

The main concern, therefore, is the *nonelectronic and electronic services that a company wants or has to provide internally as shared services or procure as external electronic services*. What exchanges can do, however, is bundle the services. The decisive factor is that all members of an ecosystem have the same understanding of the collaborative process and the software components it uses, in other words, that they establish m:n relationships. At the same time, business networks can increase coordination costs while diluting strategic intent, so investment must be holistically assessed for its various layers of impact.

Networkability is at the heart of almost all the business concepts described in this book so far. As such, we predict it will feature as a key competency in business models for the coming decade. Companies can provide services for repeated use in internal processes and for collaboration with business partners.

> Business software suites will greatly improve networking capabilities.

Management must decide:

- Which ecosystems to serve
- Which standards and exchanges to use
- Which enterprise architectural commitments brings the highest degree of networkability
- Which electronic services to build up internally and which to buy

Servicization

As firms face the market, services are typically viewed as the "opposite" of products: assembled widgets sit on warehouse shelves while haircuts cannot; they are *perishable*. The widget can be shipped while the nurse's flu shot must be delivered in person; this service trait is known as being *inseparable.* If the customer buys the widget, it can be felt, weighted, and measured in ways that legal advice, for example, cannot; many services are *intangible.* Finally, for all the efforts to standardize service, the same desk clerk on different nights, and different clerks at different outlets on the same night, will all deliver different service experiences. This means that, compared to ball bearing or semiconductor quality, services are *heterogeneous.*

Particularly because of digitization, however, services are transcending many of their previously assigned characteristics, so products and services can best be understood on a continuum (see Exhibit 7.6). Telephone service is created in heavily capitalized facilities much like factories and is not easily called heterogeneous: automobiles vary in quality far more than modern landline telephony. Voice communication is also tangible in vivid ways, and voicemail makes it less inseparable in time. Offshore programming and call centers belie the notion that services lack portability. Financial instruments, called products in that industry, are neither necessarily inseparable nor heterogeneous.

At the same time, previously obvious distinctions have multiplied in kind and blurred in character. Exhibit 7.6 illustrates one way of organizing the outputs of a modern economy at an abstract level. For our purposes, the main point is that products and services, rather than being viewed as opposites, can be combined in many ways, most notably in the digital domain.

Digital product–service hybrids can be understood as a subset of customizable hybrids. Even outside the realm of digital hybrids, adding services to products is becoming much more common among manufacturers. Exhibit 7.7 shows the increasing value-add that accompanies the transitions from something as simple as documentation or shipping all the way to outsourcing.[21] The implications of IT for such servicization efforts can be significant.

Managing the Ecosystem

For a long time, the impact of IT was felt mainly by internal processes. It is now beginning to transform collaborative processes between different companies. As a result, power balances will shift both internally and across company boundaries:

- If Wal-Mart mandates "Wal-Mart compliance," as it did with RFID, its suppliers must come to grips with the processes and standards used in the Wal-Mart ecosystem.
- If a marketplace for electronic goods provides a product catalog with offers from multiple manufacturers, products and prices will be easier to compare.

EXHIBIT 7.6 Products and Services Are Not Opposites but Lie on a Spectrum of Economic Transactions

Commodities		Products			Hybrids		Purchased Services			Public Services
Standard	Engineered	Capital	Intermediate	End-user	Standardized	Customizable	Standardized Delivered	Custom Delivered	Co-created	Government
Coal, apples, pork bellies	Farmed salmon, genetically modified seed corn	Pizza oven, crane, oil drill, city bus, milling machine	Ball bearing, micro-processor, upholstery fabric, sheet metal, newsprint	Sweater, motorcycle, applesauce, television	"Power by the hour" jet engine contract, office furniture lease-back, fast food, safe deposit box	Anti-virus software, iPod/iTunes, home mortgage, chemotherapy	Car wash, train ticket purchase, stock purchase, security guards, movie theater, electricity	Haircut, surgery, house painting, site survey, furniture movers	Tennis lessons, corporate audit, enterprise software implementation	Road building, meat inspection, drug approval, military, police, public education, driver licensing

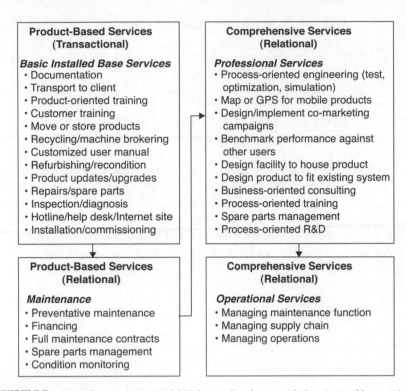

EXHIBIT 7.7 Manufacturers Can Add Value to Products with Services of Increasing Complexity

Source: Adapted from R. Oliva and R. Kallenberg, "Managing the transition from products to services," *International Journal of Service Industry Management* 14, no. 2 (2003): 160–172.

- If a drinks manufacturer coordinates campaigns, schedules, and sales with its packaging suppliers, bottlers, and logistics service providers, it will be in a better position to deliver product and also reduce stocks. But switching partners will also become more difficult.
- If a midsize bank concentrates on product development, marketing, and customer advice, but outsources the settlement side of the business to financial service providers, it may become dependent on these providers.
- If a bank's electronic services allow private customers to complete a wide range of tasks, from financial management to document storage, customers will be loath to switch to a different bank—even if the bank starts charging for e-banking.

- If a specialist in building control installs customer-specific installations and therefore holds the system configuration and logic, it will be extremely difficult for customers to hire a different provider to service or operate the control systems.

> Ecosystem formation and management is becoming a core CEO task.

FORMS OF COORDINATION   Airlines are in a phase of consolidation, which is taking several different forms. Alliances support the rise in code-sharing agreements, which allow airlines to offer customers a much wider network of destinations than before: code-sharing is a textbook example of aggregation. Flight-booking systems were introduced some time ago and let airlines market flights through a variety of channels. Another form of coordination is to outsource infrastructure services such as catering and aircraft maintenance to units with bigger economies of scale. Takeovers, such as Delta's acquisition of Northwest, are a means of securing markets and critical resources such as landing rights. In some cases, airlines are benefiting from synergies that go beyond the above measures, as in the case of regional economic growth for example.

> IT is supporting many different forms of collaboration, including mergers and acquisitions, alliances, bilateral collaboration, and outsourcing.

Given the experiences of recent years, companies may well wonder which style of value chain is the most effective and whether this will change over time. A frequent flyer program can span several airlines without the need for mergers. With IT, companies can connect in real time and work with other enterprises just as efficiently as with internal departments. As a result, other issues come to the fore, such as the allocation of expenses and revenues and, more specifically, market power.

> IT gives executives new options for organizing their ecosystems.

CONFLICTING CHANNELS   The shift of power in the value chain is becoming a critical factor. Conventional value chains like that for household appliances—spanning electrical goods manufacturers, wholesalers, installation engineers, and building owners—are inefficient. Electronic networking can easily eliminate one or two steps, bringing savings of up to 20 percent off the retail price—more than would be achieved by moving production to low-wage countries. But an electrical goods manufacturer who bypasses wholesalers risks being cut from their product range.

This danger is even more apparent in the automotive value chain. Suppliers of components like spark plugs and engine oil could sell spare parts without going through the vehicle manufacturer's expensive and inefficient sales channel. But in doing so, they would risk losing contracts to provide the initial parts for new vehicles.

All parties in the value chain develop ways of avoiding and negotiating channel conflicts. Manufacturers resort to dual-brand strategies, regionally segmented sales channels, and complementary services for products. The latter solution gives them direct access to end customers, and, with that, the chance to win customer loyalty. One example is the life-cycle concept applied by vehicle manufacturers. They have designed specific vehicle diagnosis tools available exclusively through a centralized service at their own plant. The tools let them accompany vehicles throughout their entire life cycle and thereby gain access to the end customer rather than the dealer.

The intermediaries, the wholesalers and retailers, respond with counter-strategies. They add more value by offering new solutions. Instead of just distributing and storing goods, they offer customers credit or provide more in-depth advice, for instance by exploiting regional differences. For example, vehicle registration requirements vary in the European automotive market, while selling fertilizers requires knowledge of local soil conditions. A second line of attack is to build up market power through size. Electronics wholesalers including Arrows and Avnet have established a strong global position through multiple acquisitions.

Powerful manufacturers like IKEA, Cisco, and Hyundai act as orchestrators; they organize the value chain from their business perspective and form ecosystems. They offer intensive support for sales and service partners by providing services to accompany products, such as diagnosis tools. Including third-party services in their range is another way of supporting retailers and service staff as they strive to satisfy customers. Of course, this makes intermediaries more dependent on manufacturers. The channel conflict will reappear at some stage, such as when manufacturers start charging for complementary services if only to cover their own additional costs. Ultimately, the question of collaboration or confrontation is always a question of alternatives, and consequently, of the balance of power.

Channel conflicts do not resolve themselves; they demand strategic responses.

PARTNER RELATIONSHIP MANAGEMENT Software companies and plant engineers have particularly complex products, which call for collaboration among multiple companies to satisfy all aspects of the customer process. For example, if a retailing chain decides to redesign its logistics processes, it first needs a logistics consultant for the retail sector, a process consultant to select standard software, a software vendor, and perhaps an additional consultant for a special solution to handle the logistics of fresh produce. It will also need a specialist in customer cards with expertise in buying patterns and sales forecasts, a logistics partner, and someone to operate the IT infrastructure. Together, all of these companies form the ecosystem for the "Retail" logistics process.

Intel's rise from a microprocessor manufacturer to the PC industry's standard setter began in the late 1980s with the realization that the PC architecture at that time was hampering the company's growth and innovation strategy.[22] Intel wanted to generate more demand for its microprocessors by introducing short innovation cycles. The communication standard for the different components in a PC had already become too slow to exploit the potential of existing Intel processors. No market player was willing or able to advance the PC architecture defined by IBM in the early '80s.

Intel therefore decided to introduce a new standard that would encourage companies to advance PC technology and thereby increase demand for new, faster processors. But the secret to success lay not in the enterprising decision to create a new standard, but in the move to establish and foster an ecosystem:

- Intel defined a communication standard capable of bringing to bear even more powerful microprocessors in the future.
- The company opened its standard license-free to all parties in the value chain: PC manufacturers like IBM, hardware suppliers, and software vendors like Microsoft. As a result, the standard soon achieved wide circulation.
- Inviting future users to participate in the process of defining the standard ensured high market acceptance. Besides Intel, members of the special interest groups included industry giants like IBM, Compaq, HP, and Microsoft.
- The company held quarterly compliance workshops (known internally as PlugFests) with 100 to 200 enterprises to give partners in the ecosystem a chance to test their products extensively for compliance with the standard. Intel's workshops encouraged innovative partner products, which in turn increased demand for more powerful microprocessors.

In the same period, other manufacturers of PC processors were unable to establish an equivalent ecosystem to push their processors, even though some had developed fully functional architectures that were considerably more advanced.

GXS, Volkswagen, EADS, Nokia, and Sony, along with many other leading providers, stand to gain significantly from becoming the orchestrator within their ecosystem. Partner relationship management ranges from forging alliances to serve specific market sectors, to exclusive developments and the joint collection and use of expertise, to employee training. A manufacturer of window motors is part of several automotive ecosystems. One of the ways vehicle manufacturers invest in collaborative processes is to provide their suppliers with training and consulting services for their processes, with a view to building themselves the most efficient ecosystem.

Partnerships continue to function for as long as they benefit the partners involved and there is mutual confidence in a sustained business relationship. The IT industry in particular, but also the travel and automotive industries, provide many examples of stable collaborations as well as rapidly changing ones.

> The ecosystem can become more important than the product.

Every enterprise has to battle for its position in the value chain. Large companies orchestrate their own ecosystems and attempt to win as many smaller partners as possible through excellent partner relationship management strategies. Smaller companies may try to join the two or three ecosystems that promise to prevail in the long term, or they could cast their lot with a single large customer. In either case, they depend on good relations with the orchestrators.

GETTING STANDARDS ACCEPTED   Customers want to be able to select and combine products and services freely from different manufacturers and be sure their investment is sound. They dream of a day when all providers will agree on one standard, allowing for universal compatibility. And they want suppliers to give them alternatives. An electronic travel service needs a single standard that will enable it to integrate all hotels, transport firms, sporting event organizers, and other elements into its customer offerings.

Many companies have made the Windows operating system and Microsoft's office software companywide standards. These proprietary standards that are tied to specific products provide the basis for seamless processes. Another prerequisite for consistency is that the software is used in the same way (process standards) and, usually, that the same data (one-time data entry) is used throughout the company.

People using standards want as much freedom as possible. They want the standard that allows them to combine the most components without restriction. But to do so, they have to limit themselves to one standard and become dependent on the standard setter. These dynamics are typical of network effects.

> Standards can simultaneously reduce risk and increase dependency.

When choosing a standard, the people using the standard want to be able to combine all the products developed for the standard, as is now the norm with products based on Microsoft Windows, for instance. In return, they have to accept the limitations and dependencies of the standard. But many market players still complain that Microsoft Word has become the de facto standard, making it difficult or impossible for other products to gain a foothold in the market. They protest that consumers no longer have any real alternatives. But the very same market players chose Microsoft Word in part because they wanted to exchange their text documents with everyone else.

The standard setter's first concern is to make its product accessible to as many customers as possible. Next, it will attempt to win over providers of value-added products and services by way of open standards, or it may use closed proprietary standards to prevent its solutions from being replaced by competing ones. Every standard setter creates an ecosystem with the companies whose products and services support the standard.

With Acrobat, Adobe gave a classic lesson in standardization. The PDF format has become the globally accepted standard for exchanging nonchangeable electronic documents. Adobe does not charge for Acrobat Reader but does collect license fees for Acrobat Professional (for creating documents).

If the buyer's decision is strongly influenced by the ecosystem, the standards, and the services available for a product, but the market has yet to decide on a standard setter, different ecosystems have to fight for individual standards.

With mobile telephony, several ecosystems surrounding Windows Mobile, Google, Apple, Research in Motion, and Symbian all offer overlapping capabilities. Shifting alliances, innovations, and acquisitions make this market extremely dynamic:

- The manufacturers of these operating systems are competing for both application developers and customer market share.

- The cell phone manufacturers must fight for adoption by the carriers, and wrong bets have severely affected both Sony Ericsson and Motorola in recent years.
- In terms of recruiting developers, all eyes are on the Apple App Store, which downloaded 1.5 billion third-party applications in the first year of operation.
- Google is innovating in both applications, such as mapping and mobile search, and hardware, as its Android operating system is powering several promising devices from HTC among others.
- Nokia moved decisively, making its Symbian operating system open-source and buying digital mapmaker Navteq for $8.1 billion in 2007.

With such a massive market in play, and such rapid innovation in the industry, the price for a bad strategic decision or poor execution can be steep. Some companies, therefore, try to join several promising ecosystems, but pay dearly for this type of risk mitigation in terms of investment and complexity.

> Ecosystems are often based on one standard.

Realizing the Vision

Over the past 15 years, numerous studies on business networking have shown over and over again that both industry and academia have extremely high expectations of electronic collaboration in value chains. These studies also make clear that while many of the visions have already been implemented successfully, realizing all the visions will still take some time: both theory and practice have a long way to go until the picture is stable.

Barriers

Among the many impediments to flexible business networking, five stand out.

- *Inefficiency caused by outdated IT.* Too many companies are still using software that does not support collaborative solutions, even though improved versions are available that offer such capabilities. At the same time, the ubiquitous spreadsheet, the basis of many management practices, is unable to support even modest collaboration.

- *Inadequate m:n capabilities.* A lack of standards for IT applications and processes means separate solutions for each business partner and, consequently, greater outlay.
- *Inadequate networking capabilities among business partners.* Small and midsize businesses in particular often lack the know-how and infrastructure for machine-to-machine communication. Even things as basic as good Web sites, a prerequisite of many forms of collaboration, are rare in most markets.
- *Power shifts.* Enterprises are concerned that electronic channels will diminish their power in existing relationships with partners, that increased transparency will render them more interchangeable, or that the tightly integrated relationship will make them dependent. The culture of collaboration is still taking shape.
- *Security risks.* Increasing vulnerability can offset the benefits of networking. Expanding from 1:1 interactions to m:n capability brings increasing complexity, and thus more risk.

Enablers

The technology and economic landscapes are both rich in tools for driving change across a business network:

- *Electronic services.* A new industry is providing electronic services that range from credit reports and payments to navigation and monitoring for physiological functions. In some cases, companies provide such services in-house; in others, they draw the services from external providers. In both cases, these services eliminate the need for company-specific development and thus facilitate new business concepts across an entire process. Coordination services, especially master data management (directory services, product catalogs, and so on), are particularly important for collaborative solutions, allowing companies to build complex processes with both extensive visibility and low cost of deployment.
- *SOA-enabled software suites.* The heirs to yesterday's ERP packages incorporate more and more aspects of open platforms. Development tools, process templates, and a network-centric underlying architecture contribute to "future-proofing" efforts as enterprises migrate to shared standards and interorganizational processes.
- *Service-oriented architectures.* Interoperable, reusable computational services (such as "view order" or "book reservation") can be made available to support agile development of new capability, all the while enforcing management mandates including security, performance, and cost of ownership. These services can be published to industry standards (for published APIs, for example), creating economies of scale

across an ecosystem or vertical segment, and combined with services from other sources written to the same standards. Although the vision of composite applications, created in modular fashion from resources published by a variety of organizations (an "Internet of services" to parallel the "Internet of things"), remains in the future, it will build on foundations that have been laid in the past decade.

- *Interoperability*. All software vendors have given high priority to making their software open (capable of communication). Software is gradually becoming able to deliver on some of the promises made by Internet firms at the end of the nineties.
- *Internet and mobility*. Communication channels with ever broader bandwidth, via cable or wireless, are constantly making new solutions economically feasible. Bringing data to people in motion, meanwhile, opens many more business processes to cost-effective automation and information enrichment.
- *Customer pressure*. Customer expectations of suppliers' electronic services create pressure to upgrade standards, systems, and processes.
- *Ecosystem*. The business partners' technical and personnel conditions are creating more room for electronic collaboration. Healthy ecosystems facilitate cooperation.
- *Embedded systems*. Collaborative solutions without human intervention are faster, more accurate, and more reliable.
- *Portals*. Internet browsers triggered the greatest wave of inter-enterprise networking. While they allow companies to offer customers and suppliers electronic services quickly and without the need for complicated integration activities, portals rely heavily on human-powered management, content updating, and exception-handling processes. But portals always equate to human intervention and thus integration gaps in the process.

Checklist

- ☐ What do you contribute to the value chain? Which services make you valuable to your business partners?
- ☐ How do the laws of networking affect your business areas?
- ☐ Who are your critical partners? Which customers or suppliers will force their processes on you over the next five years?
- ☐ Which aspects of your value chains are most inefficient?
- ☐ Which other companies are involved in the customer processes that you work in?
- ☐ Which internal services would you be better off buying from the market than delivering yourself? Research? Payroll?

☐ Which business units in your value chain will IT make redundant? Trade levels? Storage and logistics? Production locations?

☐ Which internal services could you offer to other companies, and thereby distribute your fixed costs better?

☐ Which standards and electronic services will dictate your networking capabilities in 2010?

☐ Which five electronic services are the most important in your value chain and which will be most important five years from now?

CHAPTER 8

IT's Role in Business Model Transformation

Management Summary

Driving change of any sort in a business is always difficult, but at the fundamental level of the business model, such change requires commitment, insight, and leadership. In addition to these intangible qualities, business model transformation relies heavily on a company's IT infrastructure, information-handling processes, and information services organization. Several forces are changing the role of the information services or systems (IS) group in many companies.[1]

First, the economic slowdown is forcing cutbacks in many areas, and IS is no exception: Double-digit annual budget cuts are common, forcing CIOs to rework their basic planning assumptions. Whether it is by offshoring to reduce development and support costs, or virtualizing hardware to increase efficiency, or renegotiating software licenses, cost pressures are driving behaviors that are unlikely to revert to old patterns once revenues begin to pick up.

Second, technology trends point toward less infrastructure intensiveness on several fronts. Whether in the environmental awareness behind "green" IT, the popularity of powerful mobile devices such as smartphones and netbook PCs, or the attractiveness of cloud computing for certain classes of applications, IT shops are lightening their hardware footprint.

Third, every index related to threats and vulnerabilities points to increased pressure from "bad guys": National security is threatened by highly skilled and powerful cyber-attacks, privacy breaches continue to multiply, and worms, Trojans, and other tools are becoming more clever (see Exhibit 8.1). When both human error and active malice threaten power grids and other life-critical systems, not to mention cure business functionality, the chief information officer's (CIO) priorities can be shifted away from innovation toward reducing downside risk.

171

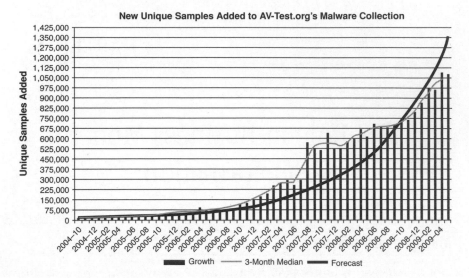

EXHIBIT 8.1 Malicious Code Signatures Are Increasing Dramatically, Indicating Higher Skill Levels among Attackers

Source: AV-Test.org.

Finally, the place of the IS group in the larger organization continues to vary widely. The pendulum between centralization (with its lower costs and clear lines of authority) and decentralization (emphasizing flexibility and speed) swings back and forth, often in the same company. IS budget allocation, whether through charge-backs or other mechanisms, remains problematic: the question of whether IS is a cost center or a profit center is often unsettled.

In addition, the CIO him- or herself may also be faced with changing reporting relationships as different organizational charts position IS under the CFO (chief financial officer), CEO (chief executive officer), or COO (chief operations officer), or distribute it through lines of business. Outsourcing adds further complexity to the organizational dynamic. The bottom line is that IS must change the business, and run the business, ensuring performance and business continuity. Risk management of various kinds extends across both portfolios of activity.

In light of these changes within IS organizations, how can they best support the necessity of business model transformation in industries ranging from aerospace to utilities? Six business concepts emerge from our research:

1. *Alignment of business and technology architectures.* The architecture, or underlying logic, of the business must be supported by the information

systems organization, particularly along the axes of centralization and standardization.

2. *Management of IT risk.* Whether it comes in the shape of security, outsourcing, or project management, risk management has become a core competency of leading IS organizations.

3. *Program and project management.* Management ensures that the right projects run in the right sequence, with the necessary resources, and achieve the promised results.

4. *Information quality assurance.* With more processes relying on accurate data, and the stakes of error higher than ever, information quality cannot be overemphasized.

5. *Cost-effective baseline principles.* Whether in software or hardware, the world of information technology is evolving and presents new models of design and resource utilization. These models can simultaneously enhance performance, cost-effectiveness, and business capability.

6. *IS and customer satisfaction.* For all of the technical demands of the department, the IS organization is valued on how well it delivers service to its clients in the business. Familiar measurements can be borrowed from marketing practice to rate customer satisfaction.

The performance of the IS organization is deeply connected to the success of business model transformation across the dimensions shown in Exhibit 8.2:

- *Product and service.* Given the connection of an enterprise's value to the customer's processes, the smooth yet secure connection of enterprise systems to customers and partners can be a key differentiator.
- *Customer access.* Customers can be anywhere, connected through a variety of technologies, at any time. System availability takes on new dimensions in a 24/7, mobile scenario; batch processes can become problematic because systems cannot go offline without consequences.
- *Ecosystem.* As we saw in the networkability discussion in Chapter 7, 1:1 mapping across an ecosystem fails to scale to the demands of most modern industries. The role of standards emerges as a priority, and leadership in the standards process can pay major dividends.
- *Customer retention.* The more functionally rich and, therefore, complex the product and the closer the partnership, the more difficult it is for the customer to switch to a different manufacturer or ecosystem. In addition, IT connects customers to suppliers in a wide variety of ways, allowing the supplier to identify new product, upsell, and other opportunities as they emerge.
- *Emotion.* A company's customer-facing systems will generate an emotional response, whether it is wariness, appreciation (for foreign-language

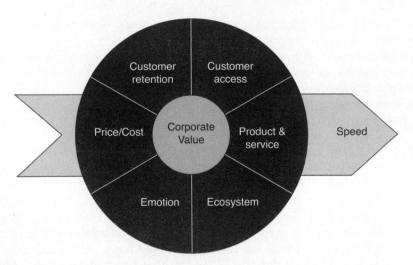

EXHIBIT 8.2   The IS Organization Influences Every Facet of Business Model Transformation

support, for example), irritation, or respect. Internally, many matters of information policy and system performance generate heated emotional responses, whether in regard to information sharing, wait times on the help line, or changing behaviors for log-in, system access, etc.

- *Price/cost.* Effective use of information technologies can directly affect margins, whether through more effective procurement, lower inventory levels, or faster time to market. Measuring the effectiveness of these investments, however, can be difficult: while IT costs of between 3 percent and 20 percent of a firm's revenues are common (depending on the industry), tracing the customer loyalty, competitive, and efficiency impacts of those budgets is rarely a direct exercise.
- *Speed.* The IS organization operates on multiple time scales: How fast does a query get a response from a database? How soon can a broken laptop be replaced? When will the application be ready for user testing? When will the changes to the product catalog be posted to the Web site?

Vision

In many regards, the most essential systems become invisible: We only notice electricity when the power goes out, or mobile telephony when our battery dies. The ideal of Information Services is that systems work so smoothly and reliably that they silently orchestrate an organization's processes. Security is sufficiently visible to inspire confidence, but not so onerous as to deter users from a given activity. Data can be relied on to be accurate, timely, and complete without user validation. Change in enterprise systems is gradual and seamless, much as users rarely notice upgrades to Google's internal systems. IS budgets reflect value received, rather than arbitrary allocations, and users can scale their requirements up or down to align with changes in the market and partner ecosystem.

High-Performance IS Organizations

Given the intense cost and competitive pressures affecting virtually every industry, both the efficiency and the effectiveness of many corporate IT shops are increasing. The three examples described next illustrate the larger trend.

Valero Energy Corporation

Valero has rapidly emerged as North America's largest independent petroleum refiner and marketer and an innovative force in the industry. It owns and operates 15 refineries, 7 ethanol plants, and associated pipelines and terminals in the United States, Canada, and the Caribbean. With 5,800 retail and wholesale sites under its brands, it also has a substantial retail presence in the United States, Canada, and the Caribbean.

A strategy of growing the refinery operation through acquisition of distressed assets has led Valero to increase refining capacity from 200,000 barrels per day in 1997 to 2.8 million in 2009. The Valero IS organization has played a critical role in this acquisition process: system integrations that can take 12 to 24 months in many M&A scenarios needed to be completed in no more than 90 days. Monitoring of key business processes, including margins and inventory levels in volatile oil and gasoline markets, was one reason integration needed to be completed so quickly.

Using a Service-Oriented Architecture, Valero created a layer of enterprise-wide services and blended these 200 services into 45 composite applications. This capability allowed the acquired companies to remain on their existing manufacturing and logistics systems while adding new consolidated functionality in weeks, rather than months. The acquired businesses could focus on optimizing their operations and utilizing Valero's integrated core of systems instead of having to replace all of their legacy systems. Valero does not strive for full integration of every acquisition or across every process. The fast and light model has one set of costs and benefits, while the managers realize that full-scale integration, with its longer timetable and higher costs, delivers a different mix of capabilities.

The confidence in the Valero integration process paid off, as Valero's acquisitions have continued at a faster rate than competitors could sustain. Visibility into merged entities improved. In one example, optimized operations using an application that continually measures and provides alerts on energy consumption has captured over $100 million per year in savings.

Intel

Intel Corporation has been at the forefront of the computing revolution from the beginning, developing generation after generation of microprocessor. Remarkably, the company still delivers on the promise of cofounder Gordon Moore's prediction that computing performance will double roughly every two years. The original prediction boldly looked ahead 10 years, to 1975. No other industry has ever sustained such a long record of dramatic innovation.

The Intel IS organization, known as Intel IT, occupies a unique position in that it is a beta site for the company's own products. Co-CIO Diane Bryant came to the role from a server product group; she holds four U.S. patents and so is familiar with the need for customer input into product development. In her new role, Bryant must satisfy the considerable computing demands of chip design and engineering: Intel's compute clusters are among the biggest of their type in the world. According to Bryant, 85 percent of Intel's servers support the engineering computation needed to design a 2 billion–transistor chip, and they run at 90 percent utilization—a handsome figure for any data center.[2]

At the same time, Intel is a manufacturing company under economic pressure. The need to be cost-effective has taken center stage in recent years, with 30 percent IT headcount reductions being one outcome. The hardware side has also come in for a significant rethinking, as the number of worldwide data centers is reduced by an order of magnitude: from more than 100 to fewer than 10 at some point in the future. Savings in 2008 approached $100 million from this one initiative.[3]

Like BMW, Intel IT utilizes a hybrid organizational model, aligning specific types of expertise with the appropriate business units while centralizing enterprise-wide operations.[4] Wherever they are deployed, the people of Intel IT are a particular focus: they constituted the top strategic priority entering 2009 with specific initiatives addressing "organizational health," training, and leadership development. Resource allocation and project management excellence also drew leadership's attention.

In addition to such traditional efforts, Intel has also aggressively embraced social media, including instant messaging, a Twitter-like enterprise tool, and blogging. The uptake has been rapid, bridging internal and external resources successfully: on Open Port, a series of external communities for end users, more than 75 percent of all content comes from end users as customers come together to solve real-world problems.[5] Going forward, Intel hopes to add video and audio as well as to gain leverage from the same tagging and search dynamics that underlie such popular services as Flickr and Delicious. At the same time, solving the challenges in social media related to privacy, liability, security, and intellectual property issues remains a top priority.

Since 2000, Intel IT has published a comprehensive, professionally designed performance report patterned on a corporation's annual report, making public many key operating metrics. To give some idea of what the organization is achieving, consider some specific examples:

- The IS organization has a budget of $1.2 billion.[6]
- Intel IT comprises 5,700 people at 66 sites in 28 countries.
- The cost per help desk incident dropped 16 percent between 2007 and 2008, to roughly $17.
- Customer satisfaction with the help desk was 89 percent, in the midst of company-wide cost-cutting.
- Intel spent more than $12,000 per employee, or 3.12 percent of revenue, on IT in 2008.
- Ninety-two percent of projects met committed release dates.
- The Web site delivers more than 100 million page views per month.[7]

In any organization, such performance would be noteworthy, but even more important is the fact that Intel measures its performance so closely in the first place: apart from server uptime and other technical metrics, many organizations lack the visibility into the business of IT, something at which Intel clearly excels, as the sophistication of its performance reporting illustrates.

UK Green ICT

In the context of a broad mandate to make its central government offices carbon neutral by 2012, the government of the United Kingdom has established a series of environmental sustainability targets for all departments. In addition to reducing the visible and significant contribution of computers and printers to those offices' environmental footprint, the effective use of information and communications technologies (ICTs) can assist other efforts to reduce environmental impact, for example through videoconferencing to reduce travel or bar codes to help with asset tracking and end-of-life disposal. Green ICT both addresses environmental policy goals and, when done well, saves money and increases agility as it enables other functions to decrease their environmental footprints and operating costs.

The UK Chief Information Officer faces a series of environmental performance targets:

- As of January 2009 carbon footprint became a consideration in all new equipment purchases.
- The Central Government's office estate will be carbon neutral by 2012, supported by the IS organization's lowering of power consumption.
- Most boldly, "By 2020 Government aims to comply with and where possible lead and go beyond global best practice for sustainability across the whole ICT life cycle. This will cover carbon neutrality and sustainable processes for use of materials, water, accommodation and transport, in the manufacture, use and disposal of ICT."[8]

The IT organization was immediately responsible for turning policy aspirations into operational documentation. In doing so, it had to strike a balance between completeness and specificity, on one hand, and the substantial size of the organization on the other. When an asset is sold, how is its environmental impact treated? What is the environmental footprint of an electronics-scrapping operation? How is power consumption measured across shared racks of servers at an outsourcer? How is the measurement accomplished by vendors within contract terms that predate the Green ICT initiative? Most importantly, in the absence of industry standards for many metrics, how could the IT organization and its vendor community develop meaningful measures on the fly, across the many units?

A vast information collection instrument was developed and then scaled back to 310 questions—still a substantial document, but a necessary step. Based on the scorecard that resulted from the questionnaire, a current scoreboard, or high level report, highlighted the 18 actions that departmental CIOs needed to deliver. Among these were longer utilization of hardware, "sweating the asset" until the end of its normal life; heavier reliance on LCD monitors and laptops where possible; more two-sided printing, less color printing, and less printing overall; and better power management of PCs without active users nearby. Data centers and networking closets received similarly detailed treatment, and the recommendations will serve as the baseline for future grading of subsequent actions and metrics.

As the first government to commit to a firm timetable toward carbon neutrality, the United Kingdom will face more issues than other organizations that follow its lead. At the same time, the entire government is engaged with the IT organization on a shared pursuit, necessitating ever-closer collaboration. More importantly, utilizing ICTs in the pursuit of a greener environmental footprint, in carbon but also in heavy metal capture, in water consumption, and in other impacts, will help the United Kingdom attain a leadership position in what may be the twenty-first-century's greatest challenge.

Concepts of IS Organizational Performance

Six broad themes underlie the development of IS organizations that effectively support both operational and strategic objectives. They are as follows.

Alignment of Business and Technology Architectures

Beginning in the early 1990s, a large body of academic work and industry literature attempted to identify the key lens for measuring the performance of an IS organization. One school of thought involved assessing the degree of fit, or alignment, between IS activities and the organization's strategic objectives.[9] This perspective had many adherents, and one effect of the intellectual trend was to shift the assessment of IS organizations from a pure cost and service level perspective to a broader set of considerations. It was also in these years that the title of Chief Information Officer came into wide usage, moving the IS function from its data processing niche potentially into the business mainstream as a market differentiator.

Strategy, however, is only as good as execution, and strategic alignment on a whiteboard is very different from high performance on loading docks, in customer service, or in managing receivables. Jeanne Ross, Peter Weill, and David Robertson of MIT's Center for Information Systems Research have proposed the notion that a company's information infrastructure and embedded process knowledge constitute a *foundation for execution,* an automated core of a company's capabilities. As they point out, however, digitizing a process can render it less flexible, which means that great care must be taken to preserve agility at the same time that instantiating key activities in software can improve service levels and deliver cost benefits.[10]

A tool by which business and IS management can collaborate in this regard is what the authors call the *operating model*, which makes explicit the degree of *standardization* and *integration* required by the business model. This simple framework precedes an enterprise architecture, specifying in business terms how the key business processes must be supported and at what cost. Integration allows a company to present a single face to the customer, but requires multiple business units to use common data standards and practices. Standardization brings cost savings and efficiencies, but limits the opportunity to customize practices to specific markets or customers. Making the costs and benefits clear at the time priorities are established begins the dialog that can most effectively allow IS to support the business.

A global chemical company, for example, needs to be highly standardized: it must deliver the same product to the same specifications all the time everywhere in the world, particularly to global customers. The level of integration is also high: When that chemical company serves a customer from its Brazil plant, the Chinese or German business units might need to see the order to recognize volume discounts, for example, or issue product recalls.

Consider, in contrast, a multiline bank. Because home mortgages, credit cards, small business loans, and corporate treasury have very different process requirements, standardization would be low. Centralization, however, should be high as customers with multiple services will want unified statements. At the opposite extreme would be a franchise operation in which international subsidiaries ran independently but used nearly identical practices. In this setting, standardization would be high and integration would be low: The Canadian operation would have little reason to see detailed operating information from its Australian counterparts. Finally, some businesses, particularly small ones, can operate perfectly well with neither standardized nor integrated processes.

Mapping the two axes onto a grid gives the construct shown in Exhibit 8.3 in which business and IT executives can begin with a common understanding of the business's market differentiators, regulatory constraints, and assumed level of investment.[11] In doing so, the operating model facilitates alignment of strategic intent and execution capability.

Management of IT Risk

Risk can affect an IT organization across multiple dimensions, and we discuss project management later in this section. For now, let us take offshoring as an example: When U.S. firms replace onshore technical and other resources with lower-cost labor in offshore markets, the logic is typically financial. Five years after some of the biggest such decisions, however, it has become clear that the calculations were incomplete.

Let's start with a generic decision to shift 3,000 applications programmers from onshore to offshore in 2004. The calculation assumes a 10 percent cost of capital, a 34 percent tax rate, and 2 percent savings per year as salaries both in the United States and abroad grow at similar rates. The base case presumes a net present value of $400,000 savings per job, times 3,000 workers, for a $1.2 billion projected cash saving. Given the realities of activist shareholders and relentless cost-cutting, it would be difficult, and perhaps an invitation to a shareholder lawsuit, to decline those kinds of cost savings.

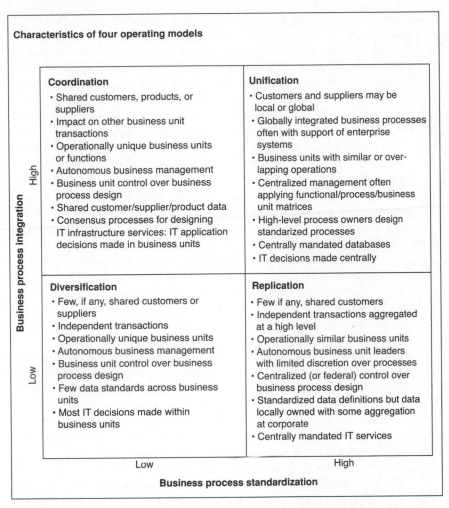

Characteristics of four operating models

Coordination	**Unification**
• Shared customers, products, or suppliers	• Customers and suppliers may be local or global
• Impact on other business unit transactions	• Globally integrated business processes often with support of enterprise systems
• Operationally unique business units or functions	• Business units with similar or overlapping operations
• Autonomous business management	• Centralized management often applying functional/process/business unit matrices
• Business unit control over business process design	
• Shared customer/supplier/product data	• High-level process owners design standarized processes
• Consensus processes for designing IT infrastructure services: IT application decisions made in business units	• Centrally mandated databases
	• IT decisions made centrally
Diversification	**Replication**
• Few, if any, shared customers or suppliers	• Few if any, shared customers
• Independent transactions	• Independent transactions aggregated at a high level
• Operationally unique business units	• Operationally similar business units
• Autonomous business management	• Autonomous business unit leaders with limited discretion over processes
• Business unit control over business process design	• Centralized (or federal) control over business process design
• Few data standards across business units	• Standardized data definitions but data locally owned with some aggregation at corporate
• Most IT decisions made within business units	• Centrally mandated IT services

Vertical axis: Business process integration — High / Low

Horizontal axis: Low / High — **Business process standardization**

EXHIBIT 8.3 The Operating Model Allows Business and IS Leadership to Operate from a Common Understanding of High-Level Process Requirements

Source: © 2005 Massachusetts Institute of Technology. This work was created by MIT's Sloan Center for Information Systems Research. Used with permission.

As the past five years have unfolded, however, some incompleteness in the analysis has emerged. Seven additional factors might be addressed in future considerations:

1. *Inflation.* Compensation growth in India in the past five years significantly outpaced that of the United States, to the point where Indian

wage inflation ran in the double digits for some of those five years. That compares to flat wage growth in the United States.

2. *Emotional intangibles.* The years with high wage inflation coincided with high turnover at some offshore firms. The resulting instability contributed to lower performance gains than some onshore clients were expecting. At the same time, onshore perceptions of offshore practices, particularly in help desk and customer-service settings, led to vocal backlash against such companies as Delta airlines. According to Interbrand, Dell lost 13 percent of its brand equity, and 10 ranking positions, in the aftermath of a highly visible reaction against offshore support.[12]

3. *Coordination costs.* Another factor widely underappreciated in many cost projections was the increase in coordination costs. Highly compensated, and extremely busy, financial services experts at various firms, for example, have told us that they overestimated offshoring's value. In particular, they and their teams spent far more time generating and refining requirements documents for a team of programmers on the other side of the world as compared to the in-house resources across the hall who knew the baseline terminology and assumptions of the process, firm, and industry in question. Producing code and generating business value through technology are not the same thing.

4. *Technology shifts in enterprise applications.* The rise of such technologies as software as a service, virtualization, and cloud computing is challenging old models of application development and deployment. In addition, scripting-based programming practices have the potential to transform software still further. Ten-year payback scenarios that hold a traditional computing model constant are likely to prove problematic in the late years of the model.

5. *Currency dynamics.* Both the Indian rupee and the U.S. dollar have undergone significant currency fluctuations, dwarfing that 2 percent cost savings assumption. In one year alone, a dollar went from buying 39 rupees to crossing the 50 barrier, a swing of about 30 percent (in this instance, in the U.S. firm's favor).

6. *Corruption.* The cost-saving calculations implicitly assumed an apples-to-apples comparison of contract law, financial accountability, and other facets of firm governance. But when Satyam, one of India's leading offshore firms, disclosed that its founder and CEO had orchestrated a billion-dollar accounting fraud, attention turned to the differences between Indian and U.S. models of corporate governance. Auditors from Price Waterhouse,[13] who have been suspended from the firm and jailed by authorities, earned "exorbitant audit fees" and are alleged to have falsified key discrepancies between sales figures and bank deposits.

7. *Political risk.* The 2004 NPV model apparently priced risk at zero, a flawed assumption when India is experiencing political tensions with its nuclear neighbor Pakistan, itself a potential "failed state" in the words of the U.S. Joint Forces Command. The Mumbai attacks of 2006 and 2008 provide further evidence that the country is facing a significant threat, in this case from nonstate actors. The story continues to unfold, up to 2009. Various insurgent factions staged attacks connected to India's month-long election; 17 deaths were reported on the first day of polling alone.

At the least, the past decade of offshoring have proven that the logic of the business case depends as much on what one leaves out as on the numbers assigned. As the process of globalization evolves, unexpected consequences, for both good and ill, will continue to challenge firms—and individuals—on all sides of the equation.

Program and Project Management

Along with its work to maintain the infrastructural skeleton of an organization, projects comprise the lifeblood of any IS organization. Projects that together can support a larger objective may be managed as a program, which requires higher levels of investment, greater complexity, and more people (and kinds of people) involved in management. Program and project management both have well-developed sets of principles, practices, and practical tools (such as planning models or reporting templates), but both rely heavily on the skill of the particular humans involved. In our experience, good project/program managers are valued extremely highly by business, nonprofits, and government alike: nearly every organization identifies a shortage of strong project managers, and the difficult career development path for such managers, as major organizational challenges.

While some facets of project management carry over from construction, for example, IT projects are unique in that code is intangible. Unlike a building, whose progress is visible, the course of a large software project is determined much less by code-writing than by testing, which by definition cannot be completed until code is available. The failure of many infamous software projects originated in misguided efforts to accelerate progress by shortening the unit and system testing phases. Fred Brooks, a widely acknowledged figure in software project management, also pointed to "gutless estimating" as a crucial flaw: project managers who neglected to include sufficient testing time in their original schedule courted project failure in many instances.[14]

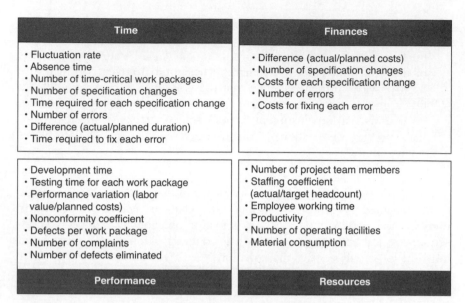

Time	Finances
• Fluctuation rate • Absence time • Number of time-critical work packages • Number of specification changes • Time required for each specification change • Number of errors • Difference (actual/planned duration) • Time required to fix each error	• Difference (actual/planned costs) • Number of specification changes • Costs for each specification change • Number of errors • Costs for fixing each error
• Development time • Testing time for each work package • Performance variation (labor value/planned costs) • Nonconformity coefficient • Defects per work package • Number of complaints • Number of defects eliminated	• Number of project team members • Staffing coefficient (actual/target headcount) • Employee working time • Productivity • Number of operating facilities • Material consumption
Performance	Resources

EXHIBIT 8.4   Key Metrics for Project Management Are Familiar

Brooks' most famous dictum is related to the intangibility of code. Because of the high coordination costs within programming teams, adding more members to a team slows down progress because the original members must spend so much time informing and checking in with a greater number of resources. Thus, what has come to be known as Brooks' Law asserts that "adding manpower to a late software project makes it later."[15] As counterintuitive as it sounds, the statement has proved its wisdom repeatedly in the 30 years since he first made the observation.

Project failure remains high despite the fact that commercial software projects are nearly 50 years old. As Exhibit 8.4 illustrates, the four basic dimensions for both projects and programs can be readily measured, but frequently are not. In addition, a key role in project failure relates to the quality and composition of teams. Process experts from the line of business, while essential for project success, are often judged as too valuable in their primary role to be loaned to the project team. Thus weaker players can contribute to incorrect or incomplete understandings of process metrics and mechanics: Bad information in the planning and specification phases can be extremely expensive to address later in the project life cycle, once assumptions have hardened.

Finally, IS risk management tends to be measured in project dollars, but business impact may affect the share price, either positively or negatively: Oxford Health Plans, an innovative health maintenance organization that depended heavily on IT, lost 62 percent of its share value in a single day, in part due to news that a key business process could not be supported. To mitigate against such extreme scenarios, the risk management process should include both project dollars and business impact dollars. In short, if IS is committed to deliver business value, it must also measure the impact, at market rates, of failing to do so.

In the end, while software is intangible and its workings complex, the key factors in project failure are human ones: inadequate quality or numbers of project managers, B- or C-level players from the business process side, incomplete specifications, escalation of commitment (the myth of sunk costs), inattention to testing, and other decisions can frequently be found when failures are analyzed in depth. This practice is not as common as it might seem: Failures are still not used as learning opportunities inside many corporate cultures. Instead, they are made invisible in attempts to preserve careers or other organizational benefits.

Information Quality Assurance

Despite cost pressures and standardization efforts, information volumes continue to multiply: As of 2008, Intel's enterprise storage capacity was growing at a compound annual rate of 35 percent, an unsustainable trend.[16] More, however, does not equate to better, as a single question might have multiple answers, and determining why the answers differ can occupy hours of decision-makers' time. As of 2006, a Harris survey found that 75 percent of respondents had made business decisions that proved to be wrong because of flawed data. Only 10 percent always had all the information they need to be confident in their decisions; respondents reported spending as much as 30 percent of their workweek verifying the accuracy and quality of the data they use to make decisions.[17]

Quality assurance can be understood from the perspective of five questions:

1. Does the information accurately reflect an underlying ground truth? If not, what manipulations have been performed, as in statistical sampling, for example. Were inventory counts done by hand, based on POS data, or derived from the warehouse system?
2. Is the information consistent? Do the Malaysian division's results reflect pre-tax or after-tax profits? What about the Brazilian results? When were currency effects calculated?
3. Are the underlying assumptions visible? What was the last day included on month-end results? What costs factored into the ROI calculation?
4. Has the information been tampered with or otherwise corrupted? This can be either malicious, from either inside or outside actors, or

accidental, as when versions of a spreadsheet get out of synch in an e-mail trail.

5. Is the information timely? As we have seen, being up-to-the-minute may be undesirable if multiple perspectives must be reconciled. Timeliness should be relatively equal across multiple reports.

The holistic nature of information quality problems and solutions can be seen at BT (formerly British Telecom).[18] Because the market was changing rapidly and the company was frequently reorganizing, business processes were permanently designed "behind reality." This gap between process design and the demands of customers was typically closed by increased manual activities and workarounds—neither of which contribute to better data quality. Business processes were designed for an "ideal world," in which, for example, customers do not cancel orders. Based on that assumption, business processes did not include any rollback mechanisms.

New sales and communications channels including the Internet required substantially improved data quality. Other main drivers causing BT to deal with the issue of data quality resulted from its functional organization, which did not support true end-to-end business processes. Business units did not know where the data they were using came from, and which other units in subsequent process steps were using the same data for what purpose. As a consequence, employees did not focus on entering seemingly unnecessary data correctly, which resulted in poor data quality in subsequent process steps. For example, repair personnel were sent to wrong locations because of incorrect customer address data, resulting in unnecessary costs for BT and a poor experience for the customer. Although employees often recognized problems in business processes, they did not perceive them as data quality problems. Too often, such problems were considered to be purely IT system related and not material to the business.

In response, the Group Chief Information Officer initiated a series of high-visibility projects with rapid payback: Cleaner name and address records reduced postal charges and then customer master data was standardized. A company event was held at which both the CEO and external speakers stressed the importance of information quality in the achievement of BT's business objectives, and project teams presented impressive return on investment proof points. The message was heard and acted upon: business unit requests for data quality projects increased significantly. By 2003, more than 50 such projects had delivered overall business value in excess of £600 million.

Among the keys to the success of the program were a heavy emphasis on organizational change: attitudes often matter more than systems in information quality initiatives. In addition, the reliance on market "pull" from the business units rather than supply "push" from the IS organization increased buy-in as executives pursued monetary and strategic benefits rather than following what might be perceived as technical directives of limited value. Finally, project performance was monitored on a long-term basis to prevent old behaviors from creeping back into practice: information quality is a long-term organizational pursuit rather than a one-time system installation.

Cost-Effective Baseline Principles

As the technology landscape evolves, the industry frequently uses the language of the Machine Age to describe its aspirations. Code should not be "hand-crafted," but rather be generated in "factories" and be "industrial strength." Computing was thought to behave like a "utility," much like water or electric power. The way to navigate the infinite World Wide Web is via a search "engine."

Despite the appeal of such characterizations, many fall short: The Information Age is qualitatively different, and runs at a different scale, compared to the world of 100 years ago. It has taken considerable experience to generate fresh understandings of the way forward that are not handicapped by the limitations of metaphor. We see three basic principles that support cost-effective delivery of information services:

1. *Second-generation SOA.* Starting in 2002 or so, vendors invested heavily in the development of service-oriented architectures, or SOA. This effort involved systematic approaches to standards-based interfaces across operating environments, applications, and data in both technology organizations and business processes. The ideal of SOA was simultaneously to deliver the cost and efficiency benefits of standardization and to support the need for flexibility required by local change and rapid adaptation. Interoperable, reusable services would be made available to support agile development of new capability, all the while enforcing management mandates including security, performance, and cost of ownership.

   While much progress was made in realizing the potential of SOA, it was widely regarded with disappointment. In common with all other technology innovations, SOA did not provide a "silver bullet," solving challenges of cost, performance, flexibility, and robustness. As the name suggests, an "orientation" required many changes to mindsets, budgeting, expectation management, and other behaviors in and across enterprises. Few products could deliver the promised benefits without the more subtle and difficult changes to code-writing, data-handling, and business processes: the key gains come from deeper change that must come mostly from within the organization.

In the credit and jobs crisis following 2008, IS budgets were cut dramatically, customer expectations changed (sometimes overnight), and corporate priorities were focused on essential matters of economic survival. In this environment, many facets of SOA proved their worth: sound data structures, well-designed code, and flexible mappings paid off in M&A spinouts or combinations, budget discipline, and competitive nimbleness. New technologies, such as software as a service, mashups, and cloud computing, are built on many SOA premises. As the economy improves, the lessons will persist, and what might be called "deployed SOA," often in the form of services-based business suites, will continue to deliver competitive and operational benefits.

2. *Mobility*. The ability to capture and process data where it originates or is used will radically change many processes. The price/performance ratio of technology for mobile communications, or "mobility" for short, is improving at a rapid pace, and driving economic competitiveness across the globe. A pack of highly capable handheld mobile computing platforms from such manufacturers as Apple, Google, Nokia, and Research in Motion is growing rapidly, but in addition to smartphones, so-called netbook PCs represent another fast-growing market segment poised to drive, and capitalize on, mobility. The distinction between telephones and PCs is getting fuzzier every year, and the iPhone presents a clear case in point: Running a Unix variant, it can be spoken at, but performs best moving and manipulating images and data.

Enterprise mobility emerges against the backdrop of a powerful demographic force. The distribution of countries with mobile teledensity (cell phones per 100 people) over 100, for example, is most surprising. According to International Telecommunications Union figures from 2008, more than 60 countries qualify. Estonia, for example, had 188 mobile phones for every 100 people. Italy was at 148, Singapore 138, and Argentina 116.

The geographic spread of greater-than-100 teledensities also comes as a surprise. Qatar and the UAE represent the Middle East/North Africa, Aruba and Trinidad and Tobago the Caribbean, and Singapore Asia. About 100 years ago, the economist Thorstein Veblen posited that there are penalties for technological leadership, largely because any generation of technology imposes switching costs on the adoption of something newer. Many states are proving his point as they leapfrog poor wireline infrastructure by building wireless capacity at stunning speed: Lithuania had a fixed line teledensity of only 32 as of 2000, but a mobile quotient of 151 only eight years later.

The phrase "Always-on People" belongs to industry analyst Chris Shipley, but the phenomenon is widely observed: Countless newspaper articles have focused on the etiquette of checking mobile message devices away from the office, whether at home, out socializing, or in business meetings. That the Research In Motion (RIM) BlackBerrry is so often called the "Crackberry" gives some sense of its addictiveness. The phenomenon is as broad as it is intense: Worldwide BlackBerry subscribers number nearly 46 million, and hundreds of millions of phones allow their owners to maintain seamless global system for mobile (GSM) communications. In 1997, by contrast, text pagers were in their earliest stages, only plumbers and doctors had beepers, and world phones were strictly a niche luxury. Now, whole negotiations are carried out in motion, with little regard for time or place. For millions of managers, the notion of being "out of the office" is almost quaint, and the blurring of work and personal time is less clear than ever before.

The phenomenon can be tracked in language. In Germany, cell phones are often called a *Handy,"* and the Japanese have named a relevant demographic the *oyayubizoku,* meaning "clan of the thumb," which is far more evocative than the American equivalent, "digital natives." Whatever they're called, these people, most of them under 30, are redefining mobile communication: Basic rules of engagement—who is expected to say (or text) what message to whom, in what contexts, with what expectations in return—are being defined in fascinating ways. The situation parallels the need for a new greeting at the introduction of the telephone, as people of manners were not supposed to speak to someone unless they had been introduced. Many languages differentiate between a telephone greeting and a spoken one ("bonjour" vs. "allô" in French), but before "hello" caught on, Alexander Graham Bell preferred the nautical expression "ahoy" as the English-language telephone greeting.

3. *Maximum asset utilization.* Physical assets such as desktops, printers, and servers have proliferated in many enterprises. Each requires financial and logistical support, and complexity in these physical environments often scales nonlinearly: 1+1 may equal 3, figuratively speaking, when considering the burden on the IS organization.

Budget pressures may be in the forefront, but there are three compelling reasons for infrastructure rationalization, utilizing a mix of reset user expectations (not every desk needs its own printer), virtualization technologies, and vendor reevaluation.

First, a simpler environment costs less to maintain and run. Fewer servers drop energy consumption, while fewer data centers save on real estate. Lower resupply and spare parts requirements lower inventory and free up working capital. Fewer software licenses require less time to audit and less time in user and support staff training.

Second, as carbon footprints and other environmental impacts such as end-of-life disposal come into sharper focus from both regulators and investors (such as corporate social responsibility groups), the role of information technology will be scrutinized. As of 2009, it is estimated that the ICT sector worldwide generates the same amount of CO_2 as commercial aviation.[19]

Third, system complexity exacts a toll in performance. Better data practices, fewer 1:1 mappings, and standardized system calls all improve the user experience and lighten the support burden. Such aspects as response time, data storage volume, and effort required for an update all improve in a rationalized environment.

Entering the 2010s, many eyes are following the growth of cloud computing, in which very large data centers exploit economies of scale related to people, power, and processing. Server utilization that typically runs about 20 percent in many corporate settings can be increased to roughly 90 percent in cloud vendors such as Amazon Web Services. As we saw at Intel, however, so-called private clouds can also deliver similar benefits, potentially at lower cost presuming the environment is sufficiently large.[20]

Importantly, cloud computing from an external vendor can both lower risk and lower costs, while shifting expenditures from capital expenditures to monthly expenses. Because scale can be purchased in individual increments as demand merits, IS organizations avoid the danger of under- or overprovisioning server clusters. At the same time, computing resources can scale down if needed, deployment time is hours rather than months, and working capital is preserved. Headcount can also be reserved for value-adding rather than undifferentiating tasks.

Extremely scalable commodity processing cycles from external providers make business sense for startups and SMEs in particular. Software delivered as a service is finding markets in enterprises of every size, while high-density data centers inside the enterprise appeal to large enterprises. In each instance, the cost, competitive, and environmental payoffs delivered by the broad range of technologies and management practices under the "cloud" umbrella will make it a factor in IT decisions going forward.[21]

IS and Customer Satisfaction

Such is the nature of being a CIO that the demands are varied: Cut costs, maintain security, assure information quality, shrink the environmental footprint, support process and business model innovation. Many of these objectives compete for resources, and while some actions such as data center consolidation or master data quality campaigns can pay dividends in multiple domains, hard decisions still have to be made.

One common trait of successful CIOs, however, is their understanding of IS as a service business, with dynamics in common with hospitality, retail, or education: Customer satisfaction can be measured, improved, and documented. Thus, while network uptime or data center cost savings can be useful measures, many IS organizations poll customers on help-line wait times and resolution rates, employee friendliness, and the proactivity with which solutions are offered. Technical capabilities, such as wireless coverage or system uptime, also can generate spirited responses.

Within many of these organizations, IS employees are encouraged to rotate through line of business positions, learning the process, data, and profitability landscape from the inside. Similarly, line of business employees at both the executive and managerial level are valuable assets who can enhance their own careers as well as IS service levels by doing a tour in the IS shop. Project managers in particular have been encouraged to work in IS on a short-term basis, both building their capabilities and mentoring younger IS colleagues.

Realizing the Vision

IS is to a company in the Information Age what the production line was to a company in the industrial age. It provides and enables the infrastructure for implementing the business model.

Barriers

As we have seen, both human and technical barriers impede the performance of an IS organization. The role of the CIO is in transition as the technologies, costs, and skills involved in IT continue to evolve:

- *Information overload.* Data is accumulating at many points in an organization: enterprise resource planning (ERP) system databases, documents in office software, datasets for technical design and realization, data from intelligent devices, floods of e-mails, voice mails, and management broadcasts in multiple forms. In particular, Internet access to almost any information outside of the company has caused an information overload that has already been described in detail. As organizations grow in size and complexity, managers often find themselves spending more and more of their limited time coordinating activities in discussions and meetings.

- *Information deficiency.* The fact that people are simultaneously crying out for more information almost sounds absurd. But it is true that many processes could be accelerated and countless inefficiencies avoided (relating to inventory levels or targeting the wrong customers, for instance) if capturing data were not so expensive, if companies could access all data recorded somewhere electronically already, and if the significance of existing data were clear to all involved.

The final three barriers share a common thread, in that they all contribute to unmanageable system complexity:

- *Stand-alone systems.* Islands create integration gaps—situations in which *people* form the interface between IT applications, say by entering an e-mail into the order entry system or by copying product information from an article database to a product catalog. Integration gaps slow down the flow of information, render processes more prone to error, and increase the complexity of procedures because people have to make inquiries and resolve problems.

    The CEOs we surveyed see harmonizing stand-alone systems as the most urgent task of the coming years—"silos" still impede creation of a uniform business process platform. Best-of-breed approaches, where companies take the best solutions from different vendors' software packages, entail persistently high outlay for machine interfaces and integration gaps, which is why many organizations look for homogeneous application architectures wherever possible.
- *Inadequate networkability.* This refers to the ability of any number (m) of suppliers to speak the "same language" with any number (n) of customers at the interfaces between processes and systems. Heterogeneous worlds have particularly serious implications when enterprises start to collaborate electronically. For instance, an automotive supplier has to adapt to the development and production practices of the individual vehicle manufacturers, mastering multiple collaborative processes and different IT applications: Many interorganizational interfaces are one-off efforts. But different manufacturers demand different collaborative development processes. Inadequate m:n capabilities loom as the biggest hurdle on the way to more efficient inter-enterprise processes.
- *Insufficient flexibility.* Many companies complain of losing flexibility. Process and office software can present barriers, for example, if customer data cannot be changed in different IT applications in parallel without becoming inconsistent. If the outlay required to standardize article data stands in the way of an enterprise-wide product catalog, for example, potentially artificial departmental budget priorities may impede the pursuit of agility at the corporate level because different

entities will call the same thing by different names or describe similar things using inconsistent terms.

Enablers

A small number of basic information technologies (including ERP and the Internet) have enabled the level of information intensiveness we know today along with the associated economic changes. Joining these are a few technologies (such as social software and content management) currently migrating into enterprise adoption, while another group of new technologies (such as the "Internet of things" made possible by cheap sensors, or new forms of information display) is about to be realized on a broad scale:

- *Global networkability.* As processes span more companies, the ability to securely share the right data across an ecosystem in machine-to-machine transactions will continue to pay dividends in cost savings, quality of execution, and strategic flexibility. As volatility and change remain facts of life, and increase in their impact because of increasing interconnection and complexity, reliable m:n mappings will become essential business capabilities. Standards, electronic services, and exchanges drive networkability.
- *Electronic services.* A common language is the basis for any kind of collaboration. Standards enable all sorts of IT applications to "communicate" with one another. An emerging industry which delivers many of its services almost exclusively in electronic form over the Internet deserves particular attention. This industry includes services for payment transactions, searching for and paying for parking, credit reports, and authentication of people on the Web. Electronic services are the intermediaries in a networked economy.
- *Sensors, networks, and "the Internet of Things."* Connected sensors and processors are rapidly increasing the functions of technical devices, most notably in cars, but also in measuring devices, lamps, sneakers, and medical apparatus. While most of the technology for embedded systems (sometimes called ubiquitous computing) is already available today, it is still too expensive for many applications. Miniaturization, standardization, changes in basic technology, and above all, the large quantities of sensors (produced by the million) will make an almost infinite range of applications profitable in the coming years. At the same time, considerable work remains to be done at the level of standards and applications to make all these sensors work properly, work securely, and work together.
- *Knowledge management.* Data warehouses, content management solutions, search engines, and applications for teamwork are gradually

beginning to meet at least some of the high expectations regarding the way existing knowledge is used and how the information overload is managed. The field of analytics and visualization is advancing in particularly promising directions. In addition, so-called "enterprise 2.0" solutions exploit the same power of crowds that has proven itself in Wikipedia, delicious, YouTube, and Flickr.[22] Information markets, corporate social networks, automated document discovery, and other tools are reinventing enterprise knowledge management.

- *New application areas.* The primary use of the new technologies mentioned above is not in business processes, but in products and services for the intelligent home, entertainment (from TV to games), health care, retired people, traffic management, vehicles, and location-based services. Many companies are finding new business areas for these IT applications. As more and more enterprises begin to use the new IT applications in their processes, there will be a greater need for integration and networking capabilities.

Checklist

- ☐ How do you assess the value of IT projects? Before and after?
- ☐ Does IT give your business sufficient incentive to innovate?
- ☐ Who is responsible for the quality of the three most important business processes?
- ☐ Do you, as business managers, deal with the right IT issues?
- ☐ Have IT and business drawn up a written service level agreement?
- ☐ Do business managers receive a statement with a breakdown of IT services and service users for their area of responsibility?
- ☐ How do you compare your IT costs with alternatives on the market?
- ☐ Which criteria do you use to assess the performance of the IT department and the CIO?
- ☐ What have stoppages in your processes cost over the past three years?
- ☐ Have you compared the price/performance ratio of your applications with other companies (benchmarking)?

Conclusion

IT-Driven Innovation in the 2010s

This book was born in the aftermath of the credit and real estate crises of 2008. In the process of writing it, we have had to reexamine many of our foundation assumptions about globalization, about growth, about the place of information technology in the modern enterprise and in the economy. Many case studies and recommendations were surpassed by late-breaking events in the world of commerce. More than once there were concerns that the world was moving fast, and that the emerging world might operate on different rules compared to where we started.

As we reflect on the concepts, case studies, and recommendations in the preceding chapters, however, we happily come to the opposite conclusion: Not only will IT-driven innovation continue to drive customer value and, thereby, enterprise value, that same mode of innovation will matter increasingly for larger entities as well. Enterprise profitability will continue to matter, of course, but so too will the health of an entire ecosystem: With the anticipated success of Windows 7, Dell and HP will sell more computers, Samsung and Sharp will sell more displays, and Intel and AMD will sell more processors.

Above the level of an ecosystem, entire industry verticals face pressing problems that can only be addressed with the assistance of IT-driven innovation. Health care is the most obvious example, but airlines, financial services, telecom, and retail could just as easily be mentioned. We are more convinced than ever that the concepts of networkability and flexible, cost-effective IS management will reshape not just individual companies but new, connected assemblages of resources.

As they confront aging populations, environmental and climatological challenges, war, new demands on their institutions of education and training, and the ever-rising expectations of their citizens, governments at all levels can no longer operate at accustomed levels of efficiency, speed, and cost. Whether it is electronic medical records, better tracking of terror suspects, or "smart" electrical grids, to take but a handful of examples, the major governmental initiatives of the coming decade are all IT-intensive.

Organizations of every size pursuing every activity are able to benefit from a convergence of factors. Computing capacity is at once more powerful and more mobile than ever before. A new generation of amazing devices has become a part of everyday existence, carried on one's person. At the same time, enormous data centers provide an effectively infinite array of applications over the wire or the ether, at any scale, from Flash games to protein-folding visualizations. One need not be a systems administrator, application developer, or data center manager to take advantage of as much or as little computing power as a person or an organization needs.

This convergence of mobility, virtualized computing resources, and standards on which to develop and run applications is not important only for its convenience and its cost-effectiveness. In a time of great market uncertainty, demographic change, and global interconnectedness, organizations at every scale need to be able to adapt to changing contexts and circumstances: as we have seen at such diverse firms as Nortel, Bear Stearns, and Chrysler, the penalty for inadequate agility can be steep. Thus the benefit of today's communications and computing models extends far beyond cost savings at the departmental or even enterprise level.

Seeing the needs and opportunities at every level of magnification, as it were, is possibly the most significant obstacle to innovation. The tools are in place and will only get better, lighter, cheaper, more secure, more widely interconnected. At this juncture, we thus have no shortage of challenges, a pretty impressive tool box, and a generation of "digital natives" all over the world who bring energy and optimism. The only missing factor is visionary, pragmatic leadership to mobilize the latter to confront the former: One dramatic shortage in a world often characterized by plenty is innovative people to lead the way to a brighter future.

Notes

Preface

1. Hakan Hakansson and David Ford, "How Should Companies Interact in Business Networks?" *Journal of Business Research* 55 (2002): 133–139.
2. To take but one example from January 2009, in the Gartner Executive Programs IT Survey of CIOs, the highest percentage of CIOs (54 percent) listed customer intimacy as their number one goal in technology and process projects (http://blogs.gartner.com/michael_maoz/2009/01/10/as-cio-youve-said-crm-is-your-differentiator-now-what/).
3. On the early stages of reengineering, see Thomas Davenport and James Short, "The New Industrial Engineering: Information Technology and Business Process Redesign," *Sloan Management Review* 31, no. 4 (1990): 11–27.
4. Jeanne Ross, Peter Weill, and David Robertson, *Enterprise Architecture as Strategy: Creating a Foundation for Business Execution* (Boston: Harvard Business School Press, 2006).

Chapter 1

1. Mark W. Johnson, Clayton M. Christensen, and Henning Kagermann, "Reinventing Your Business Model," *Harvard Business Review,* December 2008, 51–59.
2. Kevin Kelly, "The Value of Search," October 16, 2007, http://www.kk.org/thetechnium/archives/2007/10/the_value_of_se.php.
3. Sunil Gupta and Donald R. Lehmann, "Customers as Assets," *Journal of Interactive Marketing* 17, no. 1 (2003): 9–24.
4. Eugene W. Anderson, Claes Fornell, and Sanal K. Mazvancheryl (2004), "Customer Satisfaction and Shareholder Value," *Journal of Marketing* 68, 172–185.
5. Lerzan Aksoy, Bruce Cooil, Christopher Groening, Timothy L. Keiningham, and Atakan Yalçın, "The Long-Term Stock Market Valuation of Customer Satisfaction," *Journal of Marketing* 72 (2008): 105–122.

6. Information on global trends comes from *The Economist*, McKinsey Global Institute, the European Roundtable, and proprietary research. See, for example, Eric Beinhocker, Ian Davis, and Lenny Mendonca, "The 10 Trends You Have to Watch," *Harvard Business Review*, July-August 2009, 55–60.

7. Jian-Ye Wang and Abdoulaye Bio-Tchané, "Africa's Burgeoning Ties with China," *Finance & Development*, March 2008, http://www.imf.org/external/pubs/ft/fandd/2008/03/wang.htm.

8. See Anne-Marie Slaughter, *A New World Order* (Princeton, N.J.: Princeton University Press, 2004).

9. U.S. Census Bureau, International Data Base (IDB), http://www.census.gov/ipc/www/idb/pyramids.html.

10. National Oceanic and Atmospheric Administration (NOAA), Mauna Loa Monthly Mean Carbon Dioxide, http://celebrating200years.noaa.gov/datasets/mauna/image3b.html.

11. Barry Ritholtz, Big Bailouts, and Bigger Bucks," *The Big Picture*, November 25, 2008, http://www.ritholtz.com/blog/2008/11/big-bailouts-bigger-bucks/.

12. In the CEO study, we asked 17 CEOs and nine other managers in Germany, Switzerland, and Japan about their business models and IT agenda. Later, Weiying Zhang of Beijing University developed 15 Chinese case studies that usually included CEO interviews.

13. Rogelio Oliva and Robert Kallenberg, "Managing the Transition from Products to Services," *International Journal of Service Industry Management* 14, no. 2 (2003): 160–172.

14. C. I. V. Kerr and P. C. Ivey, "A Strategic Review of the Large Civil Aeroengine Market and the Paradigm Shift to a Service," *Aeronautical Journal* 105, no. 1047 (May 2001): 287–293.

15. See, for example, M. Pynnonen, "Customer Lock-in in ICT Services Business: Designing and Managing Customer Driven Business Model," in *Proceedings of the Portland International Conference on Management of Engineering & Technology* (2008), 818–828.

16. Keith Provan, Amy Fish, and Joerg Sydow, "Interorganizational Networks at the Network Level: A Review of the Empirical Literature on Whole Networks," *Journal of Management* 33 (2007): 479–516.

17. J. Borzo, "Business 2010 – "Embracing the Challenge of Change," in *A Report from the Economist Intelligence Unit*, Economist Intelligence Unit (London 2005), 22.

18. Johnson, Christensen, and Kagermann, "Reinventing Your Business Model." See note 1.

19. On information technology and new business concepts, see, for example, Nicholas Carr, *The Big Switch: Rewiring the World, From Edison*

to Google (New York: Norton, 2008); Thomas L. Friedman, *The World Is Flat* (New York: Farrar, Strauss, and Giroux, 2005); Nicholas Negroponte, *Being Digital* (New York: Knopf, 1995); and Shoshanna Zuboff, *In the Age of the Smart Machine* (New York: Basic, 1988).

20. Jim Carlton and Lee Gomes, "Apple Computer Chief Gil Amelio Is Ousted," *Wall Street Journal*, July 10, 1997.

21. Jai Singh, "Dell: Apple Should Close Shop," *CNet,* October 6, 1997, http://news.cnet.com/Dell-Apple-should-close-shop/2100–1001_3–203937.html.

22. Arik Hesseldahl, "Apple's Cheap to Build Nano," *BusinessWeek Online,* September 19, 2007.

23. Philip Elmer-DeWitt, "How to Grow the iPod as the MP3 Player Market Shrinks," *Fortune*, January 29, 2008, http://apple20.blogs.fortune.cnn.com/2008/01/29/beyond-the-incredible-shrinking-ipod-market/.

24. Paul Brown, "What's in Store for iPhone App Developers?" *Guardian,* May 28, 2009, http://www.guardian.co.uk/technology/2009/may/28/apple-iphone-app-developers.

25. For more information regarding Apple's attention to detail on the iPod, see Steven Levy, *The Perfect Thing: How the iPod Shuffles Commerce, Culture, and Coolness* (New York: Simon & Schuster, 2006).

26. The term was coined by *Wired* editor Chris Anderson in reference to the flipside of the "winner-take-all" behavior of power law distributions. See Chris Anderson, *The Long Tail: Why the Future of Business Is Selling Less of More* (New York: Hyperion, 2006).

27. Arik Hasseldahl, "A Memorable Deal for Apple and Samsung?" *BusinessWeek* August 26, 2005.

28. Michael E. Porter, "What Is Strategy?" *Harvard Business Review*, November–December 1996.

29. Kevin Allison, "Apple Ushers in New Mac Generation," *Financial Times*, August 13, 2007.

30. Cisco Visual Networking Index: Forecast and Methodology, 2009–2014, June 2, 2010, http://www.cisco.com/en/US/solutions/collateral/ns341/ns525/ns537/ns705/ns827/white_paper_c11-481360_ns827_Networking_Solutions_White_Paper.html.

31. See also Clay Shirky, "It's Not Information Overload, It's Filter Failure," video available at http://web2expo.blip.tv/file/1277460/.

32. Randall Stross, "Struggling to Evade the E-Mail Tsunami," *New York Times,* April 20, 2008.

33. See Michael Lesk, "How Much Information Is There in the World?" *Athenaeum Reading Room,* http://evans-experientialism.freewebspace.com/lesk.htm.

34. Charles Babcock, "The SOA Gamble: One in Three Companies Are Disappointed, Our Survey Finds," *Information Week*, September 8, 2007.

35. John Foley, "A Definition of Cloud Computing." *InformationWeek* Plug into the Cloud, September 28, http://www.informationweek.com/cloud-computing/blog/archives/2008/09/a_definition_of.html.
36. Andrew P. McAfee, "Enterprise 2.0: The Dawn of Emergent Collaboration," *Sloan Management Review,* 47, no. 3 (2006): 21–28.

Chapter 2

1. B. Joseph Pine and James Gilmore, *The Experience Economy* (Boston: Harvard Business School Press, 1999), 20–22.
2. See T.S. Baines, H.W. Lightfoot, O. Benedettini, J.M. Kay, "The Servitization of Manufacturing: A Review of Literature and Reflection on Future Challenges," *Journal of Manufacturing Technology Management* 20 (2009): 547–567.
3. COSCO statistics derived from Cosco Group, "Mission Statement," http://www.cosco.com.cn/en/about/index.jsp?leftnav=/1/1.
4. "COSCO Container Lines Co. Ltd. Customer Success Story," Sybase fact sheet, August, 2009.
5. Themelis quoted in "Talking Rubbish: A special report on waste," *The Economist*, February 28, 2009, p. 14.
6. Min Ding, Gerald Susman, and Anthony Warren, "Adding Services to Products: An Entrpeneurial Challenge," Farrell Center for Corporate Innovation and Entrepreneurship working paper, http://www.smeal.psu.edu/fcfe/more/white/.
7. Gary Marchionini, "Exploratory Search: From Finding to Understanding," *Communications of the ACM* 49 (2004), 41–46.

Chapter 3

1. Julia Finch, "Tesco Pursues Promiscuous with Revamped Loyalty Card," *Guardian,* May 8, 2009.
2. Clay Shirky, "Half the World," *Clay Shirky's Writings about the Internet*, September 3, 2002, http://www.shirky.com/writings/half_the_world.html.
3. Telefónica. "Informes de responsabilidad corporative" (Corporate Responsibility Report) 2006, http://www.telefonica.com/es/about_telefonica/html/publicaciones/responsabilidad2006.shtml
4. Telefónica, *2007 Annual Report*, p. 7.
5. Telefónica. "Informes de responsabilidad corporative" (Corporate Responsibility Report) 2007, p. 15.
6. N. Dawar and M. Vandenbosch, "The Seller's Hidden Advantage," *Sloan Management Review* 45, no. 2 (2004): 83–88.

7. Stephen Lin and Enrico Senger, "Xiameter Case Study," Institute for Information Management and the Glassmeyer/McNamee Center for Digital Strategy, web.iwi.unisg.ch/org/iwi/iwi_pub.nsf/wwwPubl CaseStudyEng/C573468F59CB3531C1256E860036F150.

8. Michael Maoz, "As CIO, You've Said CRM Is Your Differentiator. Now What?" *Gartner Blog Network,* January 10, 2009, http://blogs.gartner.com/michael_maoz/2009/01/10/as-cio-youve-said-crm-is-your-differentiator-now-what/.

9. Arthur Andersen Global Research Programme 2001.

10. Bill Snyder, "CRM's Holy Grail: How SOA Can Unlock a 360-Degree View of the Customer," *CIO,* October 29, 2008, http://www.cio.com/article/457927/CRM_s_Holy_Grail.

11. Adam Stein, "San Francisco Tests Dynamic Curbside Parking," *WorldChanging,* June 12, 2008, http://www.worldchanging.com/archives/008113.html.

12. Sewell Chan, "U.S. Drops Plan to Auction Landing Slots at 3 Airports," *New York Times,* May 13, 2009.

13. H. Salomann, M. Dous, L. Kolbe, and W. Brenner, "Customer Relationship Management Survey—Status Quo and Future Challenges," Institute of Information Management, University of St. Gallen, 2005.

14. Francis Buttle, *Customer Relationship Management* (Oxford: Butterworth-Heinemann, 2008), p. 79.

Chapter 4

1. Fareed Zakaria, *The Post-American World* (New York: Norton, 2009), p. xi.

2. For the degree of confusion in practice regarding the term "innovation," see Nizar Becheikh, Réjean Landry, and Nabil Amara, "Lessons from innovation empirical studies in the manufacturing sector: A systematic review of the literature from 1993–2003," *Technovation* 26 (2006): 644–664.

3. *Mechanical Turk* is a tool in Amazon's suite of Web services used for image recognition and other tasks at which humans outperform computers: the system basically asks people for help with pattern recognition and related tasks. See http://aws.amazon.com/mturk/.

4. *Procter & Gamble 2008 Annual Report*, p. 7.

5. For more on Connect and Develop, see Larry Huston and Nabil Sakkab, "Connect and Develop: Inside Procter & Gamble's New Model for Innovation," *Harvard Business Review* March 2006, 58–66; and A.G. Lafley and Ram Charan, *The Game-Changer: How You Can Drive Revenue and Profit Growth with Innovation,* (New York: Crown Business, 2008).

6. LEGO and MINDSTORMS are trademarks of the LEGO Group.
7. Mark W. Johnson, Clayton M. Christensen, and Henning Kagermann, "Reinventing Your Business Model," *Harvard Business Review,* December 2008, 56.
8. See, for instance, N. Dawar and M. Vandenbosch, "The Seller's Hidden Advantage," *Sloan Management Review* 45, no. 2 (Winter 2004): 83–88.
9. See K.W. Zimmermann and H.-M. Hauser, "The Growing Importance of Embedded Software—Managing Hybrid Hardware-Software Businesses," Boston Consulting Group, 2004.
10. U.S. Department of Energy, *Assessment of the Market for Compressed Air Efficiency Services* (2008), http://www1.eere.energy.gov/industry/bestpractices/compressed_air_ma.html.
11. See U.S. Food and Drug Administration, (FDA), *Combating Counterfeit Drugs—Safe and Secure: A Report of the U.S. Food and Drug Administration* (February 18, 2004), 9–13; and Thorstein Staake and Elgar Fleisch, *Countering Counterfeit Trade: Illicit Market Insights, Best-Practice Strategies, and Management Toolbox* (Berlin: Springer, 2008).
12. See J. P. Andrew and H.L. Sirkin, "Innovating for Cash," *Harvard Business Review* (September 2003), pp. 76–83. The wireless business owners numbers are reported in *Picture Business Magazine,* May 2009.
13. See H. Salomann et al., "Customer Relationship Management Survey," Institute of Information Management, University of St. Gallen, 2005, p. 61.
14. On modularity, see also Carliss Baldwin and Kim Clark, *Design Rules* (Cambridge: MIT Press, 2000).
15. See Gary Lilien et al., "Performance Assessment of the Lead User Idea-Generation Process for New Product Development," *Management Science* volume 48 (2002): 1042–1059.
16. Clayton Christensen, *The Innovator's Dilemma* (Boston: Harvard Business School Press, 1997), p. xxv.

Chapter 5

1. For examples, see "Perils of the Sea," *The Economist,* April 16, 2009; and "Perils on the Sea," *The Economist,* June 30, 2004.
2. See Yoshi Sheffi, *The Resilient Enterprise: Overcoming Vulnerability for Competitive Advantage* (Cambridge: MIT Press, 2005).
3. See Henry Chesbrough, *Open Innovation: The New Imperative for Creating and Profiting from Technology* (Boston: Harvard Business School Press, 2003).
4. "Unlocking Innovation in China," Economist Intelligence Unit, 2009, p. 8.

5. See also H. L. Lee and S. Whang, "Winning the Last Mile of E-commerce," *Sloan Management Review* 42, no. 4 (2001): 54–62.
6. Beth Bacheldor, "Dow and Chemtrec's RFID-Based Rail Safety Project," *RFID Journal*, April 6, 2007.
7. Alfred Angerer, *The Impact of Automatic Store Replenishment on Retail* (Wiesbaden: DUV, 2006), 64–68.
8. H. L. Lee, V. Padmanabhan, and S. Whang, "The Bullwhip Effect in Supply Chains," *Sloan Management Review* 38, no 2 (1997): 93–101.
9. NuImage Awnings, http://www.nuimageawnings.com/.
10. Bruce Richardson, "Zappos: Leveraging Customer Service, Culture, and Next-Gen Fulfillment," AMR Research commentary, March 2009, http://www.amrresearch.com/Content/View.aspx?pmillid=22422.
11. "New Automated Order Fulfillment System," *Warehouse & Logistics News*, January 28, 2009.
12. The classic statements remain W. Alderson, "Marketing Efficiency and the Principle of Postponement," *Cost and Profit Outlook* 3 (September 1950): 15–18; and L. P. Bucklin, "Postponement, Speculation and the Structure of Distribution Channels," *Journal of Marketing Research* 2 (February 1965): 26–31. The synonym "pull principle" is widely used. It emphasises that processes are triggered by (customer) demand rather than services being produced based on planning ("push").
13. "Just-in-Time Lobsters," *The Economist*, June 15, 2006.
14. See T. Davis and M. Sasser, "Postponing Product Differentiation," *Mechanical Engineering* 117, no. 11 (1995): 105–107.
15. E. Feitzinger and H. L. Lee, "Mass Customization at Hewlett-Packard: The Power of Mass Customization," *Harvard Business Review,* January–February 1997, 116–121.
16. See R. R. Fullerton and C. S. McWatters, "The Role of Performance Measures and Incentive Systems in Relation to the Degree of JIT Implementation," *Accounting, Organizations & Society* 27, no. 8 (2002): 11–25.

Chapter 6

1. Simon Jacobson, Jim Shepherd, Marianne D'Aquila, and Karen Carter, *The ERP Market Sizing Report 2006–2011*, AMR Research, 2007, http://www.sap.com/solutions/business-suite/erp/pdf/AMR_ERP_Market_Sizing_2006-2011.pdf.
2. SAP AG, *SAP 2008 Annual Report,* http://www12.sap.com/about/investor/reports/annualreport/2008/pdf/SAP_2008_Annual_Report.pdf.
3. Unless otherwise noted, all facts for the Saudi Aramco discussion come from the company's 2008 Annual Review and "Case study: Saudi Aramco

brought together by SAP," *BusinessIntelligence Middle East*, September 5, 2006, http://www.bi-me.com/main.php?c=34&cg=&id=5500&t=1.

4. Francesco Guerrera and Carola Hoyos, "Saudi Aramco revealed as biggest group," *Financial Times*, 15 December 2006.

5. Vestas, "Corporate Governance," http://www.vestas.com/en/investor/corporate-governance.aspx.

6. Vestas, "Strategy," http://www.vestas.com/en/investor/overview/strategy.aspx.

7. Vestas, "Culture: The Willpower," http://www.vestas.com/en/about-vestas/strategy/culture.aspx.

8. Yves Doz and Mikko Kosonen, *Fast Strategy: How Strategic Agility Will Help You Stay Ahead of the Game* (New York: Pearson/Wharton, 2008), pp. 56–58.

9. Robert Kaplan and David Norton, *The Execution Premium* (Boston: Harvard Business School Press, 2008).

10. Willie Pietersen, *Reinventing Strategy: Using Strategic Learning to Create and Sustain Breakthrough Performance* (New York: Wiley, 2002), 139.

11. See M. Blair, "New Ways Needed to Assess New Economy," *Los Angeles Times*, November 13, 2000.

12. John Pfister, "Reducing the Cost of Sarbanes-Oxley Compliance through Common Controls," *ISACA Journal* 5 (2006), http://www.isaca.org/Journal/Past-Issues/2006/Volume-5/Pages/Reducing-the-Cost-of-Sarbanes-Oxley-Compliance-Through-Common-Controls1.aspx.

Chapter 7

1. Thomas L. Friedman, *The World Is Flat: A Brief History of the Twenty-first Century* (New York: Farrar Strauss Giroux, 2006).

2. See Jeffrey Word, ed., *Business Network Transformation: Strategies to Reconfigure Your Business Relationships for Competitive Advantage* (San Francisco: Jossey-Bass, 2009).

3. For a comprehensive assessment of the role of services in manufacturing, see Andy Neely, "Exploring the Financial Consequences of the Servitization of Manufacturing," *Operations Management Review*, forthcoming. Available at http://ssrn.com/abstract=1339189.

4. Also known as 4PL. In contrast to third-party logistics providers (3PL), a 4PL does not own any physical resources like warehouses.

5. Unless otherwise noted, all material on IKEA comes from Enrico Baraldi, "Strategy in Industrial Networks: Experiences from IKEA," *California Management Review* 50, no. 4 (Summer 2008): 99–126.

6. Sharp Corp., *Sharp Corporation 2009 Annual Report*, p. 15.

7. Douglas Schweitzer, "A 'gem' of an approach to staying competitive," *Computerworld Blogs*, October 6, 2008, http://blogs.computerworld. com/a_gem_of_an_approach_to_staying_competitive_0.

8. For more on De Beers, see "How to Succeed in the Multi-faceted Diamond Business: The Gospel According to De Beers," published April 18, 2007 in Knowledge@Wharton, available at http://knowledge. wharton.upenn.edu/.

9. Derek Gottfrid, "Self-service, Prorated Super Computing Fun!" *New York Times Open* (blogs), November 1, 2007, http://open.blogs.nytimes. com/2007/11/01/self-service-prorated-super-computing-fun/.

10. Amit S. Mukherjee, "The Fire That Changed an Industry: A Case Study on Thriving in a Networked World," *FT Press*, October 1, 2008, http:// www.ftpress.com/articles/article.aspx?p=1244469.

11. Interview with Mary McDowell, Chief Development Officer, Nokia, October 23, 2009.

12. Mark Borden, "Nokia Rocks the World: The Phone King's Plan to Redefine Its Business," *Fast Company*, September 2009, http://www. fastcompany.com/node/1325729/print.

13. See also Stan Liebowitz and Stephen Margolis, *Winners, Losers, and Microsoft* (New York: The Independent Institue, 2001).

14. See Hal Varian and Carl Shapiro, *Information Rules* (Boston: Harvard Business School Press, 1998).

15. Chris Anderson, *The Long Tail: Why the Future of Business Is Selling Less of More* (New York: Hyperion, 2006).

16. On the difference between "mediocristan" and "extremistan" as two intellectual worlds related to Gaussian versus power-law distribution assumptions, see Nassim Nicholas Taleb, *The Black Swan: The Impact of the Highly Improbable* (New York: Random House, 2007).

17. See Jean-Charles Rochet and Jean Tirole, "Platform Competition in Two-Sided Markets," *Journal of the European Economic Association* 1, no 4 (2003): 990–1029; and Thomas Eisenmann, Geoffrey Parker, and Marshall W. Van Alstyne, "Strategies for Two-Sided Markets," *Harvard Business Review*, October 2006.

18. "Canada's Fastest Growing Companies," *CB Online*, http://list. canadianbusiness.com/rankings/profit100/2009/intro/Default.aspx?sp2 =1&d1=d&sc1=9.

19. See *RosettaNet*, http://rosettanet.org.

20. See Cedric Read and Hans-Dieter Scheuermann, *The CFO as Business Integrator* (New York: John Wiley & Sons, 2003), pp. 91ff.

21. R. Oliva and R. Kallenberg (2003). "Managing the transition from products to services," *International Journal of Service Industry Management* 14, no. 2 (2003): 160–172.

22. For a detailed explanation, see Annabelle Gawer and Michael Cusumano, *Platform Leadership: How Intel, Microsoft, and Cisco Drive Industry Innovation* (Boston: Harvard Business School Press, 2002), 15–130.

Chapter 8

1. In this chapter, information technology, or IT, refers to technologies such as computing hardware, database software, and networking infrastructure. Information services or information systems (IS) refers to the organizations within the modern enterprise that deliver those technologies.
2. Ed Sperling, "CIO Chat: Intel's Insides," *Forbes.com,* August 18, 2008, http://www.forbes.com/2008/08/17/cio-intel-bryant-tech-cio-cx_es_0818intelqa.html.
3. *IT@Intel 2008 Performance Report,* p. 3.
4. Sperling, "Intel's Insides." See note 1.
5. Tom Parish, "Making Social Media the Corporate Norm for a Fortune 500 Company: Diane Bryant, Intel's CIO" (podcast), *Enterprise Leadership,* June 25, 2009, http://www.enterpriseleadership.org/blogs/podcasts/2009/06/25/making-social-media-the-corporate-norm-for-a-fortune-500-company-diane-bryant-intels-cio.
6. Cliff Saran, "Interview: Intel CIO Discusses Datacentre Efficiency," *Computerweekly.com,* April 30, 2009, http://www.computerweekly.com/Articles/2009/04/30/235871/interview-intel-cio-discusses-datacentre-efficiency.htm.
7. All statistics from Intel IT's 2008 Performance Report.
8. Her Majesty's Cabinet Office, "Greening Government ICT: Efficient, Sustainable, Responsible," [2009]. http://www.cabinetoffice.gov.uk/media/270265/one_year_on.pdf.
9. See for example John Henderson and N. Venkatraman, "Strategic alignment: Leveraging information technology for transforming organizations," *IBM Systems Journal* 32, no. 1 (1993): 4–17.
10. Jeanne W. Ross, Peter Weill, and David Robertson, *Enterprise Architecture as Strategy* (Boston: Harvard Business School Press, 2005), 3–5. All material in this section comes from this source.
11. Ibid., p. 29.
12. Brand equity calculation is based on Interbrand, "Best Global Brands: 2008 Rankings," http://www.interbrand.com/best_global_brands.aspx?year=2008&langid=1000. Dell fell from 21st to 31st between 2005 and 2007; the tech support issue made mainstream news outlets in 2005.

See, for example, "Hanging Up on Dell?" *BusinessWeek,* October 10, 2005.

13. The firm, known as PriceWaterhouseCoopers in most regions, kept its two-word title in India.

14. Fred Brooks, *The Mythical Man-Month: Essays on Software Engineering* (Boston: Addison-Wesley, 1995).

15. Ibid., p. 25.

16. Sperling, "Intel's Insides." See note 1.

17. April 2006 Harris Interactive survey of information quality, commissioned by Business Objects. See the press release at SAP, "Information Workers Beware: Your Business Data Can't Be Trusted," June 26, 2006, http://www.sap.com/about/newsroom/businessobjects/20060625_005028.epx.

18. Thanks to Dr. Boris Otto, who leads the Competence Center on Corporate Data Quality at the University of St. Gallen, for contributing information related to data quality at BT.

19. Gartner, "Gartner Estimates ICT Industry Accounts for 2 Percent of Global CO2 Emissions," *Gartner Newsroom* (press release), April 26, 2007, http://www.gartner.com/it/page.jsp?id=503867.

20. Ludwig Siegele, "Let It Rise: A Special Report on Corporate IT," *The Economist*, October 25, 2008.

21. Michael Armbrust, Armando Fox, Rean Griffith, Anthony D. Joseph, Randy H. Katz, Andrew Konwinski, Gunho Lee, David A. Patterson, Ariel Rabkin, Ion Stoica, and Matei Zaharia, "Above the Clouds: A Berkeley View of Cloud Computing," EECS Department, University of California–Berkeley Technical Report No. UCB/EECS-2009–28, February 10, 2009, http://www.eecs.berkeley.edu/Pubs/TechRpts/2009/EECS-2009–28.pdf.

22. Andrew P. McAfee, "Enterprise 2.0: The Dawn of Emergent Collaboration," *Sloan Management Review* 47, no. 3 (2006): 21–28.

About the Authors

Prof. Dr. Dr.-ing. E.h. Henning Kagermann was CEO and Co-CEO of SAP AG, the world's largest provider of enterprise software, from 1998 until 2009. Under his leadership, SAP's annual revenues grew from $3.4 billion to $17.1 billion.

A member of the supervisory boards of Deutsche Bank AG, Deutsche Post AG, and Munich-Re, and a board member of Nokia and Wipro, he currently serves as president of acatech, the German Academy of Science and Engineering. More recently, he was the coauthor of "Reimagine Your Business Model," which won the 2009 McKinsey Prize for best article in *Harvard Business Review*.

Prof. Dr. Hubert Osterle codirects the Institute of Information Management at the University of St. Gallen (Switzerland). He teaches and performs research in the areas of business models for the information age, business networking, and independent living for elders. The Institute of Information Management works in close collaboration with leading enterprises in Switzerland, Austria, and Germany to develop academically sound solutions for strategic problems relating to information management.

In 1988 Prof. Osterle founded the Information Management Group, an international consultancy focused on the implementation of innovative business models and processes, and in 2004, the Direct Management Institute at the University of St. Gallen.

Prof. Dr. John M. Jordan teaches IT strategy to undergraduates, MBAs, and executives at the Smeal College of Business, Penn State University. His research focuses on emerging technologies and their impact on business strategy, design, and practice.

He is the coauthor, with David Hall, of *Human-Centered Information Fusion* (Norwood, Mass.: Artech House, 2010) and has written a monthly technology newsletter, *Early Indications*, since 1997. Before returning to the academy, he attained the rank of Principal at Ernst & Young's Center for Business Innovation and Capgemini's Office of the Chief Technologist.

Index